WITHDRAWN

WARWICK STUDIES IN PHILOSOPHY AND LITERATURE

General Editor: DAVID WOOD

In both philosophy and literature, much of the best original work being done today exploits the connections and tensions between these two disciplines. Modern literary theory increasingly looks to philosophy for its inspiration, as the influence of deconstructive and hermeneutic readings demonstrates.

The University of Warwick pioneered the study of the intertwinings of philosophy and literature, and its Centre for Research in Philosophy and Literature has won wide respect for its adventurous programme of research and conferences. The books published in this new series present the work of the Centre to a wider public, combining a sense of new direction with traditional standards of intellectual rigour.

Books in the series include:

THE BIBLE AS RHETORIC: Studies in Biblical persuasion and credibility
Edited by Martin Warner

EXCEEDINGLY NIETZSCHE
Edited by David Farrell Krell and David Wood

POST-STRUCTURALIST CLASSICS
Edited by Andrew Benjamin

THE PROVOCATION OF LEVINAS
Edited by Robert Bernasconi and David Wood

THE PROBLEMS OF MODERNITY: Adorno and Benjamin
Edited by Andrew Benjamin

NARRATIVE IN CULTURE
Edited by Cristopher Nash

WRITING THE FUTURE
Edited by David Wood

Forthcoming:

PHILOSOPHERS' POETS
Edited by David Wood

JUDGING LYOTARD
Edited by Andrew Benjamin

NARRATIVE AND INTERPRETATION: The recent work of Paul Ricoeur
Edited by David Wood

ABJECTION, MELANCHOLIA, AND LOVE

The Work of Julia Kristeva

Edited by

JOHN FLETCHER
and
ANDREW BENJAMIN

ROUTLEDGE
London and New York

First published 1990
by Routledge
11 New Fetter Lane, London EC4P 4EE

Simultaneously published in the USA and Canada
by Routledge
a division of Routledge, Chapman and Hall, Inc.
29 West 35th Street, New York, NY 10001

Filmset in 10/12 Plantin
by Mayhew Typesetting, Bristol, England
and printed and bound in Great Britain by
TJ Press (Padstow) Ltd., Padstow, Cornwall

British Library Cataloguing in Publication Data
Abjection, Melancholia, and Love : the work of Julia Kristeva. —
(Warwick studies in philosophy and literature)
1. Literature. Criticism. Kristeva, Julia 1941–
I. Fletcher, John. 1948–   II. Benjamin, Andrew
801'.95'0924
ISBN 0–415–04155–4 (Hbk)
0–415–04190–2 (Pbk)

Library of Congress Cataloging in Publication Data
Abjection, Melancholia, and Love.
(Warwick studies in philosophy and literature)
Includes bibliographies and index.
1. Kristeva, Julia, 1941–   –Criticism and interpretation.
2. Psychoanalysis in literature.   3. Psychoanalysis and
literature.   4. Feminism in literature.   5. Feminism and
literature.   I. Fletcher, John, 1948–
II. Benjamin, Andrew E.   III. Series.
PN56.P92K757 1989   801'.95'092 89–10308
ISBN 0–415–04155–4 (Hbk)
ISBN 0–415–04190–2 (Pbk)

Contents

The Corpse of Christ in the Tomb by Hans Holbein, courtesy of Oeffentliche Kunstsammlung Basel Kunstmuseum.

Notes on Contributors

Elizabeth Grosz is a lecturer in the Department of General Philosophy at the University of Sidney. She has published widely in the fields of Semiotics, Feminism, and Psychoanalysis. She has co-edited (with Carol Pateman) *Feminist Challenges* (Australia: Allen and Unwin, 1986).

John Lechte is a lecturer in Sociology at Macquarie University. He has published on Rousseau, Psychoanalysis, and Pacific Studies. He is the author of *Politics and the Writing of Australian History* (Melbourne, 1979) and *Julia Kristeva* (London, 1990) in the Routledge Contemporary Critics series.

Makiko Minow-Pinkey works for Oxford English Limited and its journal *News From Nowhere*. She is the author if *Virginia Woolf and the Problem of the Subject* (Brighton: Harvester, 1987).

Victor Burgin is Professor of Art History at the University of California, Santa Cruz. His most recent work is *The End of Art Therapy* (London: Methuen, 1988).

Cynthia Chase is a Professor of English at Cornell University. She has published widely in literary studies.

Leslie Hill is a lecturer in French Studies at the University of Warwick. He is the author of *Beckett's Fiction: In Different Words* (Cambridge, 1990). He is currently completing a book on Duras.

Alison Ainley is a graduate student in the Department of Philosophy at the University of Warwick where she is currently working on a thesis on feminism and ethics. She has written on

Levinas, Nietzsche, and Kierkegaard, and has written poems included in *The Eric Gregory Anthology* (London: Salamander, 1987).

Tina Chanter is Assistant Professor of Philosophy at Louisiana State University. She has written articles on Levinas, Derrida, and Heidegger. Her Stony Brook Ph.D. dissertation focused on Time in the philosophy of Levinas and Heidegger.

Noreen O'Connor is Director of the Friends World College European Centre, the Philadelphia Association (London), and is in the Psychotherapy Training Programme of the Philadelphia Association.

Julia Kristeva teaches at the Université Paris 7. Her most recent book is *Etranger à nous-mêmes*. (Paris, 1988).

Maud Ellman is a lecturer in English at the University of Southampton. She is the author of *The Poetics of Impersonality* (Brighton: Harvester, 1987).

Acknowledgements

The author and publishers would like to extend their grateful thanks to Faber & Faber Ltd, and Harcourt Brace Jovanovich, Inc. for permission to quote from T.S. Eliot, *The Wasteland*, and Ezra Pound, *The Cantos*.

Introduction

JOHN FLETCHER

This volume began with the Conference held at the University of Warwick in May 1987 on the work of Julia Kristeva. It is both more and less than the occasion itself. The eight papers read at the Conference have been supplemented by three others from Elizabeth Gross, Tina Chanter, and John Lechte.[1] Despite the inclusion of her paper in the present volume, the element of the event that could not be recorded was the presence of Julia Kristeva herself. Her inexhaustible intellectual stamina and generosity were made unstintingly available, not only at the Conference itself, in her detailed responses to the papers presented, but in the week of her stay at Warwick as Visiting Fellow at the Centre for Research in Philosophy and Literature leading up to the Conference. In a series of public lectures,[2] seminars and discussion groups with undergraduate and postgraduate students as well as academic colleagues, we were privileged to listen to and engage with one of the most innovatory and widely ranging thinkers of our time. Most striking was the way an already formidable set of interests in linguistics, semiotics, philosophy, literary criticism, and art history had been displaced and regrouped around her experience as a practising psychoanalyst. Earlier themes and preoccupations were re-posed and readdressed from the transforming and productive experience of analysis. Most illuminating and moving was Kristeva's continual witness, in both her spontaneous and considered responses, to the implications across a wide range of disciplines of the analytic experience, with its transferential and therapeutic dimensions, in an academic world massively ignorant of psychoanalysis and its effects.

The volume begins with Kristeva's own essay, 'The Adolescent Novel'. Here she reflects on a privileged homology between novelistic writing and the experience of adolescence as an 'open structure'. What she calls 'the polyphonia of the novelistic genre' (p. 22), alluding to Bakhtin's theses on the novel, owes 'its more than oedipal pliancy, its dose of perversity' to the distinctive transitional character of adolescence, open to the repressed and to an awakened pre-genitality, which it attempts to integrate within a reorganization of psychic life. The adolescent moment in Kristeva's account has a porousness in which the boundaries of sexual difference and identity, fantasy and reality, are more easily traversed, and which lends itself to a range of 'post-adolescent' cultural uses. Kristeva comments on the historical emergence and constitution of a form of novelistic writing concerned with the loves of page-boys, and in particular the first novel in French prose *Little Jehan de Saintré* (1456) by Antoine de la Sale. In a text marked by the residues of earlier literary genres and the search for new conventions of narration, Kristeva singles out the play of different roles and relations around the figure of the adolescent – child, brother, lover, favourite, page-boy – and the duplicity and ambivalence that characterize the young lover's relations with the Lady. In a striking and suggestive formulation she describes the adolescent Saintré as 'the perfect androgyne, the innocent and justified pervert' (p. 14). It is the seductiveness of such an unformed and immature figure, in whom the '*topos* of incompleteness' (p. 14) is rich with possibility, that is Kristeva's theme. The productive openness of adolescence and its narratives allows the constitution of a distinctive literary regime and gradually a distinctive psychic space of interiority. She sums up in compressed form the trajectory she is to follow through the eighteenth-century French novels of adolescence, Dostoievski and finally the mid-twentieth-century paedophilic romance of Nabokov's *Lolita*, when she writes:

> It must be noted that this ambivalence is the origin of psychology, that without the logic of pretence and betrayal, there is no psychology, that ambivalence and psychology are synonyms for the novelistic as opposed to the *epic* and the *courtly* romance. (p. 14)

Kristeva's account might be partially paralleled in the English tradition if one thinks of the great verse romances of the late fourteenth century, *Gawayne and the Grene Knight* and Chaucer's *Book of Troylus*, where the beginnings of a distinctive 'novelistic' interiority is first registered in a semi-naturalistic dialogue and limited polyphonia emerging from the longer, formal set speeches and stylistic formulae of the romance and the epic. In both cases it is the *adolescent* experiences of initiation, trial, longing, and ambition in a partly feminized male figure and of betrayal and duplicity in the Lady that map out a distinctive subjectivity in moments of crisis, choice, and transition and that enable a heightened literary attentiveness to these subjective fluctuations and intensities.

Kristeva's theme is a productive point of entry into the history of narrative and its psychic economies, and she leaves it with a provocative question, long overdue in much traditionally normative psychoanalytic theory:

This interrogation of the adolescent and writing has in fact led us to perversion and its rapport with the writer. How to understand perversion in a way that is at once faithful and non-complacent: this is what, perhaps, the history of novelistic writing could discover for us. (p. 22)

The relation between perversion and creativity in psychoanalytic thought, from Freud's *Leonardo da Vinci* (1910) to Chasseguet-Smirgel's recent collection of essays,[3] has been one of the themes most full of promise and yet most disappointingly marked by an uncritical and often reactionary retreat to normative and pathologizing positions. One may hope that Kristeva's refocusing of the question of 'perversion' around writing and the 'open structure' of the adolescent – 'the innocent and justified pervert' – will revivify and redirect psychoanalytic reflections on the psychic sources and dimensions of literary and symbolic creativity.

One group of essays is concerned with art, literature, and representation. Those by John Lechte and Leslie Hill engage with the way Kristeva's work has conceptualized the work of art, especially literature and painting, as a signifying practice, and with her notion of the avant-garde. Lechte's essay addresses in particular Kristeva's more recent preoccupations with the significance of melancholy, the capacity for love and her insistence on 'symbolic production's power to constitute *soma* and to give an identity' (p. 25). Leslie Hill's consideration of the category of the avant-garde in Kristeva's work problematizes the relations between the semiotic and the symbolic in her reading of avant-garde texts and raises the question of the possible obsolescence or surpassing of the category in her more recent concern with aesthetic activity as a sublimation of subjective and cultural crisis.

The essays by Cynthia Chase, Makiko Minow-Pinkney, Maud Ellman, and Victor Burgin make use of Kristevan categories – the abject, the semiotic chora and her interpretation of primary narcissism – to elaborate readings of particular texts or to advance meta-critical or speculative debates. Cynthia Chase's essay is a dense meta-commentary within an inter-textual field constituted by Kristeva's reworking of Freud's concepts of 'primary narcissism' and 'the father of personal pre-history',[4] which is mobilized in an engagement with Neil Hertz's commentary on Paul de Man around the distinctions between figure and grammar, the cognitive and the performative dimensions of language. In her essay on Virginia Woolf, Makiko Minow-Pinkney focuses persuasively the question of the woman writer as an outsider in language through a reflection on the semiotic process at work in texts such as *Mrs Dalloway* and *The Waves* in its relation to a patriarchal symbolic order within which the texts are held.[5] It is through Kristeva's theory of abjection that Maud Ellman develops her dazzling reading of *The Waste Land*, scanning the rhythm of expulsion and obsessional re-inscription of its abjected Babel of dead voices and writings. Retrieving, as she puts its, 'the "waste" beneath the redevelopments' of modern critical explanations, she attends to the text's own abjection and mysogyny, its parasitism (is it necrophiliac or necrophobic?) on the corpse of literature. As her recent work on Pound and Joyce makes clear,[6] Ellman is our most elegant and original practitioner of a psychoanalytically informed tracing of the textual body and its visceral economy of flows, circulations and passages, thus giving an extended (and often startling) meaning to Kristeva's notion of 'the subject in process'. It is also through the theory of abjection (which is proving a fertile theoretical incitement to literary and aesthetic reflection) that the panoptic sweep of Victor Burgin's survey of the history of visual space and its representations explores the psychic investments of the visual field, and poses the question of the relation of our geometries to our desires.

Another group of essays has shared concerns with both philosophical and feminist issues. Both Noreen O'Connor and Alison Ainley are concerned with conceptions of otherness and its place in inter-subjective relations and transactions as formulated within the tradition of phenomenology and especially in the work of Emmanuel Levinas. Noreen O'Connor writes also as a practising psychotherapist in the psychoanalytical tradition and her essay is concerned with the function of speech within the peculiar inter-subjective dynamic of the analytic situation. She suggests connections between the metaphysical hunger for a single origin or ground – whether Being, God, Tradition, or History – and its reduction of the uniqueness of the individual speaking being, and Kristeva's analysis of narcissism, abjection, and the desire for the phantasm of the archaic mother, the failure of separateness and otherness to emerge and so the capacity to love. In welcoming Kristeva's analysis she nevertheless challenges the heterosexual assumptions that often underpin much psychoanalytic theory and especially the way such an analysis can be used to pathologize homosexual love *tout court*. Turning around the Kristevan problematic of otherness and maternal separation she wonders:

Psychoanalysts devote a lot of attention to elucidating the difficulty of separating from the mother. My question is, why is it that psycho-analysts have such difficulty in separating from the Father? (p. 51)

Alison Ainley's essay on 'The Ethics of Sexual Difference' also invokes Levinas in a reflection on the function of otherness for both terms of her title, and considers especially the problems produced by the designation of the feminine as other. She deploys Kristeva's conceptualization of the feminine as a position rather than an essence and her redefinition and relocation of ethics from a traditional identification with the impersonality and abstraction of the Law (Freud's inexorable paternal superego with its return of an accusation against women) to a revalued maternity as the site of caring and an opening to a different conception of otherness.

Tina Chanter's essay shares similar concerns with Alison Ainley's. She uses Kristeva's reflections on temporality and the phases of feminism in 'Women's Time' to consider an early British feminist activist and MP, Eleanor Rathbone, and her arguments about feminist strategy based on a distinction between the goal of equality with men and political goals associated with the needs specific to women, especially in relation to maternity. Like Ainley, she argues for taking the risk of essentialism in basing an ethical or political thought on the attempt to grasp the specificity of women's experience as distinct from men's.

Elizabeth Gross's essay is a reflection on the categories of the semiotic and abjection in Kristeva's thought. She is concerned with the way they enable an account of the formation of a symbolically coded and psychically integrated body and with the role of such a corporeality in the production of a subject of discourse and enunciation. Like the essays by Ainley and Chanter, Gross returns to the centrality of maternity and Kristeva's various descriptions and theorizations of it, and especially to the sexual differentiation of bodies and subjectivities as a continuing, unresolved problem for theoretical reflection. If the semiotic and symbolic constitution of the body plays such a role in the formation and deformation of discourses, Gross asks sceptically, 'does the subject's sexuality become subordinated to the neutrality and sexual indifference of the "I"?' (p. 101).

The cumulative effect of the essays gathered in this volume is to render apparent once again the extraordinary fertility and productivity of Julia Kristeva's thought for a diverse range of theoretical projects and disciplines.

Notes

1 Unfortunately it was not possible to record the discussion in which Kristeva responded at length to a series of prepared questions put to her by Jacqueline Rose, whose recent collection of essays contains perhaps the most rigorous and extended reflection on her work in English, and by Toril Moi whose work as editor and commentator constitutes the most useful introduction to her work for the English language reader.

Jacqueline Rose, 'Julia Kristeva – Take Two', in *Sexuality in the Field of Vision*, London, Verso, 1986; *The Kristeva Reader*, ed. Toril Moi, Oxford, Basil Blackwell, 1986; Toril Moi, *Sexual/Textual Politics*, London, Methuen, 1985.

2 'The Melancholic Imaginary', reprinted in *New Formations*, no. 3, Winter 1987.

3 S. Freud, *Leonardo da Vinci and a Memory of his Childhood* (1910) in *The Pelican Freud Library*, vol. 14: Art and Literature, ed. Albert Dickson, Harmondsworth, Penguin, 1985; Janine Chasseguet-Smirgel, *Creativity and Perversion*, London, Free Association Books, 1985.

4 S. Freud, *The Ego and the Id*, Chapter III, *The Pelican Freud Library*, vol. XI, *On Metapsychology*, ed. Angela Richards, p. 370.
5 Her arguments are elaborated at greater length in her recent book *Virginia Woolf and the Problem of the Subject – Feminine Writing in the Major Novels*, Brighton, Harvester Press, 1987.
6 'Floating the Pound: the Subject of Pound's Cantos', *Oxford Literary Review*, vol. 3, no. 3, Spring 1979; 'Disremembering Daedalus: "A Portrait of the Artist as a Young Man"', in *Untying the Text: A Post-Structuralist Reader*, ed. Robert Young, London, Routledge & Kegan Paul, 1981. An earlier version of the present essay is to be found in *The Poetics of Impersonality: T. S. Eliot and Ezra Pound*, Brighton, Harvester Press, 1987.

· 1 ·

The Adolescent Novel

JULIA KRISTEVA

To Write Adolescence

Like a child, the adolescent is one of those mythic figures that the imaginary, and of course, the theoretical imaginary, gives us in order to distance us from certain of our faults – cleavages, denials, or simply desires? – by reifying them in the form of someone who has not yet grown up. Certain epochs were in love with childhood . . . that of Rousseau aspired, through *Emile*, to the liberal stability of a new social contract. The epoch of Freud and the first Freudians sought the knowledge, comprehensive yet sure, of the polymorphous perversions. Other epochs recognized themselves willingly in the problematic incompleteness of young page-boys, picaros, delinquents, or terrorists – from Casanova to Milos Forman to Mad Max. Our epoch seems to be closest to these last. Whatever real problems are posed by the adolescents of our time, it appears, from the point of view I will take today, that to speak of the 'adolescent' and even more so of 'adolescent writing' consists in interrogating oneself on the role of the imaginary and its efficacy in the care of the patient, as well as for the analyst.

I understand by the term 'adolescent' less an age category than an open psychic structure. Like the 'open systems' of which biology speaks concerning living organisms that live only by maintaining a renewable identity through interaction with another, the adolescent structure opens itself to the repressed at the same time that it initiates a psychic reorganization of the individual – thanks to a tremendous loosening of the superego. The awakening of pre-genitality follows, and an attempt to integrate it within genitality.

8

In the aftermath of the oedipal stabilization of subjective identity, the adolescent again questions his identifications, along with his capacities for speech and symbolization. The search for a new love object reactivates the depressive position and the manic attempts at its resolution – from perversion to toxicomanias, global religions, and ideological adhesions.

Just as there are 'as if' personalities, there are 'open structure' personalities. These integrate the 'as if', as well as other traits which can manifest themselves within perverse structures – without there necessarily being any precise perversions. The evolution of the modern family and the ambiguity of sexual and parental roles within it, the bending or weakening of religious and moral taboos, are among the factors that make for these subjects *not* structuring themselves around a fixed pole of the forbidden, or of the law. The frontiers between differences of sex or identity, reality and fantasy, act and discourse, etc., are easily traversed without one being able to speak of perversion or borderline – and perhaps this would only be because these 'open structures' find themselves immediately echoing the fluidity, i.e. the inconsistency, of a mass media society. The adolescent is found to represent *naturally* this structure that can be called a 'crisis' structure only through the eyes of a stable, ideal law.

One could refine the description of this 'open structure' . . . . Let us insist rather on the value that writing can extract from it. I will note within writing at least three registers:

1 *The semiologically productive activity of written signs*
 Understood through its linguistic substratum, this activity adds however the motor element, along with its muscular and anal mastery as well as the aggressive appropriation of the other's body *and* one's own, all within a narcissistic, masturbatory gratification.

2 *The production of a novelistic fiction*
 An imaginary activity, this fiction borrows from the available ideologies or codes of representation that filter personal fantasies. The filtering here can become a repression of unconscious contents and give rise to a stereotyped writing of clichés; on the other hand, it can permit a genuine inscription of unconscious contents within language, and give to the adolescent the feeling of utilizing, at last and for the first time in his life, a living discourse, one that is not empty, not an 'as if'.

3 *The screening from another's appraisal*

Through its solitary economy, writing protects the subject from phobic affects – and if it enables him to re-elaborate his psychic space, it also withdraws that space from reality testing. The psychic benefit of such a withdrawal is obvious, but does not bypass the question of managing the rapport with reality for the subject himself – and of course within the treatment in so far as it utilizes his texts.

I will briefly evoke the case of an 18-year-old patient, a 'borderline' case whom I treat in psychotherapy once a week. Incapable of phantasmatic elaboration, playing the adult through delirium and sexual acting-out (she aspires to be in the police force and is constantly seducing all varieties of officers, national guardsmen, etc.), she had no other discourse at the beginning of her treatment but accounts of this desire-delirium, and her actings-out, all intimately related. On the level of transference – and to affirm that she too, like me, could write of love – Anne began to draw comic strips representing the lives of policemen and their sexual adventures. Little by little, onomatopoetics give way to bubbles enclosing words and dialogues of increasing complexity, and to her telling me that 'these cop stories, they're like a dream, a novel.' At the next stage, Anne imagines herself a writer of love songs – but in English. One will note the utilization of drawings, and then the foreign language, to reach a more and more exact representation of unconscious contents. The sending of letters to the analyst is the following stage, expressing more directly the psychic pain and lament. Inside the sessions where she brings her writings, Anne's discourse modifies itself, becomes more complex, her claims less immediately aggressive, more depressive perhaps, but in that sense more refined. Writing has taken the place of the 'forces of order': a writing as 'guardian of the peace', provisional of course, but which seemed to me to afford Anne a respite for adapting to the memory of her past . . . .

In this case, but also in the most banal situations, I will see writing as a semiotic practice that facilitates the ultimate reorganization of psychic space, in the time before an ideally postulated maturity. The adolescent imaginary is essentially amorous and the love object – susceptible to loss – reactivates the depressive position. From the basis of this objectal position, adolescent writing (written sign + fantasy filtered through the available imaginary codes) reactivates the process of the appearance of the symbol, a process that Hanna Segal attributes to the depressive position and which she sees as taking the place of the 'symbolic equivalents' of the paranoid position. During adolescence, this reactivation of the symbol or *depressive reactivation* is accompanied by a more or less free phantasmatic elaboration, which permits an *adjustment of drives* subjacent to the phantasms *and of the signs* of spoken or written language. In this sense, imaginary activity, and imaginary writing even more so (through the narcissistic gratification and phobic protection that it affords) gives the subject an opportunity to construct a discourse that is not 'empty', but that he lives as authentic. I will add to Hanna Segal's position[1] that if it seems to me incontestable that adolescent writing draws in on itself in a reactivation of the depressive position, it is yet from a *manic* position that it sustains itself. Refusal of loss, triumph of the Ego through the fetish of the text, writing becomes an essential phallic compliment, if not the phallus *par excellence*. It depends, for this very reason, on an ideal paternity.

Our society does nothing to prohibit such a phallic affirmation during adolescence. On the contrary, the adolescent has a right to the imaginary, and it is perhaps by an invitation to imaginary activities that modern societies replace or perhaps sweeten the initiation rites that other societies impose on their adolescents. The adult will have the right to this only as a reader or spectator of novels, films, paintings . . . or as artist. I do not see, moreover, what would prompt writing if not an 'open structure' . . . .

Novelistic Writing

One could maintain that the novelistic genre itself (and not writing as such, which allies itself even more to the battle of the subject with schizophrenia or depression) is largely tributory, in its characters and the logic of its actions, to the 'adolescent' economy of writing. It would be, from this point of view, the work of a perpetual subject-adolescent which, as a permanent testimony of our adolescence, would enable us to retrieve this immature state, as depressive as it is jubilatory, to which we owe, perhaps, some part of that pleasure called 'aesthetic'.

To demonstrate this affirmation, namely that the novelist presents himself as an adolescent, that he recognizes himself in the adolescent, and is an adolescent, I will take the theme of the adolescent in novels. He will appear to us as a key figure in the constitution of the novelistic genre in the West.

The Betrayed Page turns Traitor. Ambivalence, a Novelistic Value

Mozart immortalized the figure of the page-boy who, like a happy Narcissus, sighs in *The Marriage of Figaro*, night and day, without knowing whether this be love. It has been perhaps not enough stressed that the themes of the first modern novels, just after the Middle Ages, consist in the loves of page-boys. These loves thus constitute the very thread of novelistic psychology.

It is often considered that the first novel in French prose which is neither an epic nor a courtly lyric is a text by Antoine de la Sale (born 1385 or 1386, died 1460), entitled *Little Jehan de Saintré* (1456). We are right in the middle of the fifteenth century; the author is living through the Hundred Years War, the Battle of Orleans (1428), the death of Joan of Arc (1431). A feverish ecclesiastical activity attests to the symbolic upheaval of the time: the Council of Basel (1431–1439), the Council at Constance (1414–1418). Even if these events do not enter directly into the text, the novel still attests to the transition from the Middle Ages to the Renaissance, by the residue of an erudite medieval discourse, and by the appearance of new discourses within that.

Having finished his preliminary studies in Provence, Antoine de la Sale starts as a page-boy in the Court of Louis II, king of Sicily. He is 14 years old. Around 1442, he is both a writer (he compiles historic, geographic, juridical, ethical, etc., texts) and a tutor (he writes textbooks for his students). Then, as if by a synthesis of his own history as a page-boy and the students for whom he writes his didactic literature, he creates the personage of Jehan de Saintré. I will insist first of all on the unpolished and merely 'hinge' character of this first French novelist – who is so clumsy as to leave clearly visible the threads with which he wove his novel: classical erudition, borrowings from courtly literature, the utilization of theatrical dialogue are all blatant in this novelistic text. These stereotypes or cliches reveal an author still without authority, constantly in search of a master discourse. Added to this adolescent trait is an ambiguity within the novel between text, theatre, and reality; each speech is announced by a title, such as 'Author', 'Actor', or 'Lady'. These indices signify both a certain distance *vis-à-vis* fiction (as if the author were conscious of employing contrivances and wanted to show us this), and the reification of the text in a spectacle (as if he wanted to make us see these word-creatures in the hallucinatory or real form of actual bodies). Thus, a writing that does not give up the efficacy of drama – of psychodrama – but transposes it into the quiet exercise of reading. But what seems to me to centre this inaugural text around the adolescent structure is the very specific relationship of the little page-boy with the Lady, and with her lover the Abbot. Little Jehan loves the Lady. Now, the Lady maintains a traitor's discourse: she tells Jehan one thing, and the Court another – and she directly exposes herself as a traitor to her young suitor by her relations with the Abbot. The novel is thus a confrontation, after the fact, with the oedipal situation – such that during adolescence, little Jehan himself learns duplicity. His incestuous love for the Lady will transform itself into an imaginary identification with her. Jehan will gradually forge for himself a double language: he will at once love and despise the Lady, and will end by punishing her. The story consummates itself at that point, but not the novel – this continues in the shape of a résumé of the hero's adventures up until his death.

The importance of this novel – and its novel character – rest in the triumph of the adolescent over his incestuous object, through the imaginary assimilation of the latter's discourse. In effect, an entire revolution of mentalities is at play within this little adventure. Up to this point, heroes and villains had been monovalent. In the *Song of Roland* and *Tales of the Round Table*, they follow the course of an irreconcilable hostility, with no possible compromise. Roland and Ganelon have nothing in common; they are mutually exclusive. It is the same within the courtly tradition. Now, there is nothing of the sort with our adolescent or his universe. Child and warrior, page-boy and hero, deceived by the Lady, but conquering the soldiers, cared for and betrayed, loving the lady and loved by the king or by his brother-in-arms Boucicault, never fully masculine, child-lover of the Lady, but also comrade-friend to his tutors and to the brother with whom he shares his bed, Saintré is the perfect androgyne, the innocent and justified pervert. It must be noted that this ambivalence is the origin of psychology, that without the logic of pretence and betrayal, there is no psychology, that ambivalence and psychology are synonyms for the novelistic as opposed to the *epic* and the *courtly* romance. As if the fifteenth-century French writer needed – in order to write loss, and betrayal – to first imagine this in-between space, this *topos* of incompleteness that is also that of all possibilities, of the 'everything is possible' . . . from which follows the triumph over the Lady and over the Abbot, so that a new genre henceforth lives: the adolescent novel. The writer, like the adolescent, is the one who will be able to betray his parents – to turn them against him and against themselves – in order to be free. If this does not *mature* it, what an incredible loosening of the Superego, and what a recompense for the reader – this child, who, himself speechless, aspires only to be adolescent.

The Eighteenth Century: Which Sex? Or: How a Psychic Life is Built

The psychoanalyst has a tendency, it seems to me, to consider the psychic space as an interiority within which, through an involuntary movement, the experiences of the subject end by withdrawing in on psychic life – inner psychic space. The very principle of analysis, founded on speech and the moment of introspection, no doubt favours such a conception – a conception that gives itself, definitively, as the model of an ideal functioning leading (or able to lead) to a definitive and complete integration and elaboration.

Now, for the historian of literature, it is clear that 'psychic interiority' is a creation that affirms itself magnificently in the nineteenth-century psychological novel. Seventeenth-century man, on the contrary, has no inside or, at least, there exists a representation of seventeenth-century man without interiority. Completely faithful to baroque inconstancy, versatile, this individual without interior, this 'man without a name' (as is said of Don Juan in Tirso di Molina's play) finds his truest reflection in baroque spectacles – those of 'the enchanted isle', where the sparkling of the water and the sumptuousness of the other stage props – which were in fact often burned afterwards – must have told the spectators that nothing is true outside of God, but that all is 'staged', or 'put on'. Two centuries later, the nineteenth-century realists will have ceased to understand this kaleidoscopic and inauthentic psychic space. They will make a clumsy effort to tame it by postulating that such an improbable and careless ludism is a matter, no doubt, of a 'second nature'(!) . . . The transition from baroque man, with his neither inside nor outside, to the psychological man of the Romantics, Georges Sand and Stendhal, occurs in the eighteenth century. More precisely, this transition appears within the affirmation of the novelistic genre itself, which will recapture the surprises, the theatrical effects, the unlikely disguises and other 'actings-out' proper to picaresque and libertine novels and subordinate them to another order: order of the 'social contract', order of the 'natural' individual, order of novelistic composition. A remarkable fact: the adolescent character serves as a standard of measure within this involution of baroque man, who is neither within nor without, into nineteenth-century psychological man.

Of the numerous questions based around the eighteenth-century adolescent, I will limit myself to the interrogation of sexual identity. In reading the novels of this epoch, one can affirm that it is in the eighteenth century that the question of sexual difference as an unsolved problematic, or one that is *impossible* to solve, poses itself explicitly. Rousseau's *Emile* (1762) postulates a difference of sexes at the *origin* of society, but also at the moment of its perversion-perdition. The goal of the educator will be essentially to differentiate sexes and tasks, so that Emile becomes tutor and Sophie nurse. But the child is undifferentiated: 'Up to the age of puberty, children of both sexes have nothing apparent which distinguishes them; same face, same skin-tone, same shape, same voice, everything is equal: the girls are children, the boys are children, the name suffices for beings so similar.[2] 'The child raised according to his age is alone; the only attachment he knows is that of habit, he loves his sister like his watch, his friend like his dog. He is unaware of any sex, of any species, man and woman are equally foreign to him'.[3] Even worse, the risk of indifferentiation endures even when the sexual identities are assumed: 'Emile is man and Sophie is woman: all their glory lies in this. Given the confusion of the sexes that reigns among us, it is almost a marvel to be of one's own kind.'[4] In order to arrive at a stable sexual identity, the rousseauist child is subjected to a real educational voyage of which the initiation rites are not the rocambolesque adventures of adventure novels but consist rather in confronting the *feminine* in order to better protect oneself from it, and thus to become *other*; oneself. Now, if such is the goal of this education, it seems far from simple. A little story of Rousseau's, *The Fairy Queen* (1752), followed in fact by the *Letter to d'Alembert on Theatre* (1758) puts us on guard, as do other writings, against the danger of a generalized feminization ('no longer wanting to suffer from separation, unable to become men, women turn us into women'). This story delights in exploring the possibilities of sexual confusion. Confusion, and no longer infantile a-sexuality, this philosophical little story treats of sexual hybrids, of the double, and of twinhood. Rousseau gambles on writing a novel that is 'tolerable and even gay, without intrigue, without love or perversity'. Yet – and we are here at the height of perversity – he fails, for the story retraces a bizarre adventure. Two twins, brother and sister, find themselves at birth, through misunderstanding and spite, to possess the attributes of the opposite sex. This imbroglio spills into the natural order since the growing children, with the coming of adolescence, cannot assume their social functions, without some clarification. Far from being de-eroticized, the story plumbs the depths of sexual ambiguity: Prince Caprice is feminine in the extreme and Princess Raison has the qualities of a sovereign. The one and the other embroil themselves within an intrigue of about-faces and absurdity, hybrids and madness. The ambivalence is such that no logical or pedagogical means seems able to put an end to it. Only providence, an accident, makes things return to order. Rousseau, moreover, has his characters repeat a number of times that this order, on the whole, seems completely arbitrary to them. You must 'rave' is what he in fact recommends ('the best method you have for curing your wife is to go crazy with her' says the fairy to the King); or again: 'In spite of these oddities, or thanks to them, all will return to the natural order'. Rousseau long hesitates before publishing this eulogy of the confusion of sexes which depends, at bottom, on the fantasies of the mother, and which must resolve itself providentially at the end of adolescence. Man and woman, brother and sister, child and adult, the adolescent figure in Rousseau's work next becomes one apparently without perversity. Such is the idyll of the rural and incestuous societies of Valais, peopled with ambiguous adolescents ('his voice breaks, or rather he loses it; he is neither child nor man, and cannot assume the tone of either of them')[5] who become 'husband and wife without having ceased to be brother and sister'.[6] Rousseau mitigates on the whole the twins' extravagant perversion in *The Fairy Queen* by the mirage of a golden age. More wanton, Diderot makes of *Rameau's Nephew* (1773), and *Jacques the Fatalist* (1777), the adolescent prototypes of those who will contest paternity, normality, and religion. To illustrate one last process of integration/disintegration of the personality and its sexual identity – through the figure of the adolescent – I will have recourse to a lesser-known eighteenth-century text: Jean-Baptiste Louvet's *The Loves of the Knight of Faublas* (1787–1790).

Faublas excels in the art of disguise, which enables him not only to change his sex at will, but to accumulate false names in a polynomia that far exceeds that of Stendhal. Son of the Baron de Faublas, but having lost his mother very early, this young man is without identity – or he accumulates them so frantically that he seems to take pleasure less in sexual inversions than in the rapidity of betrayals that leave him with no guilt whatsoever. Disguise is his art, not his essence: he changes place like the figures in a ballet, displaces himself between masters and mistresses, brothers and sisters. Such a sexual amphibian, a series of masks, he indifferently names himself Faublas, Blasfau, Mlle de Portail, the Knight of Florville (thus assuming the pseudonym that Mme de B., one of his mistresses, uses when she dresses as a man). He is the son of the Baron, the brother of Adelaide, then the daughter of the Baron, the sister of Adelaide, the daughter of Portail and then his son in order to become brother to himself . . . . In search of what 'dead mother'? Such a vertiginous disguising is a powerful screen against madness. It is sufficient in the end that two of his mistresses die (like his mother. . .), for him no longer to be able to *play-act* between them and, the game over, the masks fall and uncover not nudity, but an emptiness, nobody, adolescent insanity. In fact, Faublas, now free since the disappearance of his mistresses, does not hedge toward a select spouse: without the masks that allowed him to attain false mothers, he has no place to be. Quite symptomatically, Faublas' madness stops the narration and it is his letters (fragments, for the most part) that relate his irrationality. And it is when his father finally puts things back in order, by imposing himself on his son, that Faublas is cured and the final cry resounds: 'He is ours again'. The masked lunatic becomes a true adolescent who belongs to his own people.

Sexual ambiguity, disguise, polynomia: Faublas is a punk in the eighteenth century. Once his game ends, madness follows. This means that the conscience is already affirming itself according to which the baroque game (Don Juan, Casanova) can – and must – cease. An interiority is in this case opened which is initially delirium, chaos, or emptiness. It will have to be ordered: by putting in place the figures of the Father and his accomplice the doctor, but also by the putting into place of the novelistic discourse. Because after the letters that relate the breakdown of madness (speechlessness, shouting), the narrative reappropriates and integrates psychic events. Disguises give way to the narrative of dreams, reconciliations, analogies. Writing becomes associative and interpretative. One will likewise note that incestuous acting-out, in Restif de la Bretonne, for example, is accompanied or announced by a text that becomes increasingly twisted into the order of representation itself: dreams that respond to each other, signs, allusions, discourses that summon their complementaries (as with *The Perverted Peasant Boy* (1775) and *The Perverted Peasant Girl* (1784)).

Thus, whether it be by the extravagance of perversion, or its naturalness, the eighteenth-century adolescent appears as a key personage: not only the emblem of a subjectivity in crisis, but also a means to display the psychic breakdown up to the point of psychosis and at the same time to re-collect it, to unify it within the unity of the novel. This unity is already polyvalent, and yet centred around an author who has in view the globalizing interpretation that could contain all the disguises, all the games. The novel that follows thus, takes up without mediation the relating of this adolescent, ambivalent, hybrid, disguised, 'baroque' universe of which the author speaks: the novel prolongs adolescence and replaces its acts with their narratives and interpretation.

Father and Son: Of the Paternal Body and Name

Dostoievski's *The Adolescent* (1874–1875), often considered a minor text of the great writer, is situated between well-known masterpieces like *The Devils* and *The Brothers Karamazov*.[7] I will retain Dostoievski's concern for adolescence. In 1874, Dostoievski writes in his *Notebooks*: 'A novel on children, uniquely on children, and about a child-hero'. Later, in 1876, *A Writer's Journal* specifies the definitive choice: 'as the test of his thought', to take 'a boy already beyond childhood: the still immature man who timidly and all alone desires to make as quickly as possible his first step into life'. One will note: 'as the test of his thought' as a writer, an adolescent hero must be chosen. In addition, in the preparatory notes for the novel, one follows the identification of the writer with the adolescent, by the occurrence of the decision to write in the first person: 'A young man offended, with a thirst for vengeance, and a colossal love for himself'; '"The Adolescent, confession of a great sinner, written by himself"'; grievous solution of the problem: to write in one's own name. Begin with the word "I". . . . An extremely concise confession'. Dostoievski sees first of all in the adolescent 'a true bird of prey . . . the lowest vulgarity allied with the most refined generosity . . . seductive and repulsive. . . .' Little by little, this type becomes Arkadi's father, and the novel describes Count Versilov – the seducer and atheist who represents decadent high society and who is nonetheless fascinating, the Adolescent's biological father. Beside him, a saintly paternity, fully symbolic: this is Makar Dolgorouki, the moujik, the legal father, who gives his name to his wife's illegitimate son before devoting himself to a mystical nomadism propagating Christ's word over the holy land of Russia. In this context, which is both historic and familial, the adolescent has an 'idea': power of money (he wants to be rich like Rothschild), the power of a triumph over women and inferiors that brings money and then, in the end, 'that which is acquired through power and cannot be acquired without it: the consciousness, calm and solitary, of his force'. A purely symbolic force, moreover, since the adolescent has no desire to use it: 'If only I had the power . . . I would no longer need it; I am certain that, from myself, of my own, I would everywhere occupy the lowest place'. And there he is, giving himself to reveries: 'I will be like a Rothschild who eats only a piece of bread and a slice of ham, and I will be sated with my conscience'. This symbolic, phallic affirmation of triumph connects the adolescent posture to the symbolic imaginary power of the writer: 'And mark it well, I need all of my evil will, only to prove to myself I have the power to renounce it'.

Such an aspiration, megalomanic even in humility, must confront the divided father-figure: the saint and the seducer. In terms of these two, the adolescent will place himself in a love-hate attitude, fascinated by the erotic life and religious scepticism of Versilov but also religiously admiring of the mystical renunciation of the peasant Dolgorouki. He will be by turns the wife of Versilov and the alter ego of Dolgorouki, running the gamut of his homosexual passion for an elusive father. For let us not forget that in this duo of fathers, Arkadi is never, at bottom, sure of having one. Not only would there be something like *two* 'fictional origins' battling to place definitively in doubt the existence of the father, but this implicit rejection of the father by the writer-adolescent is accompanied by a love for the father that seems to reproduce, in a profane way, Christ as the corporeal and spiritual appurtenance of the Father. The Son, separated from the Father and aspiring to reunite with him, is undoubtedly a fecund theme for orthodox Russian theology, and one that is at the very least ambiguous – if one refers to the Catholic dogma of the consubstantiality of the Father and the Son. For the orthodox Dostoievski, this consubstantiality (what I call the '*filioque*') seems not to be given right away; everything happens as if the adolescent had to prove, within his adolescent being aspiring to symbolic autonomy, this identification with paternity that is as much libidinal as symbolic. A subtle elaboration of homosexuality doubtless follows, which takes into account all the love-hate ambivalence of the father-son relation. Let us recall that in his study on Dostoievski, Freud sees him perhaps too hastily as a 'parricide'. It is possible, on the contrary, to decode even up to the epileptic symptom a pre-verbal expression of a sustained contradiction: love + hate, an insoluble that produces the subject within a motor discharge (as it can produce others within an acting-out). The novelistic elaboration by the adolescent of his struggles with the Body and Name of the father can be seen, from this point of view, as an attempt to dis-ambiguate (if only by naming the components) the obscure relation of the young Dostoievski to his tyrant father – who was killed by the moujik rebels, and who seems to have unleashed the first convulsive symptoms reactivated, as is known, by the even more tyrannical treatment of the penal house. . . . *The Brothers Karamazov* will resume the themes of the father and guilt, of brothers and the homosexuality *between* them and always *through* the intermediary of the father-figure, who remains the pivot of desire. Yet it is in *The Adolescent* that this problematic finds its natural place and its most direct familial treatment.

The Seduction of the Unformed and Immature

At the other end of the line, when the modern novel questions itself, or questions the necessarily paternal values of necessarily adult society, the writer states explicitly his seduction by the adolescent boy or girl, as with Nabokov and his *Lolita*, or Gombrowicz in his *Trans-atlantic* (1950) and his *Pornography* (1958).[8] It is not much to say that writers thus recover the means to exhibit . . . their own more or less latent exhibitionism or homosexuality. There is a certain identification of the narrator with his seductress or seducer, even more so, since these adolescents escape all categories – even those of coded perversions – and impose themselves on novelists as metaphors for what is not yet formed: metaphor of what awaits the writer, of what calls to him, the mirage of pre-language or unnamed body. Thus Gombrowicz, although he devotes all his work to the search for narrative forms adequate to the fluidity of experience all the way up to its extinction in aphasia or absurdity (*Cosmos*, 1964), can write that 'Form does not agree with the essence of life' (*Journal*, 1953–6, p. 171); devoting himself to a glorification of the unformed and the 'inferior, immature, which are essentially particular to all that is young, that is to say, to all that is alive' (ibid., p. 259). To the adult world – even the most baroque (like the pervert Gonzalo in *Trans-atlantic*) – will be opposed in this case the fascinating world of adolescents: Ignace, Karol, Henia. 'My first task, of course, is to elevate to the highest position the minor term of "boy", of "adolescent", at all the official altars, by adding another one erected to the young god of the worst, of the less good, the inferior, the "unimportant", who is yet strong in his inferior power' (*Pornography*, p. 260). It is there that the pornography written by the writer articulates itself like the erotic game of adolescents, nothing obscure or scandalous, or even explicit, nothing but suggestions – approximations – allusions to junctions or detours. Nothing but *signs*. The pornography of the young and immature, like that of writers, of *adolescents* in short – is it the effort to name, to make an uncertain meaning appear at the frontier of word and drive? It is thus, at least, that Gombrowicz's message comes through to me.

These themes, the betrayal of the page and the page's betrayal, bisexuality and disguise, filiation, immature seducers – clearly do not exhaust the adolescent conflicts and images that punctuate the grand moments of novelistic creation. One could add here the whole literature of character 'formation' that, from Tristram Shandy to Julian Sorel and Bel Ami, retraces the intimate ties between adolescent and novel. Still, these themes seem to me sufficient for indicating how much the polyphonia of the novelistic genre, its ambivalence, its more than oedipal pliancy, its dose of perversity, owe to the open-adolescent structure. Such a writing-mimesis of a structure essentially open, incomplete – is it for the reader anything but a drug? Evoking more catharsis than any elaboration that would eventually realize transference and interpretation, novelistic writing proposes however a certain elaboration internal to sublimation. I will call it semiotic: close to the primary processes awakened in adolescence, reproducing the dramaturgy of adolescent fantasies, absorbing stereotypes, but also capable of genuine inscriptions of unconscious contents that flower in the adolescent pre-conscious. This semiotic elaboration is the container – the form – and sometimes simply the mirror of adolescent transition. Question: must we choose between sending an adolescent to analysis and writing novels for him? Or maybe writing them together? Or having him write alone? The question is hardly serious, even adolescent. From which follows another: is analysis grandmotherly or adolescent? Perhaps, after all, it is never the one without the other – if we wish to remain attentive to an open structure.

This interrogation of the adolescent and writing has in fact led us to perversion and its rapport with the writer. How to understand perversion in a way that is at once faithful and non-complacent: this is what, perhaps, the history of novelistic writing could discover for us. The analyst who is already aware of the fact that his benevolent attention is not exempt from a certain perversion can continue this interrogation by submitting it to his own technique: the closure of the psychoanalytic framework of the flexibilities, the utilization or not of different signs of speech, the taking into consideration of real events outside of their intra-transferential import, etc. These are some of the technical problems that suggest to the analyst the taking into consideration of these 'open structures' that adolescents are ... among others. . . .

Notes

1 Cf. 'Notes on Symbol Formation', *International Journal of Psy.*, XXXVII, 1957, part 6.
2 J.J. Rousseau, *Oeuvres Completes*, Paris, Tome 4, p. 489.
3 Ibid., p. 256.
4 Ibid., p. 746.
5 *Emile*, p. 490.
6 *Essay on the Origin of Languages*, p. 125.
7 Editor's note. Kristeva prepared her own translations of Dostoievski. For the sake of consistency these have been retained.
8 Editor's note. W. Gombrowicz is a Polish writer whose work is extremely popular in France. The references are to the French editions of his work. Of his works in English see: *Diary 1904–1909*, translated by L. Vallee, London, Quartet, 1988; *A kind of Testament*, translated by A. Hamilton, London, Calder & Boyars, 1982; *Possessed*, translated by J.A. Underwood, London, Marion Boyars, 1980.

· 2 ·

Art, Love, and Melancholy in the Work of Julia Kristeva

JOHN LECHTE

> Between classicism and mannerism, [Holbein's] minimalism is the metaphor of scission: between life and death, meaning and non-meaning, it is an intimate and fine reply to our melancholies. (Julia Kristeva, *Soleil noir*)

Artistic endeavour, especially in its forms of literature and painting, has always featured prominently in Julia Kristeva's writing, because for Kristeva, as a psychoanalyst, there is no fundamental discontinuity between the production of a work of art and the life of the individual. Even though this does not mean that a work of art is to be seen simply as a representation of the intentions or personality of the artist, Kristeva's position may yet seem surprising given the tenacity of our structuralist and post-structuralist heritage.

In what follows, I shall try to show that although the function of art might depend on the (psychological) state of the subject (for example, whether we are dealing with love or melancholy), Kristeva views art less as an object, and more as a process, or practice, which 'creates' the subject. In short: art is constitutive of *both* subject and object, and that is why Kristeva emphasizes the notion of 'practice' over 'experience' which presupposes an object.[1] Let us note, before proceeding, the following strong statement by Kristeva where the notion of art as constitutive of the subject, rather than constituted by the subject, is confirmed.

It's necessary to see how all great works of art – one thinks of Mallarmé, of Joyce, of Artaud, to mention only literature – are, to be brief, masterful sublimations of those crises of subjectivity which are known, in another connection, as psychotic crises. That has nothing to do with the freedom of expression of some vague kind of subjectivity which would have been there beforehand. It is, very simply, through the work and the play of signs, a crisis of subjectivity which is the basis for all creation, one which takes as its very precondition the possibility of survival. I would even say that signs are what produce a body, that – and the artist knows it well – if he doesn't work, if he doesn't produce his music or his page or his sculpture, he would be, quite simply, ill or not alive. Symbolic production's power to constitute *soma* and to give an identity is completely visible in modern texts. And moreover, all of his experience, literary as well as critical, is preoccupied with this problem.[2]

Potentially, at least, aesthetic *activity* is within the reach of every one, even if producing an object readily and broadly admired is not. However to equate art entirely with an object is to fetishize it. In this regard, another general remark made by Kristeva can further help to orient our subsequent discussion of art in her work:

Art is the possibility of fashioning narcissism and of subtilizing the ideal.
. . . In the ideal hypothesis, the artist succeeds in probabilizing, relativizing, his own production, as though it were a living system that lives only on condition of being open to the other. A life, a work of art: are these not 'works in progress' only in as much as capable of self-depreciation and of resubmitting themselves to the flames which are, without distinction, the flames of language and of love?[3]

Clearly, Kristeva's view of art is not one that is static and fetishized, but one that is above all dynamic: constitutive rather than constituted. My argument shall be that this dynamic conception of art speaks to our current crisis where the individual's symbolic and imaginary capacities have become atrophied: a growing absence of love, and an increasing presence of melancholia and depression, seem to be increasingly the lot of human beings in this *fin de siècle*. The picture presented in Kristeva's latest book, *Soleil noir*,[4] is thus where we are now; Kristeva's previously published *Tales of Love*[5] presents a picture of where we partially were, and what we may perhaps aspire to – with the help of psychoanalysis. I shall speak later in more detail about these two pictures. However, in order that they may be better understood, let me first of all recall some important aspects of Kristeva's psychoanalytic theory and its implications for a theory of art.

Separation and its Reverberation

Although psychoanalysis in Kristeva's hands does not set the individual over against society (or vice versa), it is true that the emphasis, in the first place, is on the formation of individuals and thus subjectivities, rather than on the social context. In addition, psychoanalysis in general in France, and Kristeva's version of it in particular, attaches far more weight to Freud's *Totem and Taboo* and *Moses and Monotheism* than do other disciplines – whether in France or elsewhere.[6] Kristeva finds much of theoretical interest in both these texts because they offer a framework for understanding the complex interrelation between individual and social life. In order to become a fully social being, the individual must become a competent user of language. Language both constitutes individualities, or subjects, and also the (social) link between them. This is the level of Lacan's Symbolic order. The latter is what constitutes the subjects in their inter-subjectivity. It is the means whereby each subject might be able to produce reality and fantasies in images, the means for producing the order that Lacan designated as the Imaginary. It is the imaginary which is the place of the constitution of an ego ideal. Lacan's Real, to complete the triangle, is what cannot be captured by either the symbolic or imaginary realms. The real is what cannot be symbolized, represented, or expressed in any way. If the subject only *lives* symbolically and imaginarily, the real, on the other hand, is connotative of death. Therefore, the real precedes and succeeds the subject in language and, more generally, the symbolic.

Kristeva's work presupposes that of Lacan's as far as the triangular structure of the Real, the Symbolic and the Imaginary (RSI) is concerned. It should be recognized, however, that each domain is linked to actual processes; they are not entirely abstract. And from this perspective Kristeva can be seen to go further than Lacan. For example, Lacan's subject tends to be the already posited linguistic subject – a subject of desire in search of the object of desire, '*objet petit a*'. This is a divided subject, but not the subject of scission whose stake in the symbolic realm is always under pressure from pure drive energy. Again, we can recall that for Kristeva, it is not sufficient to think in terms of what is always already constituted, but necessary also to work towards achieving the impossible task of bringing the real into the symbolic – or, at any rate, of enlarging symbolic and imaginary capacities in the attempt.

To return to the notion of actual processes, it will be the mother, the empirical evocation of the maternal chora, who also stands at the threshold of the entry of the real into the symbolic. It is the mother, furthermore, who is at the point where the drives become manifest as the material base of language, art and all subjectivity. We are now speaking about the 'semiotic' chora: it is evocative of the real, and thus death, as it is at the same time indicative of the child's initial moves to become separated from the mother. Life and death are here poised confronting each other. As drive energy is partially brought under the control of repression (that is, the symbolic), it assumes '*significance*': the voice as rhythm and timbre, the body as movement, gesture and rhythm; prosody, even word-play, and especially laughter fall within the ambit of the semiotic. Chronologically, the operations of the semiotic can be observed in children before the acquisition of language has been completed. The unarticulated sounds a baby makes thus have *significance* even if they have no specific – symbolic – meaning. The more complete the child's entry into the symbolic, the more repression constitutes an articulation of the spoken or written word. Not to have entered the symbolic at all, that is, not to have separated from the mother – as in extreme psychosis – is to be close to living death. On the other hand, not to be alerted to the material basis of the symbolic which the concept of the semiotic evokes, is to remain at the level of a static, fetishized version of language. The symbolic order embodied in the Name-of-the-Father intervenes in the idyllic union between mother and child to facilitate the child's entry into the symbolic. Such a process has its painful, melancholic side. But provided this pain can be symbolized, nothing untoward is likely to happen.

Avant-garde art of the late nineteenth and twentieth centuries has exploited the semiotic dimension of what Kristeva calls the signifying process. Mallarmé, Joyce, and Artaud have shaken the existing configuration of the symbolic and given rise, in Kristeva's interpretation, to a theory of the subject in process: a subject equally constituted by symbolic and semiotic elements. It is in this sense, therefore, that the subject is also a rhythmic reverberation in the symbolic, a reverberation which is connotative of both union with, and separation from, the mother.

The semiotic is what cannot be entirely grasped by conceptual thought, and is, says Kristeva, at the same time the basis of 'all avant-garde experience since the late nineteenth century'.[7] To be perceived at all, the semiotic cannot but have an aesthetic aspect: it is as close as one can come to language speaking. It is precisely because the semiotic dimension has been excluded from consideration that art has come to be seen exclusively as equivalent to the object produced by the artist of genius – as though an aesthetic realm only belonged to the select few. In Kristeva's terms, this would mean that only the few are truly human.

Poetic Language and Society

The underlying thesis Kristeva presents in the last third of *La Révolution du langage poétique*[8] is that to make real headway in the social and economic transformation of Western society, the very basis of the social has to be confronted. Not to do this is to risk having the same socio-economic conditions reconstituted under a new name. In effect, the symbolic is constitutive of the social as such, as it is also constitutive of (logical) negation within the social sphere. Oppositional political parties, for example, can be accommodated. Western societies tend not to recognize the semiotic level of human existence woven of drive energy, let alone the need to harness such energy aesthetically to avoid its becoming manifest in violence. We could be speaking about France in the late nineteenth century, as Kristeva is, or the highly technocratic societies of the 1980s modelled on the United States or Japan. It is what is rejected by the symbolic which here becomes crucial. In fact, 'rejection' is another term Kristeva uses for Hegel's notion of negativity (the ground of all logical operations). Negation and dichotomy have to be distinguished from negativity and heteronomy.[9] It is the drive charges of rejection which challenge the bland tranquillity of a technocratic structure based on representation. The drives themselves (life drives and death drives) are not a form of vitalism, but 'already semiotic' energy charges.

It is rejection, then, which forms the basis of Mallarmé's and Lautréamont's poetic language in late nineteenth-century France. Poetic language which, in confronting a particularly static version of the symbolic articulated in the bourgeois representative state and society in France, fulfils the ethical function of art by being a signifying practice. Poetic language here 'pluralizes, pulverizes' and 'musicalizes' all static socio-symbolic features – from the family and Catholicism to the naturalist text and the punctual, unitary subject. It challenges the order of these institutions (their rules and syntax for example) as well as institutions as such. The ethical function of art, therefore, is not the same as its ideological, or communicative function:

> This conception of the ethical function of art separates us, in a radical way, from one that would commit art to serving as the representation of a so-called progressive ideology or an avant-garde socio-historical philosophy.[10]

Consequently, the avant-garde poetic language of the late nineteenth century has a political effect to the extent that it transgresses the symbolic law of the Father. It is not another version of that law as a Hegelian negation (alluded to above) would be. As Kristeva expresses it: 'Music in letters is the counterpart of the parliamentary *oratio*',[11] an *oratio* based on the principle of Hegelian negation.

Art and Love – or Subjectivity as an 'Open System'

Separation from the mother (begun as an expulsion of an object by the drives, and completed by the entry into language) is also a precondition of love. This is what *Tales of Love* seeks to analyse and illustrate.

Love is fundamental to psychoanalysis in the transference, opening the way to the cure. The latter is, fundamentally, a defusing, or at least an assuaging, of a difficult separation from the mother. It is the separation from the mother which enables us – as Kristeva says in *Soleil noir*[12] – to become narcissists: that is, to develop an identity, an ego.

From the very beginning of its unfolding, separation is psychically painful. A sense of loss, or emptiness comes to exist where once there was a satisfying union with the mother. At this point, Kristeva refers to Freud's concept of an amalgam of the two parents in primary narcissism which becomes the basis of an 'archaic' or 'primary' identification: the 'father of individual prehistory'.[13] The father in individual prehistory emerges prior to the formation of an object which will accompany the emergence of the subject in language; it is thus prior to any ideal, but is nonetheless the *basis* of all idealization – especially in love. The father of individual prehistory which Kristeva also calls the Imaginary Father is the basis for the formation of a successful narcissistic structure – one that enables the symbolization of loss, and the formation of desire. Ovid's Narcissus before his pool is precisely not an example of the narcissistic psychic structure we have been describing. Narcissus wants otherness: he is in love with his image; but he also refuses it: he will not accept a real other to replace the image. Narcissus, says Kristeva, is 'a borderline case',[14] for the youth beside the pool is frozen at the very point of desiring an object outside himself thereby confirming his subjectivity. Narcissus' death is the sign of the failure of psychic space to form due to the failure of a sense of loss to form as the basis for love – a love which would make the other essential to one's own psychical make-up. The message here, then, is that the ego-self is also other: it is constituted through love. An ego which is not formed in this way, is exactly a de-formed ego that is not open to the world, but closed in upon itself and, like Narcissus, on the way to death.

Love is a synthesis of ideal and affect. In other words the ideal object has to be sought (desired) with passion. The pure ideal (as with the troubadours) is not enough. Passion *in* language is what we are speaking about. Metaphor as condensation in Freud's sense closely approximates the nature of love. That is, metaphor, too, is seen by Kristeva to be more than a linguistic phenomenon: but the point at which ideal and affect come together in language. Love is therefore present in poetry and art in general through the agency of metaphor. Kristeva illustrates the link between love and metaphor with reference to Baudelaire's poetry.

In Baudelaire, it is the theme of perfume which would most closely approximate the notion of metaphor as condensation – as love. According to Kristeva, perfume has 'fusional connotations that condense the intoxicated memory of an invaded maternal body'.[15] Perfume gives the Baudelairean text its great lyricism by dissolving the object, or rather by merging all objects into one: the poet's contemplation, the poet's subjectivity as a subject in process. Baudelaire's contemplation thus becomes the equivalent of condensation – of metaphor – as such. Perfume, Kristeva continues,

> is thus the most powerful metaphor for that archaic universe, preceding sight, where what takes place is the conveyance of the most opaque lovers' indefinite identities, together with the chilliest words: 'There are strong perfumes for which all matter/Is porous. They seem to penetrate glass'. (*The Flask*)[16]

Metaphor as perfume in Baudelaire, as 'synaesthesia' (displacement of sensation), is love as the dissolution of otherness, as the metamorphosis of self into . . . what? Into the metaphor as pure condensation, to be sure: the equivalent of a fusion with the mother which places individual identity at risk. Baudelaire is therefore profoundly inseparable from his art. He needs to develop a way of coping with the loss of a coherent identity which his poetry brings. Dandyism becomes this way of coping for Baudelaire.

Looked at in this context, dandyism is not simply an individual choice subject to sociological analysis. It is also a kind of desperate assertion of independence – of social survival – against the mother. Dandyism is the symbolic appropriation of the maternal position. The question still remains as to why the dandy needs to draw attention to himself ('those flowing locks, pink gloves, coloured nails as well as hair'), why, indeed, he feels the need to be anti-social, rather than social: a punk before the fact. Kristeva's answer, put very simply, is that industrial, technocratic societies do not give recognition to those who wander 'at the borders of the speakable and the visible',[17] that is, in the realm of the musicality of language inhabited by poets and all of us to the extent that, as Mallarmé said, each soul is '*un nœud rythmique*'.[18] Thus the dandy – like today's punks, according to Kristeva – seems to be saying: 'I cannot bear being without the fully articulated symbolic existence, fundamental to a full social existence'.[19]

Dandyism, then, is an attempt to bear the narcissistic wound opened up first of all by the loss of identity in 'perfume' poetry, and, secondly, in public opprobrium. To comport oneself as a dandy is to find the semblance of an identity. Put another way, the artist who dissolves identities and shatters the communicative, representative aspect of language often finds it difficult to gain recognition: that is, to be accepted as different. This type of artist is a threat to a society not open to difference, to the other – to love. New symbolic means are needed to appropriate this difference. For this is not a difference which in the end is simply another version of the same, but a semiotic difference founded on the rejection manifest in phonic rhythms and the 'timbre' of language deriving from the semiotic chora. In short, we are speaking about a fundamental otherness which, to recall our earlier remarks, transcends Hegelian negation. To the extent that the amatory condition is captured in writing as pure (semiotic) lyricism, it is a threat to the society closed to new forms of identity and social relations. As Kristeva forcefully explains:

If through a writing that is synonymous with the amatory condition – an experience at the limits of the identifiable – the writer can find no other place in the bosom of bourgeois society than that of a refugee at the side of non-productive nobility or the Church, which protects fetishes under the symbolic umbrella, we can only interpret that as an indictment of that very society rather than the evidence of the writer's error or 'failure'.[20]

To appreciate, or struggle to appreciate, the lyricism of writing, to be open to the notion that it is the product of another's *nœud rythmique*, of another *as a nœud rythmique*, is to be capable of love for this other. It is to be able to allow this other to become (symbolically) part of one's own self, thereby changing an identity. Love means being open to change in this sense. Such is Kristeva's argument in a nutshell.

Crisis in the 1980s, Kristeva shows, means that the individual is largely dispossessed of an amatory code through which a continually changing, idealizing (symbolic) dimension of love might be expressed. This is also to be deprived, like Narcissus, of the psychic space an unambiguous separation from the mother entails. Intoxication of all kinds ('from drugs to sacred music') has increasingly closed off the individual from the outside world, and taken the place of psychic space: the space of love. To the psychoanalyst, this intoxication is also a symptom of suffering which he or she feels duty-bound to ameliorate. Most of all, though, intoxication deprives the subject of the imaginary and symbolic wherewithal to be a truly living being, rather than a 'corpse under care'.

As a psychoanalyst, Kristeva is working against a deformed subjectivity incapable of love. In conjunction with developments in logic and biology (cf. the work of von Forster), Kristeva proposes that the subject be understood as an 'open system',[21] This means that rather than thinking of the outside world of the other as a threat, we should see it as a stimulus to 'change and adaptation'. Trauma, crisis, and perturbation similarly should be seen as the sources of an 'event' in the life of the subject, something which broadens horizons, and not something to be denied or resisted with a resultant atrophying of psychic space. To the extent that crisis is absorbed into the psychical structure, the latter becomes increasingly more complex and supple, increasingly more capable of love. The greater the capacity for love, the less the other becomes a threat and becomes, in his or her very individuality, a participant in an identity as 'a work in progress' central to 'the amorous state':

We . . . know the mechanisms of this transfer which makes the human psyche an *open system* capable of auto-organization on condition of maintaining a kind of link with the other: these are the *identification* of primary narcissism 'revealing' the subject, and *idealization of the word* of the other. I have called this the amorous state.[22]

Based on love, the cure in analysis gives the psyche over to the other, to difference and variation, making the other an 'event' in the life of the subject. It aims to make this loving condition permanent.

To say that the work of art has analytic effects is to imply that it has the capacity for enlarging the symbolic (artistic, linguistic, religious) and imaginary capacities of the subject who appreciates it. 'The amorous and artistic experiences as two solid aspects of the identificatory process are only ways of preserving our psychic space as a "living system" . . .'[23] – that is, as a work in progress always subject to change and renewal. Consequently, to experience art to the full, we should open ourselves up to the other as the artist s/he is. This is to appreciate art with love. Love and art, therefore, are a mutual opening up of the individual's psyche. Will it be the same for art and melancholy?

Art and Melancholy. Art of Melancholy

If love is a striving, largely fuelled by (symbolic) idealization, for a union with an object, melancholy, as Kristeva outlines it, would correspond to a tendency toward a union with Lacan's Real: that is, for Kristeva, with the mother and death. The union of mother and child is prior to separation, thus prior to the entry into the symbolic – prior to life, in effect. Melancholia, and its more temporary form of depression, would therefore be examples of an unsuccessful separation from the mother, an unsuccessful emergence of primary narcissism and the concomitant Imaginary Father. Seen in this way, the melancholic/depressive is thus not simply displacing hatred for another onto his own ego, as Freud maintained,[24] but rather is dominated by a sadness which would be

the most archaic expression of a non-symbolizable, unnamable narcissistic wound that is so premature that no external agent (subject or object) can be referred to it. For this type of narcissistic depressive, sadness is in reality the only object. More exactly, it is an ersatz of an object to which he attaches himself, and which he tames and cherishes in the absence of anything else.

Consequently, while Freud sees melancholia as a particular kind of object relation, Kristeva argues that the problem is located in the failure of the relation as such to materialize. There is no object for the melancholic, only a sadness as an ersatz of an object; or, as Kristeva goes on to say, there is only a 'Thing' ('*Chose*'), a vague, indeterminate 'something', a 'light without representation' which Nerval captures in his metaphor of a 'black sun' ('*soleil noir*').[25]

In its extreme form, melancholy verges on psychosis, and an almost total failure of the subject to form an identity in the symbolic, and this, because separation from the mother had hardly taken place. Hence, melancholia tends towards a loss of words, of taste for life – towards despair. Despair is the only meaning life has for those so afflicted. No object, then, can replace the mother; no sign can express the loss, and desire fails to emerge.

Unlike the true psychotic, the depressive has not lost the use of signs. Rather, language is always foreign, never maternal. Words have become detached from their link with energy drives; or emotions have become separated from symbolic constructions. In other words, melancholia is the reverse of love with its synthesis of idealization and affect. Melancholia holds the two elements apart.

Melancholia is considered by Kristeva to be the equivalent of a mourning for a partial loss which cannot be symbolized. The individual is that loss, weighed down by tears and silence. Kristeva refers here to the *'dénégation'*[26] of language which relates to the absence of the object. Language begins with a *dénégation*, which the depressive denies. Kristeva explains:

Signs are arbitrary because language begins with a *dénégation* (*Verneinung*) of loss, at the same time as depression occasioned by mourning. 'I have lost an indispensible object which is found to be, in the last instance, my mother', the speaking being seems to say. 'But no, I have found her again in signs, or rather because I accept to lose her, I have not lost her (here is the *dénégation*), I can get her back in language'.[27]

The melancholic's denial of *dénégation* (which is also a denial of representation) results in signs not having the force either of bringing the mother back, or of expressing the pain of loss. Rather than expressing emotion and affect, the subject *becomes* these: melancholics, in short, act out what needs to be elaborated in signs and symbols formed in response to the loss of the object (mother). This detachment of signs from an object thus corresponds to an attachment to the Thing: the object as *not* lost. A chasm now forms between the melancholic subject and its objects, and it is the psychoanalyst's task, Kristeva says, to provide a symbolic 'graft'[28] in order to connect the two domains, thereby turning the Thing into an object. Can the artist do something similar?

Soleil noir will, in all likelihood, become renowned for its analysis of Holbein the Younger's painting of *The Corpse of Christ in the Tomb* (see illustration p. vi), and we shall come to examine this in some detail. But first, art and melancholia should be generally explained.

To begin, we may suppose that the artist tends towards the melancholic pole of the psychical spectrum. Every imaginary artistic work, even those geared to provoke a strong emotional response, is executed with a certain detachment. The artist exemplifies an attachment to the Thing in the sense that there is a continuity between the artist's life – or *'comportement'*, as Kristeva says[29] – and his work; but this, not in the sense that the artist's life is represented in the work, but in the sense that the work is *part* of the artist's life. Perhaps, then, Dostoievski's excessive gambling, equivalent to an evacuation of drive energy, would be the precondition for the detachment, and, as he remarked himself, clarity of mind necessary for him to write his moving fiction. Finally, the artist would evoke the attachment to the mother through the semiotic dimension of the signifying process, where the transposition of affect becomes rhythm, alliteration, intonation, etc. The artist, unlike the melancholic, has control over the use of signs; the true artist is not naive: style (coherence) predominates. The work of art is thus the possible mark, Kristeva suggests, of a 'vanquished' depression.[30]

While the psychotic is incapable of carrying out all linguistic operations successfully, the melancholic masters signs, but not affect. In short, the denial centres predominantly on the primary inscription of affect in the symbolic. Artists, however, are not like either the psychotic or the melancholic in that they very often articulate the primary inscription of loss semiotically, and by this means the loss is given a certain form. While it is impossible to imagine that art could exist without the semiotic being at least minimally present, Kristeva argues that some of Holbein the Younger's paintings, and especially *The Corpse of Christ in the Tomb*, take us very close to a representation of the complete absence of affect in signs which characterizes the melancholic's condition. For Kristeva, therefore, Holbein's painting goes very close to illustrating the denial of *dénégation* and therefore the evacuation of affect which characterizes the melancholic's constructions. This is achieved by a 'minimalism' which isolates the figure of Christ through depicting the body entirely alone in its crypt, and by giving no hint of an idealization of the body, no sign of transcendence, or of passion (semiotic features). Indeed, the spectator cannot very easily identify with this painting. But this is not to say that the same spectator is not directly affected by it through being given a premonition of his or her own death. In short, there is no coded rhetoric in Holbein's *The Corpse of Christ in the Tomb* to alleviate the anguish induced by the intimation of death. Holbein's minimalism places the spectator in touch with death and its synonyms: the unnamable, the real, the void. *The Corpse of Christ in the Tomb*, then, evokes the sadness of separation, enables us to relive it in signs (albeit minimal), and to come as close as possible to experiencing death: a depression, in effect: a disruption in and of the symbolic.

According to Kristeva,[31] Christianity has, through facilitating an imaginary identification with the death of Christ, provided a means of bringing death into the symbolic; or at least it has provided a way for enlarging the imaginary and symbolic means available for coping with death:

In light of this identification, admittedly too anthropological and psychological in the eyes of a strict theology, man is nevertheless bequeathed a powerful symbolic device enabling him to live his death and resurrection in his physical body, thanks to the power of imaginary unification – and its real effects – with the absolute Subject (Christ).[32]

Christ is the Absolute, imaginary subject (ego) forming the border between the real (Mother) and the symbolic (Father). The subject, therefore, comes to occupy the place of art itself, the place transcending death through signs. The analyst thus points to the following scenario: to transcend death (which is also the death of the symbolic) it is necessary to identify with it for all we are worth, expanding our imaginary capacities, and thereby overcoming the unnamable basis of our depression. 'To enter heaven, travel hell', as Joyce put it.[33] We need to put hell into the symbolic, to describe it, name all its aspects, experience it in imagination, and so constitute ourselves as subjects, with an identity. We will become . . . somebody – and this, through transcending nothingness: the void, the unrepresentable.

Kristeva's point is, though, that Holbein's minimalism, depicting death, almost reaches the point of no return – death without resurrection. This is reinforced in Holbein's work, says Kristeva, by the arrival of the protestant iconoclasm leading to an extreme simplicity of signs, almost to the extinction of expressivity. *The Corpse of Christ in the Tomb* thus takes us to the limit of imaginary capacities. In fact, Kristeva argues, Holbein paints the gap in the imaginary which is death: he thereby paints the 'scission' in the psyche between 'death' and 'divine love' (Hegel) – the equivalent of a simultaneous opening-up and closure of the psyche itself. As Kristeva succinctly writes:

Between classicism and mannerism, [Holbein's] minimalism is the metaphor of scission: between life and death, meaning and non-meaning, it is an intimate and fine reply to our melancholies.[34]

Depression and Art in the 1980s

It is not inevitable, however, that the art deriving from a melancholic disposition has a melancholic content, or subject matter. For the issue is not centred on a scene of sadness, or on a melancholic or depressing story. Rather, it is a question of being able to be an artist at all, a question of coming into the realm of the symbolic and developing our imaginary capacities and thereby producing a language for – and thus against – our sadness. Kristeva's clinical experience suggests that it is not simply the case that depressives in Western capitalist societies go through a symbolic death – a death which would hold out the possibility of a rebirth – but more the case of a partial death of the symbolic itself, manifest in the cutting of links with others, and an atrophied imaginary. Here, modern society would be witness to a wasting away of the imaginary that is the equivalent of the death of subjectivity. The real, and the act as such – the destructive aspect of the death drive – then emerge in the void left by the imaginary, and society becomes increasingly marked – despite itself – by terrorism, crime, suicide, and violence of all kinds.[35] It is as though society were living the current crisis (often mistakenly thought to be purely economic) through a kind of melancholic withdrawal, and a concomitant refusal to give a name to crisis in its various modes of articulation, a nomination which would open up new possibilities for change. Indeed, there is a strong hint in Kristeva's *Soleil noir* that in the drive to establish the truth as adequation (that is, making the symbolic equivalent to the real) within a milieu of extreme iconoclasm, love and art (the basis of idealism and the imaginary) find it hard, if not impossible, to exist.

Extreme iconoclasm leads to nihilism, which Nietzsche opposed in calling for a 'revaluation of all values': that is, value has to be put back into values after nihilism has itself been discredited. Interestingly, both the melancholic, and the nihilist as Nietzsche defined him, find that the world is without meaning: nihilism is 'the radical repudiation of value, meaning, and desirability'.[36] We may further note that for Nietzsche, nihilism does not derive solely from distress, but from a view that truth is singular, unitary, monistic (the ideal form of both science and Christianity alike). For such a view of truth opens the way to its total collapse: '"God is truth" risks becoming "All is false"'.[37] Such a framework produces its own demise because there is no provision for the recognition of difference as part of truth, and of art, as constitutive of subjectivity, as part of difference. What we need is an artistic science lest we die of scientific truth. For Nietzsche, art affirms, gives a sense of power to the artist; it creates egos as much as objects, and is never pessimistic.

And so although Nietzsche may have underestimated the power that Christian art brings with it – a power of resurrection in signs – the rudiments are there, it seems to me, for linking Nietzsche's notion of a revaluation of values with Kristeva's analysis of melancholy. For art, in both thinkers, is the way to a rebirth – although this is present in a much more elaborate form in Kristeva than in Nietzsche; Kristeva, in short, is Nietzsche's heir on this point. While Nietzsche dances on the surface of things, as it were, Kristeva, the analyst, opens up new, complex symbolic domains. To know that is also to have read Kristeva with love – in the sense that her work has, like art, analytic effects.

In a discussion organized in 1983 following the publication of *Tales of Love*,[38] it was suggested[39] that Kristeva had in effect moved away from her early emphasis on the importance of the semiotic domain, only to privilege the symbolic once again. I believe that such a criticism is entirely misplaced precisely because it was never a question of *privileging* the semiotic in works like *La Révolution du langage poétique*, but of giving it equal prominence with the symbolic. It was never a question, in other words, of proposing that the avant-garde were to be heralded for their destruction of the symbolic order. Rather, it was a case of the music of language being recognized as being as fundamental as syntax in the constitution of language. Similarly, with her analysis of love and melancholy, it is still *not* a question of returning to the symbolic, or moving out of the semiotic; for Kristeva has never moved from suggesting the need for a balance to be maintained between the two. As a result, the call to recognize the importance of idealization in the formation of the subject, is a recognition that there is evidence in social life of a risk of stultifying the imaginary domain in the subject, a domain that is fundamental to ego-formation.

If, however, melancholy or depression is a feature of our contemporary experience, we have to ask whether so-called post-modernity is the breakthrough many have been waiting for. In the flight from dogma and the impossible precariousness of faith, may we, in the West, not be risking collective suicide, or at least a symbolic death? For Kristeva, the answer seems to be 'Yes', and we should thereby be awakened to the need to have a 'new loving world surface from the eternal return of historical and mental cycles'.[40]

Notes

1 See Julia Kristeva, *Revolution in Poetic Language*, translated by Margaret Waller, New York, Columbia University Press, 1984, pp. 195–7. Beginning at the point where (non-Sartrean) phenomenology left off in its reflections on the subject-object relation, Kristeva acknowledges, in her discussion of Hegel, that phenomenology nevertheless greatly refined our understanding of this relationship. What this philosophy left out of account, however, was the movement which created *both* subject and object (the thetic moment) – 'practice' as movement – so that consciousness, and therefore 'experience', remained predominant in the end. The whole of the theoretical introduction to *Revolution in Poetic Language* could be seen as a refinement of phenomenology in this sense. The moment of practice also conforms to the *aesthetic* moment given that the latter cannot, in Kristeva's terms, be reduced to an object produced by a subject.

2 Perry Meisel, 'Interview with Julia Kristeva', translated by Margaret Waller, in *Partisan Review*, no. 51, Winter 1984, pp. 131–2.

3 Julia Kristeva, '*Histoires d'amour – Love Stories*' (discussion paper), in *ICA Documents: Desire*, London, Institute of Contemporary Arts, 1984, p. 21.

4 Julia Kristeva, *Soleil noir: dépression et mélancholie*, Paris, Gallimard, 1987.

5 Julia Kristeva, *Tales of Love*, translated by Leon S. Roudiez, New York, Columbia University Press, 1987.

6 Cf., here, Stephen Frosh, *The Politics of Psychoanalysis: An Introduction to Freudian and Post-Freudian Theory*, London, Macmillan, 1987, pp. 41–2, where a sceptical (Anglo-Saxon?) view of Freud's *Totem and Taboo* is put forward – a view quite different to Kristeva's.

7 *Revolution in Poetic Language*, p. 185.

8 Cf. Julia Kristeva, *La Révolution du langage poétique. L'avant-garde à la fin du XIXe siècle: Lautréamont et Mallarmé*, Paris, Seuil, 1974, pp. 361ff.

9 Julia Kristeva, *Polylogue*, Paris, Seuil, 1977, p. 64. This is my own translation, as are all subsequent quotations from French texts.

10 *Revolution in Poetic Language*, p. 233.

11 *La Révolution du langage poétique*, p. 402.

12 *Soleil noir*, p. 38.

13 *Tales of Love*, pp. 25–6.

14 Ibid., p. 115.

15 Ibid., p. 329.

16 Ibid., p. 334.

17 Ibid., p. 339.

18 See Stephane Mallarmé, *Œuvres complètes*, Paris, Gallimard, 1945, p. 644.

19 See, in this regard, Julia Kristeva, 'Les Looks sont entrées dans Paris', *L'Infini*, no. 5, Winter 1984, p. 16.

20 *Tales of Love*, p. 339.

21 For Kristeva's treatment of the notion of the subject as an 'open system' see *Tales of Love*, pp. 13–16, 379–82; 'Événement et révélation', *L'Infini*, no. 5, Winter 1984, pp. 3–11, and 'Les Looks sont entrées dans Paris', ibid., pp. 14–19.

22 'Événement et révélation', p. 5.

23 Julia Kristeva, 'Joyce et le retour d'Orphée', *L'Infini*, no. 8, Autumn 1984, p. 5.

24 See S. Freud, 'Mourning and Melancholia', in *On Metapsychology*, *The Pelican Freud Library*, vol. XI, Harmondsworth, Penguin, 1964 and 1984, pp. 251–68.

25 Cf. *Soleil noir*, p. 22.

26 I leave this term in the French to mark its difference from both negation (which has been used to translate Freud's *Verneinung*), and disavowal. *Dénégation*, as will be seen, connotes a negation which is also an implicit affirmation.

27 *Soleil noir*, p. 55.

28 Ibid., p. 64.

29 Ibid., p. 141.

30 Ibid., p. 76.

31 Cf., in particular, ibid., pp. 143–6.

32 Ibid., p. 145.

33 Cited by Jean-Louis Houdebine in 'Joyce: littérature et religion', *Tel Quel*, no. 89, 1981, p. 69.

34 *Soleil noir*, p. 148.

35 A point reiterated by Kristeva in an interview entitled 'Les abîmes de l'âme', in *Magazine littéraire*, no. 224, July-August 1987, p. 17.

36 Cf. Friedrich Nietzsche, *The Will to Power*, translated by Walter Kaufmann and R. J. Hollingdale, New York, Vintage, 1968, p. 7.

37 Ibid.

38 See Julia Kristeva, *'Histoires d'amour - Love Stories'* and 'Julia Kristeva in Conversation with Rosalind Coward', in *ICA Documents: Desire*, London, Institute of Contemporary Arts, 1984, pp. 18–27.

39 Ibid., p. 27.

40 *Soleil noir*, p. 265.

· 3 ·

The An-Arche of Psychotherapy

NOREEN O'CONNOR

As a psychotherapist one of my principal concerns is that of allowing for plurality of expressions – the speech of individuals which
is irreducible to a unified rationality. This is a concern to maintain
differences and to reject the notion that there is one specific ideal
of being a human being whether it be a Platonic philosopher or a
Heideggerian poet shepherding Being. Many people come to
therapy because they are locked within the Same, a totality of feeling, a way of being in the world that is uneasy, unbearable yet felt
as irrevocable and fixed, not allowing for otherness. Can we list
these 'fixations', label them as symptoms of known psychic conditions and prescribe the cure and thus to living both joy and
vulnerability? This question highlights one central feature of
psychodynamic psychotherapy, namely, that it is not a practice of
ontological topologies, not the practice of a question-answer structure within the parameters of thinking the truth of Being. Within
this ontological perspective there is an operative assumption that
not only is the questioner involved in the Being that he questions
but that Being is open to understanding. This leads to the view
that in principle the enquirer is able to ground his own grounding
meaning through his relationship to Being. Here the question 'who
am I?' can be posed only as a 'what-question' because Being can
be approached only in terms of generality. Gadamer bears out this
point with his argument in *Truth and Method* that the primary
hermeneutic requirement is one's own fore-understandings as they
are drawn from previous relations to the matter in hand. This
presence of anticipation and retention as text 'contains not only
this formal element that a text should fully express its meanings,

but also that what it says should be the whole truth'.[1] Here then the primary interpretation occurs in terms of a grasp of the particular in the light of the general. The 'I' as open to question, or as able to be understood, appears in the mode of generality. This means that the universal 'I' is held in speech while its particularity escapes.

Even if the question 'who understands?' is answered by the monosyllabic 'me', without any content, nonetheless, in this context the answer must mean 'me who is known to you', 'me whose voice you find in your memories', 'me that you can situate in the system of your history'.[2] In this self-presencing of the Logos the 'who' is lost in the articulation of 'what'. For Heidegger and Gadamer the answer to the question 'who understands?' must take the form of an exposition of essence, for the question assumes that thinking and Being are within Being – the 'who' is 'one who understands'. Thus, truth must consist in the exposition of Being to itself, in the consciousness of self, where consciousness implies knowledge or possession of self. This involves a denial of difference, of otherness, because it implies a sovereign thinker who reduces everything to himself through an intellectual grasp. An ontologist might object to this and argue that what escapes categorization is precisely the uniqueness of self and other; however, by describing the relationship with the other in terms of a totality or system which is completely open to understanding or interpretation the possibility is established of the relationship as able to be possessed by the one who understands, or interprets.

Freud's principal contribution to the twentieth century was the recognition of the resourceful character of the lived speech of one individual to another who then responds in a particular manner. What emerges from this conversation is, in a sense, a new speaking of that which is not anticipated, not already known, but yet is felt to be that which is most familiar. In the *Phaedo* (62b) Plato presented us with the notion of speech emergent from the inequality or asymmetry of interlocutors. Plato postulates the Stranger (*Phaedo* 57b, 58b) as calling to the soul who dwells in her own place, alone. The role of the Stranger is such that he cannot be encompassed, yet by his call or invitation, he can highlight the presuppositions of the community. Desire emerges through the revelation of the other in his call to the autonomous subject and thereby erodes the absoluteness of Being. Desire is not just an exigence towards immortality because its objective is the other, the Stranger: 'The absolutely foreign alone can instruct us. And it is only man who could be absolutely foreign to me, refractory to every typology, to every genus, to every classification . . .'.[3]

Kristeva succinctly expresses the otherness inherent in the psychoanalytic enterprise:

From past to present, from frustration to desire, from the parameter of pleasure to the parameter of death . . . [the analyst] dazes the analysand with the unexpectedness of his interpretation: even so, however, the unexpectedness of the analysis is in any case sustained by a constant: the desire for the Other.[4]

In her paper 'Psychoanalysis and the Polis' Kristeva discusses psychoanalytic interpretation which cannot be confined to a hermeneutics. The analyst does not give meaning or reassurance of identity to her patients, she does not speak from the position of a fixed system or prescriptive morality. Kristeva stresses the subject's symbolic integration of negativism, rejection, and the death drive, through his ability to distinguish propositional statements from speaking which is addressed to another for mutual understanding. In Kristeva's view psychoanalysis challenges the foundationalism or formalism of western metaphysics. Such formalism involves shared notions of original experience and givenness. The experience is original, foundational, or ultimate because it is that to which all others refer, or to which they may be reduced, while it itself is not reducible to any other experience. Hence, whatever name is used – God, Being, History, Tradition – the origin, irreducible in its ultimateness, is both original as the ultimate experience and simultaneously originating as giving origin. The positing of a foundational structure does not provide a model for pluralist expression, for the discourse of desires, wishes, fears. This involves an acknowledgement of asymmetry of human relationships, the difference yet relationship between speakers. The desire to possess one's own origin, to be one's self as self-knowledge, is the desire to exclude otherness or difference.

Kristeva argues that analytic speech reveals the desire to return to the origin which she designates as the archaic mother. This desire subtends all speech. The archaic mother is resistant to meaning, she is unnamable. The task of the analyst is to open the space for the unnamable, to see it as a phantasm. This involves shifting obvious 'realistic' meaning from speech to allow for the emergence of what Kristeva calls the meaninglessness or madness of desire. She maintains that one is ill when one is not loved. A central assumption of psychoanalysis is that present unhappiness, suffering, occurs because of failure of communication with others, primarily parents, in the past – the child speaks and is not heard. psychoanalysis then is communication about communication. Central to this endeavour is the specification of subjectivity in terms of language and time. Against the Cartesian ego and Husserl's transcendental ego Kristeva specifies subjectivity as a process, the subject of enunciation. Philosophers are perennially questioning and reformulating the notion of time and subjectivity. Historians, archaeologists, physicists, biographers, religions, provide various theories of time in relation to the objects of their investigations. Psychoanalysis provides a theory of the genesis of the psyche – the timing of the subject in its instinctual and/or object relationships. Since 3-month-old babies cannot speak in our syntax about their relationships, psychoanalysts have provided various hypotheses, in some cases claimed to be facts, based on their work with older people about the experiences of the early stages of life. Kristeva refers to this difficulty or impossibility of gaining access to childhood in *Desire in Language* and she maintains that in Western thought a discourse on childhood involves a confrontation between thought and what it is not.[5]

The Oedipus complex has been postulated in order to explain how it is that we become sex-gendered people and how we enter the symbolic order, language. Prior to this it is assumed that the baby functions with polymorphous instinctual drives and is established in a dyad with its mother. Kristeva's originality in this area is that by positing the subject as subject of enunciation she expands our notion of language to include the pre-oedipal, pre-symbolic expression without subsuming it into the later syntactical development. She terms this early expression the semiotic relation:

The *semiotic* [is] a psychosomatic modality of the signifying process; in other words, not a symbolic modality but one articulating (in the largest sense of the word) a continuum: the connections between the (glottal and anal) sphincters in (rhythmic and intonational) vocal modulations, or those between the sphincters and family protagonists, for example.[6]

The semiotic is not simply a stage or phase surpassed in later integrations, but Kristeva emphasizes the fact that the subject is always both semiotic and symbolic. She uses the Platonic term, *chora*, to elucidate the various processes anterior to sign and syntax. The notion of the chora also helps us to consider the genesis of psychic pain, suffering, sadness. Kristeva specifies the chora as the place where the subject is both generated and negated, where the unity of the subject is fragmented by the changes and stases that produce him. Although the chora is not a 'meaning' available to representation it is, nevertheless, a modality of significance 'in which the linguistic sign is not yet articulated as the absence of an object and as the distinction of real and symbolic'[7] Kristeva specifies the symbolic as arising from the relation to the other through constraints of biological differences and historical family structures. The symbolic stage of development begins with the mirror stage to which psychoanalysts have attributed the capacities for absence and representation.

As I have already mentioned, Kristeva stresses the importance of the subject's desire to return to the resistant archaic mother and the way in which the analyst's attentiveness to the desire opens space for the unnamable. In *Powers of Horror* Kristeva offers a fascinating analysis of borderline psychosis in the context of the pre-oedipal relationship of the baby to its mother, focusing on feelings of rejection, fear, and aggression. The term 'abjection' is introduced in order to describe the revulsion and horror of the pre-oedipal attempt to separate from the mother, that is, the attempt to separate from the mother prior to the autonomy of language:

The abject is the violence of mourning for an 'object' that has always already been lost.[8]

Kristeva posits abjection as the object of primary repression. Abjection shatters narcissism when repression is released and then 'the death that I am provokes horror'.[9]

In a commentary on 'Little Hans' Kristeva elaborates the kind of communication that is effected by phobic states. Processes of condensation are integral to the production of phobias. The phobic 'object' is not an already constituted object but rather the representative of drive. Communication through phobias arises from an incapacity to produce metaphors. In this context analysis has two main tasks, first, the restitution of a memory, a language, to unnamable and namable states of fear, and second, to make the analysand aware of the void underpinning the play with the signifier and primary processes. Kristeva describes the language of phobia as one of 'want'. Here language itself has become a counter-phobic object, it barricades a discourse which has to be tracked down through that which is not spoken.[10]

Margaret Little designates borderline psychosis as a state of undifferentiation between the psyche and *soma* and the failure of fusion between ego and id. States of excitement are felt as threats of annihilation. Kristeva describes this state of being in the world in terms of experiencing a collapse of a border between one's body and the world. Here one is flooded with bodily insides – the fluidity of blood, sperm, excrement. She describes the abjection of these flows which become the sole object of sexual desire. The subject of borderline psychosis, like any speaker, fears castration but for him it is not only a part of himself that he loses but his whole life. His immersion in the bodily flow spares him the risk of a castration which is integral to a relationship with an other. Kristeva maintains that the borderline subject is asking for a rebirth in which he can find the speech that belongs to him.[11] She argues that the borderline patient has never felt loved for himself because, paradoxically, his mother loved only him, she did not love any other: 'The oedipal negation of the father is here linked with a complaint against an adhesive maternal wrapping and it leads the subject towards psychic pain dominated by the inability to love'.[12]

During psychoanalytic treatment the borderline subject identifies with the analyst. Kristeva specifies two types of identification, first, a primal one resulting from affection for the archaic mother as well as anxious guilt, and second, the introjection into the ego of an object that is already libidinal. Kristeva argues that the subject exists only in so far as he identifies with the other in so far as he speaks. The analyst while being the object of identification is also a non-object in that he evokes the analysand's non-object-orientated layers of drives. This allows for the possibility of transference with people in non-object-orientated psychic states such as a borderline state.

Kristeva traces the genesis of archaic unity in terms of the phallus desired by the mother. The identity of the mother and her desire is the unity of the imaginary father. Kristeva argues that primary identification involves a transference to/from the imaginary father and that this is correlative with the mother being ab-jected: 'Narcissism would be that correlation [with the imaginary father and the ab-jected mother] enacted around the central emptiness of that transference'.[13] Narcissism is a defence against the emptiness of separation and the representations, projections, identifications involved in it are attempts to deny that emptiness. Psychosis reveals that the representation of our speech rests upon emptiness. Kristeva warns of the analytic danger of conceiving narcissism as origin as unanalysable. This can result in the presentation of interpretative discourse as either comfortably reassuring or as a confrontational hostility; these attitudes on the part of the analyst collude with the narcissistic state. This is why Kristeva stresses the importance of opening out the more archaic operations of the psyche.

Kristeva praises Freud for challenging the western concept of subjectivity in terms of self-conscious rationality. The notion of the unconscious introduces otherness and dethrones the epistemological primacy of the ego. The question of difference, heterogeneity, arises within a discussion of what is sometimes interpreted as the solipsistic formulation offered by psychoanalysis. A common argument proposed against psychoanalysis is the self-justification of its theoretical stand; disagreements are interpreted in terms of repression and defence. Can the analysand say 'no' to the analyst's interpretation without this being interpreted as a defence? It depends on the specific situation whether the 'no' is in fact operating as a defence or whether it is an assertion of separateness. Can one assert this and remain in analysis? Is every exchange within the analytic situation a matter of transference and countertransference interpretable, at least in principle, by the analyst? If this 'no' is not transferential yet acknowledged, what then is the status of the interlocutors – do they remain analyst and analysand or is this a collapse into a humanistic conception of an exchange between two self-contained egos? In his *Letter on Humanism* Heidegger argues that all forms of humanism agree that the humanity of man is already determined with regard to an already established interpretation of nature, history and the world.[14] Furthermore, language becomes a tool, a means of communication which is determined by the public realm which decides in advance what is intelligible and what must be rejected as unintelligible. A humanistic specification of the interlocutors would, then, preclude otherness, difference. In a culture dominated by the *logos* there is no fundamental interruption, for all contestation and interruption of discourse is automatically translated in terms of the discourse itself. Hence, as Gadamer argues, it survives the death of the interlocutors who utter it as cultural heritage assuring the very continuity of the culture itself.

Levinas introduces his notion of the asymmetry of human relationships in terms of the face-to-face relation. Here the Other in his otherness cannot appear as the result of an objectifying act, that is, in the affirmation that the object of consciousness, while distinct from consciousness, is a product of consciousness.[15] Levinas proposes the model of the face-to-face relationship in order to designate the irreplaceable uniqueness of each human being where this uniqueness is precisely what escapes categorization. He argues that it is in relationship to the other person/persons that this arises. What is at issue is the specification of subjectivity as ethical, that is, as separate, other, yet in a relationship of responsibility, vulnerability. The subjects are specified as interlocutors, each inviting the other to respond, to move out of egocentricity, yet where this response is not 'meaningful', it is 'for nothing'. Otherness here is specified as that which cannot be thematized yet is the specificity of an individual in relation to me. The realm beyond intentionality, as communication, introduces otherness not as the term of a project, but as the relation with the neighbour in the sense of he who has meaning before one gives it to him. The face is not a presence announcing an 'unsaid' which lies behind and which, in principle, could be said. The face-to-face is a saying that in being said at each moment breaks the definition of that which it says, and breaks through the totality that it embraces.[16] Levinas' task is not one of distinguishing between the lived, as spontaneously operative, and efforts to account for it critically as operative totality. Even within the confines of a more traditional kind of phenomenological investigation the notion of lived experience is not treated merely as simple repetition of that which has already gone before. The work of Gadamer and Merleau-Ponty, for example, stresses that questions can be asked which challenge and which seek to overcome the insights held in our cultural store. But Levinas' central point here is that responsibility of one-for-the-Other does not occur within the tension of a naive, lived, unreflection which would be available to thematization in some manner. For the interval, or difference, which separates one from the Other, as well as the non-difference of the one-for-the-Other cannot be simply gathered into a theme, or established as a state of the soul.[17]

Kristeva claims that it is psychoanalysis that gives heterogeneity an analysable status by designating it as sexual desire and/or death wish. She interprets deconstruction as relativizing truth and thereby not adequate for theorizing the analytic process which she maintains is centrally concerned with truth (of interpretation) and the ethical. For her a practice is ethical when it dissolves narcissistic fixations 'to which the signifying process succumbs in its socio-symbolic realization'.[18]

What is the ethical stand of psychoanalysis *vis-à-vis* its claim to account for sexual difference? In 'Stabat Mater' Kristeva stresses the irreconcilable interest in both sexes in asserting their differences. To what extent does psychoanalysis allow for the unveiling of this interest? In pursuing the question of how we become men and women, of explaining heterosexuality, is there some operative assumption that we know about homosexuality, that we can explain adult desire in terms of regression or fixation? Can desire be an object of explanation? How can psychoanalysis reconcile its claim to acknowledge the specificity of each person's love and fear while its theoretical stand maintains expressions such as the following from Kristeva:

Beneath homosexual libido, which our social objectives catch and maintain captive, the chasms of narcissistic emptiness spread out; although the latter can be a powerful motive for ideal or superegotic cathexis, it is also the primary source of inhibition.[19]

. . . the girl . . . will retain the traces of that primary transference only if assisted by a father having a maternal character, who nevertheless will not be of much help in her breaking away from the mother and finding a heterosexual object. She will thus tend to bury that primal identification under the disappointed feverishness of the homosexual, or else in abstraction which, as it flies away from the body, fully constitutes itself as 'soul' or fuses with an Idea, a Love, a Self-Sacrifice.[20]

How can psychoanalysis think sexual difference if it works with an operative assumption of 'knowing' sexuality, exemplified in many cases by the refusal of major psychoanalytic institutes to accept lesbians and homosexual men as training candidates? Joanna

Ryan raised this issue in a very incisive manner recently when she addressed the first British conference on Feminism and Psychotherapy. She argues against a prevalent psychoanalytic view that adult sexuality is determined by early fantasies and identifications. Instead she stresses the notion that all adult sexuality is complex, partial, fragmentary, and only precariously established.[21]

I have argued that it is of crucial importance that there is consistency between the practical claims made by psychotherapists and their 'theoretical' claims, that is, concern for the status of their ontological, epistemological, and, most important, ethical statements. I have introduced some concepts of central importance in Kristeva's elaboration of psychoanalytical notions of time, language, and subjectivity. Finally, I have questioned the consistency of her position on the interpretation of the central issue of psychoanalysis, that of sexual desire.

Psychoanalysts devote a lot of attention to elucidating the difficulty of separating from the mother. My question is, why is it that psychoanalysts have such difficulty in separating from the Father?

Notes

1 Hans G. Gadamer, *Wahrheit und Methode*, Tubingen, Mohr, 1960, p. 278; *Truth and Method*, ed. G. Barden and J. Cumming, London, Sheed & Ward, 1975, p. 262.

2 Emmanuel Levinas, *Totalité et Infini: Essai sur l'exteriorité*, The Hague, Martinus Nijhoff, 1961, p. 275; English translation by A. Lingis, *Totality and Infinity: An Essay on Exteriority*, Pittsburgh, Duquesne, 1969, p. 299. Here Levinas argues that the Being of the existent is a *logos* that is the world of no one.

3 Ibid., p. 46/73.

4 Julia Kristeva, 'Psychoanalysis and the Polis', in *The Kristeva Reader*, ed. Toril Moi, Oxford, Blackwell, 1986, p. 311.

5 Julia Kristeva, *Desire in Language: A Semiotic Approach to Literature and Art*, ed. Leon Rodiez, translated by Thomas Gora, Alice Jardine, and Leon Rodiez, Oxford, Blackwell, 1980, p. 276.

6 Julia Kristeva, *Revolution in Poetic Language*, translated by Margaret Waller, New York, Columbia University Press, 1984, pp. 28–9.

7 Ibid., p. 26.

8 Julia Kristeva, *Powers of Horror. An Essay on Abjection*, translated by Leon Rodiez, New York, Columbia University Press, 1982, p. 15.

9 Ibid., p. 25.

10 Ibid., pp. 34–8.
11 Ibid., p. 50.
12 Julia Kristeva, 'Freud and Love: Treatment and its Discontents', in *The Kristeva Reader*, p. 251.
13 Ibid., p. 257.
14 Martin Heidegger, *Platons Lehre von der Wahrheit: Mit einem Brief Uber den 'Humanismus'*, Berne, Franke, 1954.
15 Emmanuel Levinas, *Autrement qu', être où au-delà de l'essence*, The Hague, Martinus Nijhoff, 1974, p. 40.
16 Ibid., p. 62.
17 Emmanuel Levinas, *En decouvrant l'existence avec Husserl et Heidegger*, Paris, Vrin, 1967, p. 232.
18 Kristeva, *Revolution in Poetic Language*, p. 233.
19 Kristeva, 'Freud and Love': Treatment and its Discontents', in *The Kristeva Reader*, p. 258.
20 Ibid., p. 262.
21 Joanna Ryan, 'Lesbian Therapists; Some Theoretical and Practical Considerations', presentation to the First Conference in Britain on Feminism and Psychotherapy, Leeds, April 1987, p. 12.

· 4 ·

The Ethics of Sexual Difference

ALISON AINLEY

The alignment of the figure of woman as mother and the possibility of a reconceptualized notion of ethical relations may seem to be an echo of an already existing equation. The figure of the mother is traditionally associated with the embodiment of idealized virtues of forbearance, fortitude, care and patience; an equation which, under relations of patriarchy, works ultimately not as a paradigm for other ethical relations, but as a site of constraint and exploitation. Here the qualities associated with caring, with 'access to the other'[1] via an attempt to address the vulnerabilities of his or her needs, are conscripted to the interests of the classical family structure and seem to hold that structure in place.

Nevertheless, Kristeva seems to suggest a re-examination of the equation of ethics and maternity,[2] particularly in the final parts of 'Stabat Mater' and 'Women's Time'.[3] Such a re-examination is prompted by two questions Kristeva raises in the course of 'Stabat Mater': first, the feminist question, What does this desire for motherhood correspond to? and secondly, the question taken up from Spinoza or Freud, Are women subject to ethics? The second question is important in that it draws attention to the ethical framework within which such a question may be raised at all. It is a framework which valorizes freedom and equality for all individuals, and yet simultaneously demands that the criteria for achieving those aims be those generally associated with men – a capacity for abstraction and an ability to compete in a public arena being just two examples. Such a framework disavows the inequality which seems to arise when distinctions between individuals are made, and yet also promotes certain qualities at the expense of others.

Both questions concern the specificity or non-specificity of sexual difference in the realm of ethical concerns, and, in particular, the determinations placed upon maternity in this realm. The problems arise in attempting to articulate what is involved in the conjunction of ethics and maternity in a feminist context without merely reinforcing the existing determinations.

In a famous passage from the paper 'Some Psychical Consequences of the Anatomical Distinctions Between the Sexes', Freud states:

I cannot evade the notion (though I hesitate to give it expression) that the level of what is ethically normal is different in women from what it is in men. Their superego is never so inexorable, so impersonal, so independent of its emotional origins as we require it to be in men. Characteristics which critics of every epoch have brought up against women – that they show less sense of justice than men, that they are less ready to submit to the greater exigencies of life, that they are more often influenced in their judgements by feelings of affection or hostility – all these would be amply accounted for in the formation of the superego which we have inferred above.[4]

Freud's speculation on the ethical inequality of men and women points to the contradiction inherent in, on the one hand sustaining universal ethical norms or laws, and on the other, positing determining differences between men and women, whether biological or cultural. Because Freud is following the differential development of men and women's psychic identities it makes sense in this context to consider whether this results in different apprehensions of ethics. But the next step is to assume that women's apprehension is necessarily inferior or defective. However, if rather than making this assumption, we examine the criteria of neutral ethical action assumed in this passage, it turns out to be a capacity for acting in such a way as to be free of emotion, impersonal and abstractly judgmental, capacities which are then correlated with men's behaviour. This legacy of the Enlightenment, which manifests itself in liberal moral structures, emphasizes the individual moral choice at the expense of a morality with a history or histories, i.e., one consonant with a network of social relations of power. It occludes such relations of power in the neutrality of a universal agent. It is the introduction of some form of difference, whether cultural or biological or a complex interrelation of these, which begins to raise questions about the assumptions of such a framework.

Kristeva's interest in interpreting the symbolic aspects of motherhood becomes politicized, in the sense that the premature rejection or valorization of conventional understandings of this aspect of women's experience may allow such determinations to be incorporated into existing structures. Thus Kristeva's warnings of the dangers of becoming 'either militant or victim'[5] are attempts to confront such potential incorporation. The *rejection* of motherhood in its symbolic forms, as, for example, in the figure of the Virgin Mary or as bearer of the sanctified values of the family, may position a woman as apparently counter or marginal to the central social and economic forces, leaving her trapped in the very oppositional structure which profits from this dichotomous form of dissent. Conversely, the *celebration* of motherhood as a positive aspect of women's experience which omits consideration of its constraints, may yoke it to the patriarchal reduction of women to mother. These are obviously simplified contradictions, but they do seem to leave feminism in an ambiguous relation to motherhood. However, it is such ambiguity which, Kristeva suggests, may provide some critical means to consider the complex strands comprising motherhood. Consequently, the importance of a theoretical and aesthetic practice which can confront this area lies in its ability to rupture those aspects of the socio-symbolic structure which seem most prone to becoming rigid formulations.

In *Revolution in Poetic Language*, Kristeva identifies such practice as a practice of dissent, a practice as the frontier at which ethics develops. She writes: 'The ethics that develops in the process of negativity's unfolding is not the kind of "ethics" that consists in obedience to laws.'[6] Here she seems to be suggesting that the location of ethical practice should no longer lie in the reformulation and attempted perfection of rules and laws. Instead, the disruptive effect of the subject in process/on trial as it is worked out in Kristeva's theorization points toward a different trajectory of the ethical subject. The constant transgression and renewal of the subject's positioning with regard to the process of signification *reinserts* such a subject into the transformation of community and discourse. As a consequence it seems it is the boundaries at which transformations are taking place and new practices are being forged where the focus of attention should lie.

This trajectory is presently contextualized in the work of Emmanuel Levinas,[7] in the questions which Levinas directs to the priority of a unified subjectivity in philosophy. Levinas is important in this area because he puts aside the immediate attempt to redefine any ethics concerned with the privileged relation of an ethical subject to a guiding principle, and instead occasions the introduction of the other as irreducible alterity – hence the difference, not identity, of ethical agents. In addition, Levinas also broaches the question of sexual difference in relation to the transformation of ethical life. The significance of 'the feminine' is that of an essential rupture to what Levinas calls 'the virility of the force of being'.[8]

For Levinas, the feminine appears as that which disrupts and transforms this realm, and yet also facilitates its continuance, since the exterior realm, the public realm where signification takes place, would be a closure without the undecidable or equivocal feminine 'interiority'. Consequently, the deployment of the feminine appears to be a strategic adoption of the oppositional structuring in which women are encoded as other, or as the excess which escapes, and yet also provide the boundary to that excess. For Levinas, the feminine provides the basis for rethinking ethical relations since it corresponds to the otherness established in terms of, for example, de Beauvoir's 'woman as other'[9] and yet also attempts to cut across the violence of the determining gaze by situating ethical possibility not in this determination, but in the command, or address, of the other.

The feminine is also aligned with the erotic realm, which is a dimension in which silence and equivocation put into question the distance of exteriority. Signification takes place in the space of such a distance, but the intimacy of the erotic relation disrupts such a space with silence, allusions and equivocal language uses.[10]

For Levinas, the dimension of fecundity is related to the symbolic aspect of reproduction, and hence the possibility of something which lies beyond the immediate present. It cuts through and across Levinas' characterization of voluptuousness, or the self's immersion with itself, to provide a glimpse of 'an endless recommencement of a different order of time'.[11] Nevertheless, Levinas' notion of fecundity is not intended to be elevated to the status of a continuous ideal, to which the love relation is subordinated as a part of that project. It arises through erotic desire in the dimension of interiority. But not does it remain enclosed within itself as a biological telos to be projected onto the world.

Levinas' conception of infinite time cannot be reduced to the individual desire for a child, although it is in the love relation that such a conception is hinted at.

However, the conception of ethicality towards which Levinas gestures is expressed via a love relation which, it seems, must contain the potentiality of parenthood. It is difficult to avoid seeing this assumption as an acceptance not only of a continuity of the Law of the Father expressed through successive generations, but also of a specifically heterosexual relation. By retaining this determination albeit symbolically addressed, it seems that Levinas subsumes the heterogeneity of the site of maternity under an aim which in the last analysis *escapes* that site, what he calls 'the permanent opening of a messianic perspective'.[12]

Levinas' attempt to put into question the authority of identity perceived as 'full presence' is also reflected in his relation to the authority of his authorship. Avoiding the apparent neutrality of a kind of writing which presents itself as objective, Levinas makes clear the relation between language, patriarchal power structures, and the apparent privilege of a masculine access to culture. Acknowledging that we are contained within the divisions which align women with nature, men with culture, Levinas does not avoid or occlude the entrenched values continuous with this structure. To opt out of them altogether might either become a tacit acceptance of their scope, or a utopian gesture.

Instead, in making the feminine 'other', Levinas opens up the bias of language and the bias of metaphysical desire. The question of sexual difference is brought into the arena of ontology and ethics. In this arena, where femininity is 'other' to philosophy, Levinas states his interests and hence falls into this pattern, but at the same time he addresses the relation and problematizes it. Thus the accusation of a simply reactionary attitude towards women becomes more difficult to make. Levinas attempts to reconsider the relation between women and concern for the interior space, which is both, in Levinas' terms, 'the dwelling' and 'being at home in the world'.[13] This desire for an ethics based on community both looks back to what Levinas calls 'an unrecuperated, pre-ontological past of maternity', and forwards to reconciliation.

Nevertheless, Levinas is writing in a framework articulated in terms of sexual difference. Despite the attempts to disavow the determinations inherent in the notions of an authoritative and constituted subject, placing the feminine as other – albeit radically other – means that such determinations may be implicitly retained. It is possible to see that the intentions of such a strategy – that it be read with an eye to its double edge – might be read in a different way.

Regarding this strategy, Derrida writes in a footnote: 'let us note in passing that *Totality and Infinity* pushes the respect for dissymmetry so far that it seems to us impossible, essentially impossible, that it could have been written by a woman'[14] The ambiguous use of the word 'essential' in this note adds to the questions regarding strategy. Does Derrida imply a *necessary* and strategic dissymmetry? Or does he imply that Levinas falls into essentialism? The questions concern the relation of sexual identity to textual strategy.[15]

Kristeva suggests that the site of motherhood gains its subversive potential as 'the threshold of nature and culture',[16] the woman who is both *mother*, guarantor of the community and *other*, 'the polymorphic, orgasmic body, laughing and desiring'.[17] Scientific discourse attempts to objectify the body and Christian theology idealizes motherhood while, Kristeva adds, 'Lay humanism took over the configuration of that subject through the cult of the mother; tenderness, love and seat of social conservation'.[18] Desire is conscripted into desire for a child and difference or diversity is suppressed as counter to the interests of the social order. Kristeva posits motherhood as the site of potentially reconceptualized notions of production and reproduction, as different kinds of time, a different notion of identity. In this sense it represents a possible irruption or interruption of the Symbolic, in the conjunction of stasis and dynamism, of cyclical and monumental time with the linear time of genealogy and grammar. In 'Stabat Mater', the personal, left-hand, 'other' side of the text irrupts into the historical mapping of the Virgin Mary as paradigmatic mother. Textually, this double writing corresponds to the mother as a body positioned and repositioned in language, but a body with intimations of its own splitting, separation and pleasure.

The implications of these modes of experience are contradictory ones. What Kristeva calls 'the heterogeneity not subsumed under any present law'[19] is apparently an access to a space of different subjective possibilities, and yet there is still an appeal to the specificity of women. In 'Stabat Mater' she writes:

if contemporary ethics is no longer seen as being the same as morality, if ethics amounts to not avoiding the embarrassing and inevitable problematics of the law but giving it flesh, language and jouissance – in that case its reformulation demands the contribution of women . . .[20]

In order to realize this aspect of repressed expression, some form of unified identity seems necessary, and yet Kristeva does not homogenize such identity into an anonymous general experience.

Kristeva's theorization of language as other than a homogeneous, logical, rule-bound system with internal coherences allows it to be seen as 'an articulation of a heterogeneous process, with the speaking subject leaving its imprint on the dialectic between its articulation and its process'.[21] This creates the possibility of considering aspects of language which were hitherto seen as marginal because they were considered inferior attempts at achieving 'normal' communication. Kristeva suggests that far from being secondary, such aspects of language are the sites of linguistic transformation, upheaval and dissolution. Hence the process of language as changing and dynamic allows a conceptualization of subjectivity emerging through language as rhythmical and fragmentary. The possibility of different positionalities of the subject points to an endless construction and destruction, instead of an original, formative speaker. The potential of this formulation seems to be complete disintegration, a welcome release into language to be 'broken up' into positionalities. But the implicit prospect of a loss of language ensures, mostly, the continued transgression and renewal of this frontier. In effect, positionality is the co-operation with material, cultural, and historical conditions – the patriarchal and social ordering of modern class society. It is also the interiorization of power structures seen as 'other' and, as such, a disruption of the psychic drives or impulses apparently recollected as whole. And yet, Kristeva suggests, the mobilization of the process allows for the possibility of positions in language not wholly subordinate to dominant structures.

The notion of positionality is counter to a metaphysical hypostatization of Woman, certain manifestations of which may appear in feminism in the forms of sacrifice or violence. The challenge to the notion of identity pertains even in an oppositional structure of sexual difference. Kristeva writes: 'I am not simply

ALISON AINLEY

suggesting a very hypothetical bisexuality which, even if it existed, would only in fact be the aspiration towards the totality of one of the sexes and hence an effacing of difference.[22]

Hence femininity appears to become one of a series of options in the Symbolic, not a necessary result of biological sex. The dangers of essentialism propel Kristeva away from a simple valorization of difference, but this necessitates prioritizing the individual and his or her contingent entry into language perhaps at the expense of a more generalizing theory of experience. And yet, to return to her characterization of motherhood as the threshold of nature and culture, it is clear that this threshold does not simply oppose the individual to the political, but seeks to characterize the complex dialectic operating across the assumed distinction. Motherhood, which culture may idolize as that which is most 'natural' compared to the complex sophistries of its own networks, can be seen to shift within a whole constellation of dichotomous themes regarding the natural and the cultural. This constellation calls upon a splitting of reflection from so-called immediate sensuous experience, the valorizing of objectification and the progressive and productivist thrust which has mastery as its central tenet. The corresponding themes which emerge are the characterization of nature as 'regressive', reproduction linked with a feminine realm, the concomitant devalorization of the private sphere and hence a general impoverishment of this realm. Each of these factors tacitly relies on the others for justification, while there is a systematic idealization of motherhood in the controlled role of nostalgic reminder of a more 'primitive age'.

To speak of a threshold is to suggest a potential opening, however, and it is towards a relation of love that Kristeva gestures in writing of motherhood. This perhaps utopian and risky undertaking may nevertheless present the site of maternity with new understandings and interpretations. It is, of course, open to question how much difference new understandings can make, but at the least they may occasion a different investment of meaning in an arena that not only constantly resists changes of meaning but also refuses to consider interpretation as politically significant.

The trajectory of a re-invested understanding of an ethical subject does not, at this point, lend itself to a programme of action. The direction at present is towards questioning the assumptions of traditional ethics, a questioning that can be contextualized in the problematic area of motherhood for feminism. The possibility of formulating conceptions of maternity which are not definitional of women may indicate ways of informing and perhaps transforming ethical relations. But this possibility is not divorced from both informing and transforming understandings of maternity.

Notes

1 Julia Kristeva, 'Hérétique de l'amour', *Tel Quel*, no. 74, Winter 1977, p. 47; 'Stabat Mater', translated by Leon S. Roudiez, in *The Kristeva Reader*, ed. Toril Moi, Oxford, Blackwell, 1986, p. 182.
2 See also Julia Kristeva, 'Un nouveau type d'intellectuel; le dissident', *Tel Quel*, no. 74, Winter 1977, p. 5; 'A New Type of Intellectual, the Dissident', in *The Kristeva Reader*, p. 297.
3 Julia Kristeva, 'Le temps des femmes', *33/34 Cahiers de recherche de sciences des textes et documents*, no. 5, Winter 1979, p. 16; 'Women's Time', in *The Kristeva Reader*, p. 206.
4 Sigmund Freud, 'Einige Psychische Folgendes Anatomischen Geschechtsunterschieds', *Gesammelte Werke*, 14, Frankfurt-am-Main, S. Fischer Verlag, 1948, p. 30; 'Some Psychological Consequences of the Anatomical Distinction Between the Sexes', *The Pelican Freud Library*, vol. VII, On Sexuality, ed. Angela Richards, translated under the general editorship of James Strachey, Harmondsworth, Penguin, 1977, p. 342.
5 Kristeva, 'Le temps des femmes', p. 11; 'Women's Time', p. 200.
6 Julia Kristeva, *La Révolution du langage poétique*, Paris, Seuil, 1974, p. 102; *Revolution in Poetic Language*, translated by Margaret Waller, New York, Columbia University Press, 1984, p. 110.
7 The brief characterization which follows relies principally on the section entitled 'Au delà du visage' ('Beyond the Face') in Emmanuel Levinas, *Totalité et infini*, The Hague, Martinus Nijhoff, 1961, pp. 229–61; *Totality and Infinity*, translated by Alfonso Lingis, Pittsburgh, Duquesne University Press, 1969, pp. 251–85.
8 Emmanuel Levinas, *Difficile liberté*, ed. Albin Michel, Paris, 1976, p. 53.
9 Simone de Beauvoir, *Le Deuxième Sexe*, Paris, Gallimard, 1949; *The Second Sex*, translated by H.M. Parshley, Harmondsworth, Penguin, 1984.
10 Levinas, *Totalité et infini*, pp. 233–44; *Totality and Infinity*, pp. 256–66.
11 Ibid., pp. 244–7/267–9.
12 Ibid., p. 261/285.
13 Ibid., pp. 127–9/154–6.
14 Jacques Derrida, 'Violence et métaphysique', in *L'écriture et la*

différence, Paris, Seuil, 1967, p. 228; 'Violence and Metaphysics', in *Writing and Difference*, translated by Alan Bass, London, Routledge & Kegan Paul, 1981, p. 321, note 92.

15 A number of feminist critics raise these points in relation to Derrida himself. See, for example, Alice Jardine, *Gynesis*, New York, Cornell University Press, 1986.

16 This formulation is to be found in a number of places in 'Hérétique de l'amour' ('Stabat Mater') and 'Le temps des femmes' ('Women's Time'), *passim*.

17 Julia Kristeva, *Des chinoises*, Paris, Editions des femmes, 1974, p. 105; *About Chinese Women*, London, Calder & Boyars, 1977, p. 118.

18 Julia Kristeva, 'Maternitie selon Giovanni Bellini', *Peinture*, December 1985, no. 10–11, reprinted in *Polylogue*, Paris, Seuil, 1977, p. 409; 'Motherhood According to Giovanni Bellini', in *Desire in Language*, ed. Leon S. Roudiez and translated by Thomas Gora, Alice Jardine, and Leon S. Roudiez, Oxford, Blackwell, 1984, p. 237.

19 Kristeva, 'Hérétique de l'amour', p. 49; 'Stabat Mater', *The Kristeva Reader*, p. 185.

20 Ibid., p. 49/185.

21 Kristeva, *La révolution du langage poétique*, p. 169; *Revolution in Poetic Language*, p. 189.

22 Kristeva, 'Hérétique de l'amour', p. 52; 'Stabat Mater', *The Kristeva Reader*, p. 209.

· 5 ·

Female Temporality and the Future of Feminism

TINA CHANTER

The aim of the following presentation of Kristeva's work is a limited one in so far as my attention is largely confined to only one of her essays – although I draw on other works for clarification of certain central terms. However I think that the essay 'Women's Time' is important enough to merit detailed consideration.[1] First, Kristeva's reflections upon the nature of the feminist movement, which are perhaps articulated more clearly in this essay than in any of her other works, and second, her confrontation with the problem of time, both deserve to be carefully analysed. In 'Women's Time' Kristeva brings together these two subjects, feminist history and the philosophy of time, by identifying three phases of feminism – although, as we shall see, her very conception of 'feminine' time puts into question the adequacy of thinking the story of feminism in terms of successive and mutually exclusive phases. I aim to examine Kristeva's threefold categorization of feminist history, and to ask how one particular feminist, Eleanor Rathbone, fits into Kristeva's interpretation of feminist history.

Active in public life earlier in this century, Rathbone falls into the category Kristeva classifies as the first phase of modern feminism. She was an MP, and a leading member of the women's suffrage movement. An independent MP, who was committed to social reform, with a particular interest in issues affecting women and children, Rathbone joined the Women's Local Government Society. The WLGS was effective in campaigning for women's issues in local government. Its efforts to encourage women to stand for parliament were consolidated in 1913 with the formation of the Women's Municipal Party, a non-party political feminist support group which Rathbone joined.[2]

Eleanor Rathbone includes in her essay 'Changes in Public Life'[3] a section called 'The Tasks of the Future' in which she distinguishes between two schools of feminists, identifying one as the 'old school' and the other, the one to which she is committed, the 'new school' (CP). Rathbone calls the old school the 'Me Too' feminists (CP, p. 57), a nickname which effectively conveys their determining characteristic: in Rathbone's words 'the habit of continually measuring women's wants by men's achievements' (CP, p. 58). In her essay 'Feminism and Fiction between the Wars' Marion Shaw sees a similarity between the divergent types of feminists recognized by Rathbone, and the 'split' in the contemporary 'literary world', where on the one hand there is a 'privileging' of women and, on the other hand, there is an assumption of 'their total equality with men'.[4] However, I want to pursue a different line of enquiry. Rather than develop an analogy between the two schools of feminists Rathbone recognizes and present-day literary trends, I want to cite the 'new' feminists to whom Rathbone pledged her allegiance as a precedent for what has come to be known as 'French feminism'. More specifically, I want to focus upon a feature common to both Rathbone's and Kristeva's conceptions of the future of feminism. Both Rathbone and Kristeva accept the 'risk' involved in insisting upon feminine specificity, and both indicate that there is a certain necessity in this risk. The phenomenon of women-centred feminist perspectives is not new, and neither is the suspicion of it. This suspicion, I want to suggest, is not unconnected with the risk that such a perspective involves.

In the essay 'Women's Time' Kristeva sets out to explore the way in which the feminist movement both 'inherits and modifies' a certain conception of time (WT, p. 190). This conception of time Kristeva designates the common idea of time, whereby one moment is successive upon another. This common view of time is differentiated from another view of time, which Kristeva calls, after Nietzsche, 'monumental time' (WT, p. 189). It proves to be a difficult notion, which is understood by its intricate interrelations with time as ordinarily understood (as the simple succession of moments), yet as distinct from this ordinary understanding. 'Monumental' time, together with cyclical time, is akin to feminine time. Kristeva herself acknowledges that the problematic of temporality she attempts to broach in the first few pages of her essay 'Women's Time' is one of 'unheard-of complexity' (WT, p. 193).[5] It will be useful therefore to review her analysis. Monumental time is construed both in opposition to, and as parasitic upon, and even constitutive of, the ordinary concept of time, that conception which might be called (perhaps misleadingly, because, for reasons that will emerge, it is not the exclusive preserve of men) 'male' time. Monumental time is a time 'without cleavage or escape, which has so little to do with linear time (which passes) that the very word "temporality" hardly fits' (WT, p. 191).

Successive, or linear, time is teleological, a time of progress (WT, p. 192). Kristeva sees this projective 'time of the line' as characteristic of national values, the reality of which she sees as having effectively collapsed with the crash of 1929 (WT, p. 188). The predominance of national values which, on Kristeva's analysis, obtained prior to 1929, was, she suggests, replaced by a 'symbolic denominator'. Both terms, 'national values' and 'symbolic denominator' call for further elaboration. Kristeva's construal of 'national values' draws upon the Marxian account of the three factors determining a nation, 'economic homogeneity, historical tradition and linguistic unity' (WT, p. 188). If these bastions of the nation existed in the nineteenth century as both 'dream and reality' (WT, p. 188), the support they provided became increasingly precarious after 1929, while after the Second World War they lived on solely in the imagination. The belief in the continued existence of the nation was, Kristeva says, based only on ideology, or for 'strictly political purposes, its social and philosophical coherence having collapsed' (WT, p. 188). The economic homogeneity of the nation – now merely a dream in any case, having lost any firm basis it previously had – was transformed into economic interdependence, while the other two constants of national identity, historical tradition and linguistic unity, suffered a more profound transformation. They entered what Kristeva calls the symbolic order.

It is not possible to give anything like an adequate account of the 'symbolic' here. Kristeva devotes, for example, nearly half of her major work *Revolution in Poetic Language* to the distinction between the semiotic and the symbolic, and we cannot hope to do justice to that complex discussion here.[6] Suffice it to provide a few pointers which will help to orient us in her later use of the term in 'Women's Time'. The semiotic level is characterized by motility, by the movement of energies and drives, a movement which is however always already informed by the influence of the symbolic. The symbolic, says Kristeva, 'is a social effect of the relation to the other' (RLP, p. 29; RPL, p. 29). Precisely because the symbolic order always already informs the semiotic, simply to equate the symbolic with the social, and the semiotic with the biological, would do violence to Kristeva's articulation of the relation and exchange between the two levels. Nevertheless, for those who are unfamiliar with Kristeva's terminology, Leon Roudiez, in his introduction to *Revolution in Poetic Language*, makes an observation about the division between semiotic and symbolic that proves helpful. It is one of those comments which, as Roudiez admits, is misleading in a sense, but which does at least serve to point the reader in the right direction. Although the distinction between semiotic and symbolic 'is not identical with that of unconscious/conscious, id/superego, or nature/culture, there are analogies here that could be usefully kept in mind. In all four instances there is a constant dialectical process at work, one that has its source in infancy, and is implicated in sexual differentiation. Such a dialectic comprises drives and impulses on the one hand, the family and society structures on the other.' (RPL, p. 4). Roudiez goes on to concede that there is an obvious disanalogy between the above three distinctions, and the semiotic/symbolic distinction itself. That is, unlike the distinctions it is compared to, and as illustrated by the longer quotation from Kristeva below, the sphere of operation of the semiotic and symbolic is language. Kristeva says:

These two modalities are inseparable within the *signifying process* that constitutes language, and the dialectic between them determines the type of discourse (narrative, metalanguage, theory, poetry, etc) involved; in other words, so-called 'natural' language allows for different modes of articulation of the semiotic and the symbolic. On the other hand, there are nonverbal signifying systems that are constructed exclusively on the basis of the semiotic (music, for example). But . . . this exclusivity is relative, precisely because of the necessary dialectic between the two modalities of the signifying process, which is constitutive of the subject. Because the subject is always *both* semiotic *and* symbolic, no signifying system he produces can be either 'exclusively' semiotic or 'exclusively' symbolic, and is instead necessarily marked by an indebtedness to both. (RLP, p. 22; RPL, p. 24)

66

One last characteristic worth noting in this brief excursion into Kristeva's explanation of the symbolic in its relation to the semiotic is that it is the former that includes the separation of the subject from the object. At the symbolic level, the subject posits itself as different to, or as other than, that which it names in the process of signification. In designating an object, the subject engages in 'a positing of identity or difference' which is 'the nucleus of judgement and proposition' (RPL, p. 42; RLP, p. 43).

'Symbolic denominator' as Kristeva defines it in 'Women's Time' is 'the cultural and religious memory forged by the interweaving of history and geography' (WT, p. 188) and is manifested by the 'art, philosophy and religions' of the 'socio-cultural' ensemble that might be said to constitute Europe (WT, p. 189). When Kristeva points to the gradual disintegration of national values, it is the symbolic order to which she looks as the force that replaced them. National values thus gave way to 'a new social ensemble superior to the nation', one which could 'embrace an entire continent' – in this case, Europe. The process that Kristeva sees at work in Europe is not so much a complete eradication of national values, as their transformation. 'The nation', says Kristeva, 'far from losing its own traits, rediscovers and accentuates them in a strange temporality, in a kind of "future perfect"' (WT, p. 189). Why a future perfect? Because the particular kind of cultural memory with which Kristeva is concerned is a memory of past events which were not experienced as they will be remembered – events which were 'deeply repressed' (WT, p. 189). What type of memories are being considered here? The relationships, says Kristeva, not so much of production (the mode which typifies national identity) but of reproduction – 'survival of the species, life and death, the body, sex and symbol' (WT, p. 189).

Having outlined the development of a European identity, based on symbolic denomination and represented in the artistic and spiritual expressions of the community, and replacing the preponderance of the nation, Kristeva now complicates this trans-national identity by introducing a 'double problematic' which faces the 'socio-cultural ensembles of the European type'. It is here that Kristeva specifies the two different temporalities which she identifies as linear and monumental. The 'double problematic' of the socio-cultural groupings is 'that of their *identity* constituted by historical sedimentation, and that of their *loss of identity'* (WT, p. 189). The former, the sedimentation of identity, takes shape as linear or cursive time, and the latter, the undermining of identity, is a 'monumental' movement. The European mode of reproduction is distinguished by traits specific to that particular socio-cultural ensemble (and as such its identity is constituted according to the time of the line, the time of progress, history, linear development, projects). But certain elements of this mode of reproduction and its representations are also connected 'diagonally' with other socio-cultural groupings, which may be culturally remote from it. One such element is the category, for example, of 'European women', a group which, in so far as it is defined by sex-specific traits, is paralleled with, for example, women in China. But in so far as it is distinctively European, it retains the specific characteristics of its particular socio-cultural identity. Through their participation in monumental time, European women 'echo in a most specific way the universal traits of their structural place in reproduction and its representations' (WT, p. 190). This time, along with 'cyclical' time, says Kristeva, has been traditionally associated with 'female subjectivity in so far as the latter is thought of as necessarily maternal' (WT, p. 192).

It is easy to see why Kristeva says that the word 'temporality' is hardly suitable to designate 'monumental time', for it appears to have more to do with synchrony than with diachrony, and it seems to be concerned with spatial rather than historical links. It is not surprising then that monumental rather than linear time is that which has come to be understood as female time, since, as Kristeva points out, spatial references have traditionally been associated with the feminine sensibility, with maternity, while time is attributed to masculinity, to the father.

Kristeva identifies two separate phases of the feminist movement, stages which respectively map onto the predominance of the nation on the one hand and its successor, according to her suggestion, the 'symbolic denominator' on the other hand. Accordingly, the first stage of feminist history is circumscribed by the determining features which characterize nations – the demand for equality is shaped in conformity with the parliamentary or constitutional structures of each nation, for example. Kristeva describes the political and social demands made by early feminists for the equality of women, as well as 'the rejection, when necessary, of the attributes traditionally considered feminine or maternal' (WT, p. 193) as part of an attempt to 'gain a place in linear time as the time of project and history' (ibid.). The activities of suffragists in this first phase of feminism attained, or paved the way for obtaining, improvements for women such as equal pay, equal job opportunities, improved facilities for abortion, and increased control over reproduction. This approach, says Kristeva, is both 'universalist' and rooted in the nation-state (WT, p. 193). It is universal because it '*globalizes* the problems of women of different milieux, ages, civilisations, or simply of varying psychic structures, under the label "Universal Woman"' (WT, p. 194). And it is caught up with national ideals in so far as it shares these ideals in its attempts to gain power within the particular social and political establishment.

The second stage of feminism that Kristeva identifies, not subject to national characteristics but defined by both European and trans-European experience, dates from around 1968. In so far as it is characterized by the 'distrust' of politics that followed the events of May 1968, this phase of feminism no longer aspires to secure a place in linear history. Instead of political achievements and status, feminists of this generation focused their attention on the 'specificity of female psychology' for example, appealing to cyclical or monumental temporality. Not content to demand equality with men, women demanded 'recognition of an irreducible identity, without equal in the opposite sex and, as such, exploded, plural, fluid, in a certain way non-identical' (WT, p. 194). Often growing out of art or psychoanalytic activities, discoveries by women about themselves fed into increasingly sophisticated formulations of their symbolic identities.

These two distinct generations are nevertheless distinguished from a third feminist stance by sharing a more general characteristic, a 'universalist and cosmopolitan' approach (WT, p. 190). If the first phase is broadly characterized as an age in which national values predominated, and the second era is one in which women are concerned to carve out for themselves some kind of unique and irreducible feminine identity, there is a third attitude which runs 'parallel' to these two. This contemporary approach questions the very meaning of the concept 'identity', which the two preceding phases presuppose, and refuses the metaphysical distinction between men and women as the decisive opposition.

It is essential to understand that even though Kristeva roughly indicates these three approaches as historically succeeding one another, the strategies embodying national values still continue to be exercised, and will no doubt continue until all demands for equality have been met; and the insistence upon the irreducibility of femininity is still an issue. Kristeva suggests that one reason for the emergence of this second approach, which she sees as flourishing after 1969, is that while some measure of economic, political and professional parity had been more or less achieved, the attempts by women to achieve reproductive control were less than successful, so that sexual and reproductive freedom seemed '*essential* in the struggle of a new generation' (WT, p. 196). Feminism thus became an issue about 'difference and specificity' rather than equality. Kristeva explains further,

It is precisely at this point that the new generation encounters what might be called the *symbolic* question. Sexual difference – which is at once biological, physiological and relative to reproduction – is translated by and translates a difference in the relationship of subjects to the symbolic contract which *is* the social contract: a difference then, in the relationship to power, language and meaning. (WT, p. 196)

Not only does the symbolic become an urgent issue for this second generation of feminists; the experience of temporality changes too. The time which marks their appeal to an identity which is specifically feminine is not circumscribed by linearity, that is, the time characterizing the demand for equality. This time is rather determined as 'the cyclical or monumental temporality of marginal movements' (WT, p. 195).

Kristeva expresses serious concern about the marginality that this type of feminism embraces. I do not want to dwell on the various reservations Kristeva articulates about women attempting to confirm their irreducible otherness. Let me just briefly mention two of these reservations. One is manifested for example in the threat posed by the development of 'counter-investment'. The danger, as Kristeva sees it, is that feminism indulges in the formation of counter-cultures which re-inscribe the very oppression and exploitation against which it reacts. Appropriating power, governed by dynamics which differ from those of the power it denounces, this strategy is liable to hold back rather than advance the cause of feminisim. A second problem Kristeva sees as inherent in the affirmation of a feminine identity as distinct from male power is that it tends to posit a single identity for women in general, thereby diminishing the individual uniqueness of women. Indeed plurality is the focus of Kristeva's proposed alternative, 'which I strongly advocate – which I imagine?' (WT, p. 205) she says. Concretely, this takes the form of differences not just between women but even within individual women. The success women have in combining motherhood with professional careers is an example of the way in which women are combining the two previous trends of feminism into a third strand. That success depends upon both provision of, for example, nurseries – institutions which recognize the specific needs of women as childbearers – and the effectiveness of equal opportunity policies – institutions which recognize the similarity between men and women. The third feminist attitude depends upon seeing these trends as compatible, although of themselves, each might be said to endorse opposing ideals for women.

Kristeva acknowledges that the third strategy she outlines, which undermines the concept of identity, 'necessarily . . . involves risks not only for what we understand today as personal equilibrium but also for social equilibrium' (WT, p. 209). The risk that Kristeva admits here echoes that which Rathbone recognizes. In arguing against the 'Me Too' feminists, Rathbone concedes that there is a risk (of limiting women's opportunities) in diverging from equality but goes on to endorse the need to take this risk (CP, p. 59). She supports this view by pointing out how the 'Me Too' feminists back themselves into a corner by refusing to depart from their rigid adherence to a principle of 'equality' on every point. Their position involves the impossibility of making a case for the special circumstances of women to be considered in pregnancy, maternity leave and child benefit for example. Rathbone admits further to the risk in embracing femininity when she acknowledges that it may be taken simply as a reassertion of what has been traditionally designated feminine, thus reinforcing instead of overcoming the restrictions traditionally imposed on the 'legitimate' activities of women. She says:

There may be some who, in their reaction against the sentimental conception of women, may resent the idea of utilizing rather than combating this traditional difference of outlook. There may be others who will agree that, however much it may have been exaggerated by popular presentation, it corresponds to real facts of human experience. (CP, p. 76)

It is perhaps as a way of clarifying what is at issue in such 'real facts of human experience' that Kristeva's analysis of the feminist movement during this century as threefold comes into its own. The first phase of women's experience, as we have seen, corresponds to the 'socio-cultural' grouping of particular systems of production, while the second phase takes account of the structural affinities of women who, despite their location within culturally specific modes of production, share a cross-cultural identity, so that, for example, young European women are in 'diagonal' relationship to young women in non-European countries and cultures through reproduction and its cultural and artistic representations.

Despite the different emphases of the first two phases of feminism identified by Kristeva (the first phase being largely determined by a 'national problematic' and the second being 'European *and* trans-European'), as against the third 'phase', they share an underlying conception of the 'Universal woman', a common tendency to generalize the problems of women. And in this, Kristeva sees a failure to appreciate the differences between women. Despite the avowed intent of the second phase of feminism to concentrate upon the specificity of women, as opposed to trying to aspire to male values, Kristeva sees it as ignoring the multiplicity of individual women's experiences insofar as it still appeals to a universal, albeit specific to women.

Aware that to advocate turning away from the universalism embodied in a counter-culture which is born in reaction to sexism, is in some respects a 'retreat from sexism', Kristeva nevertheless endorses the need to take this risk. She says 'The fact that this might quickly become another form of spiritualism turning its back on social problems, or else a form of repression ready to support all status quos, should not hide the radicalness of the process' (WT, p. 210).

I am suggesting a parallel between the risk endorsed by Rathbone on the one hand and Kristeva on the other hand. But far from illustrating the validity of Kristeva's tripartite division of the feminist movement, does this not put it in question? We should remember however that Kristeva does not think of the three phases she delineates as mutually exclusive of one another. She therefore does not rule out the early emergence of a tendency for feminists to embrace femininity, to celebrate difference. Nevertheless, if Rathbone belongs to the first generation of feminists, the generation characterized by political activism, there still remains the question of why she did not adhere to the general view of her time, the view that equal opportunities were the only front on which the feminist struggle could be fought? Perhaps, far from proving Kristeva's periodization of feminism as inapplicable, Rathbone reinforces Kristeva's thematization of a temporality that is specific to women. Perhaps the very marginality of women privileges them with respect to time. Rathbone testifies to the possibility of standing outside the predominant feminist view of her era. How is this possible? Perhaps through the feminine thinking that is born of being oriented towards others. The position of women on the borders of the linear time of progress gives them access to a future in a way over and above the special relationship to the future that all 'minority' groups maintain, by virtue of their struggle for change – their attempt to upset the present status quo. Perhaps the privilege might subsist in the very 'sacrificial' role demanded of women. The necessity of caring is a burden that has carried the weight of oppression, but perhaps it also holds the key, not only of reversing that oppression, but also of overcoming the power from which oppression feeds.

About maternity, Rathbone says:

Here we have an occupation in which a far greater number of persons is engaged than in any other whatever – an occupation which is essential to the very existence of society; for its poorer members peculiarly onerous, since they have no time off and no holidays. . . . Yet it is so little recognized by society that those engaged in it are described in the census as 'unoccupied'. . . . They are expected to be kept out of the wages or salaries of their husbands and fathers, under a wage-system which pays no regard to the existence or number of a man's dependants, except by paying him rather more than a woman would receive for the same job under the vague assumption that normally 'men have families to keep'. (CP, p. 61)

Rathbone sees the 'absurdity' of a situation in which the only family income society provided mothers was through the wages of husbands, thus ensuring 'the economic dependence of mothers and children' (CP, p. 61). She explains the reluctance of men to relinquish their responsibility in providing for their families in a humorous observation that deserves quoting at length:

A man likes to feel that he has 'dependants' (literally 'hangers-on). He looks in the glass and sees himself as perhaps others see him – physically negligible, mentally ill-equipped, poor, unimportant, unsuccessful. He looks in the mirror he keeps in his mind, and sees his wife clinging to his arm and the children clustered round her skirts; all looking up to him, as that giver of all good gifts, the wage-earner. The picture is very alluring. If he is benevolent, here is a field for his benevolence. If he is a tyrant at heart, the power of the purse gives him the means of domineering which meddlesome law-makers have sought progressively to filch from him. Simultaneously, he may know perfectly well that the whole thing is working out badly; that the burden he has taken on his shoulders is too heavy and that society, while applauding him for taking it, is doing precious little to help him bear it. . . .

The point behind this somewhat amusing sketch of the burdens of a man's responsibilities is a serious one: it is that, while deploring their responsibilities, men also realize that the enforced economic dependence of their wives and mothers 'is the best and by far the greatest weapon of masculine dominance'.

However, while Rathbone acknowledges the importance of economic factors in the subjection of women, she does not draw out the more general conclusion that would seem to follow from this observation. That is, she fails to demand the same standards for all women. She sees nothing wrong in arguing for a form of economic benefit based upon 'the claims of the children' (CP, p. 69) on the grounds that

on the whole it may be best to provide for the mothers through them. In the older form of the demand, we used to call it 'endowment of motherhood' and to include an allowance for the mother as well as the child. But this is open to the objection that the mother is also the housewife, and that single men and women need a housewife – someone to do their chores for them – not less than married men. . . .

This comment betrays a fundamental failure to appreciate the plight of women as a plight of all women, irrespective of class. But let us not be too quick in jumping to conclusions. We need not use this weakness as an excuse for abandoning Rathbone's line of thought altogether. Perhaps the general approach is sound, but Rathbone has not followed it through far enough. Rather than reject her approach altogether, and fall back into the position of the 'Me Too' feminists, where everything hinges on attaining equal opportunities, let us try to carry Rathbone's thought further forward. Despite the insight into specifically feminine attributes that Rathbone shows she does not follow through the implications of her important insight. There is no doubt that she does demonstrate a remarkable awareness of the feminine experience as irreducible, asking, for example, whether it can be

merely a coincidence that during those past generations when it required an immense effort for women to break through the tradition which forbade them to take part in public work, those who did break through were nearly all dominated by the same kind of motive – an overmastering desire to relieve some immense, hitherto neglected area of human suffering and injustice? (CP, pp. 74–5)

She even comments that 'One of the worst results of the subjection of women was that hardly any use was made of their special experience and knowledge in moulding the structure of society and directing its policy' (CP, p. 74). But what is lacking in her analysis is a recognition of the difference between femininity and masculinity as a difference which is not only constitutive of the very identity of female and male, but is also lived beyond that identity. Patricia Hollis notes the ambiguity of Rathbone's approach when she describes it as

Conservative, in that it reinforced stereotyping of women's nature; supportive, in that it encouraged women to come forward with the confidence that their domestic and family background was as useful and relevant to public service as men's commercial and business experience; and radical, in that it permitted women to claim public space and to expand the contours of what elected authorities were there to do, and for whom they were to do it.[7]

Olive Banks makes a similar point. Discussing her view that economic support for motherhood should be introduced she says 'Eleanor Rathbone's scheme was . . . by implication at least, a radical one. These implications were never realized in practice, however'.[8] The Women's Local Government Society, to which Rathbone belonged, is described as a 'liberal upper-middle-class society' and these values are reflected in the demands she made on behalf of women, such as financial provision for mothers in the form of family endowment.[9] As Banks says, Rathbone saw this 'primarily as a means to strengthen both the family and women's traditional part in it rather than to explore possibilities for change'.[10] I mentioned earlier that Rathbone accepts the risk that she runs in her approach to feminism. Embracing femininity leads to suspicion. For example, Rathbone says:

> There may be some who, in their reaction against the sentimental conception of women, may resent the idea of utilizing rather than combating this traditional difference of outlook. There may be others who will agree that, however much it may have been exaggerated by popular presentation, it corresponds to real facts of human experience. (CP, p. 76)

I suggest that while Rathbone is surely right to appeal to the 'real facts of human experience', she fails to clarify the status of such experience. In other words, she does not distinguish between the idea that women are 'naturally' carers and nurturers, and the fact that the social expectations imposed upon women have pushed them into certain roles. The experience of women conforms to gender expectations, and it is when this becomes confused with the natural capacity of women as a sex that the affirmation of women's experience as different from men's runs into problems. The difficulty is that social pressure has so consistently identified women as 'natural' childbearers that the concepts of 'sex' and 'gender' have, for all practical purposes, become barely distinguishable. Thus Rathbone is suspected, by the 'Me Too' feminists, of colluding with traditionalists, who think of women as destined, by nature, for motherhood.

The real danger of collusion that an attempt to affirm sexual difference carries with it is not ignored, but accepted, by Rathbone and Kristeva. Confusion will inevitably arise between 'traditional' feminine traits and a genuine 'post-feminist' plurality; but without taking this imaginative leap, and risking all, neither, perhaps, can the 'radicalness of the process' that points to a 'fundamental difference' between the sexes be realized (WT, p. 193). Imaginative, because no longer designated only from the standpoint of the opposition male/female identity, which nevertheless still predominates at every level and sphere of society, and carrying a legacy that flies in the face of feminism. About this fundamental difference Kristeva says:

> I think that the apparent coherence which the term 'woman' assumes in contemporary ideology, apart from its 'mass' or 'shock' effect for activist purposes, essentially has the negative effect of effacing the differences

among the diverse functions or structures which operate beneath this word. Indeed, the time has perhaps come to emphasize the multiplicity of female expressions and preoccupations so that from the intersection of these differences there might arise, more precisely, less commercially, and more truthfully, the real *fundamental difference* between the two sexes: a difference that feminism has had the enormous merit of rendering painful, that is, productive of surprises and of symbolic life in a civilization which, outside the stock exchange and wars, is bored to death. (WT, p. 193)

Before going on to conclude, it is worth just noting two questions raised in another recently published essay, by Juliet Mitchell, 'Reflections on Twenty Years of Feminism'.[11] 'She asks: 'Through women's marginality and hence through our flexibility can humankind as a social being move for ever upwards? Do women put the future on trial?' (p. 45). The final sentence of her essay runs 'As feminists we conceived yesterday's future' (p. 48). Can we discern a special relationship that women sustain with the future?

The suggestion that I have presented, following Kristeva's analysis of production and reproduction, linear and cyclical time, is this: precisely the 'universal' structure of care characterizing women's activities, points beyond the time of feminist activism, and towards another time. Not to a utopia as shaped according to what sexism does not permit, which would still be determined by the sexist society against which it revolts. Such utopian vision, maintaining its oppressor as its point of departure, stays within the domination of that oppressor, producing only its inverse, instead of evading the structure of its domination by seeking other ways of expression that are no longer defined and circumscribed by the terms against which it reacts. This time would no more leave behind the attempt to continue fighting for parity, where this is still left unachieved, than it would think of going somewhere else, moving on to an as yet unknown future, as if such a future could be mapped out ahead of time, and still retain its mystery. Rather it would fill in the spaces, stop up the gaps, left behind by those who would forge new paths ahead, in the name of progress. But in doing so, it would not forget how indispensable the feminist affirmation of the irreducibly feminine is, it would not forget its history. Neither would it relate to that history in a necessarily straightforward way, for it would no longer follow the march of history in a straight line. The time of the line would be supplemented, substituted for the cyclical, monumental, which may give the illusion of going round in circles, an illusory phenomenon however only if one insists on looking straight ahead. It is hardly surprising that, as women, the ones who have always been expected to take on the role of caring, we should find ourselves loath to take risks. For, until feminism is no longer cast in the very patriarchal terms it seeks to overcome, who but ourselves will take care of the casualties? Such tasks will be left to us, until feminism has the strength to think not in opposition to men as a group, but in terms of women, from the specific and positive perspective of the values that individual women have sustained. It is not necessarily these values themselves which are at fault, but the fact that women have been chained to them. To conclude, as Rathbone said in 1936, 'The cutting of women's bonds has not yet made all the difference it should, because women's limbs are still stiff from the bondage' (CP, p. 74). The stiffness has not yet disappeared.

Notes

1 Julia Kristeva, 'Le temps des femmes', *33/34 Cahiers de recherche de sciences des textes et documents*, no. 5, Winter 1979, pp. 5–19; 'Women's Time', in *The Kristeva Reader*, ed. Toril Moi, Oxford, Blackwell, 1986, pp. 188–213 (previously published in *Feminist Theory: A Critique of Ideology*, ed. N.O. Keohane, M.Z. Rosaldo, and B.C. Gelpi, Brighton, Harvester Press, 1982; first published in translation in *Signs*, vol. 7, no. 1, Autumn 1981, pp. 13–35).
2 Patricia Hollis, 'Women in Council: Separate Spheres, Public Space', in *Equal or Different: Women's Politics 1800–1914*, ed. Jane Rendal, Oxford, Blackwell, 1987, p. 212.
3 The following abbreviations are used in this chapter:
    CP   Eleanor Rathbone, 'Changes in Public Life', in *Our Freedom and its Results*, ed. Ray Strachey, London, The Garden City Press, 1936, pp. 15–76.
    RLP Julia Kristeva, *La Révolution du langage poétique*, Paris, Seuil, 1974.
    RPL Julia Kristeva, *Revolution in Poetic Language*, translated by Margaret Waller, New York, Columbia University Press, 1984.
    WT   Julia Kristeva, 'Women's Time', in *The Kristeva Reader*, ed. Toril Moi, Oxford, Blackwell, 1986, pp. 188–213.
4 Marion Shaw, 'Feminism and Fiction Between the Wars: Winifred Holtby and Virginia Woolf', in *Women's Writing: A Challenge to Theory*, ed. Moira Monteith, Brighton, Harvester Press, 1986, p. 176.

5 Kristeva observes that 'it has already been abundantly demonstrated' that linear temporality 'is inherent in the logical and ontological values of any given civilization, that this temporality renders explicit a rupture, an expectation or an anguish which other temporalities work to conceal' (WT, p. 192). Presumably Kristeva has in mind philosophers such as Martin Heidegger, when she says that linear temporality has been shown to be embedded in the 'logical and ontological values' of civilizations. However, I would say that it is not linear temporality that 'renders explicit . . . an anguish'. Rather, the focus upon anguish precisely disrupts the adequacy of the metaphor of the line to describe our experience of time. In so far as anguish throws us back upon ourselves, it is a recognition of temporality not as an infinite line of progress, but upon the interrelations that circulate between future, present and past. Perhaps then there is an implicit criticism of the Heideggerian-type analyses in Kristeva's omission to distinguish these from depictions of time as linear. Perhaps she thinks Heidegger's critique of traditional concepts of time is not far enough removed from linear temporality.

6 Julia Kristeva, *La Révolution du langage poétique*, Paris, Seuil, 1974; *Revolution in Poetic Language*, translated by Margaret Waller with an introduction by Leon S. Roudiez, New York, Columbia University Press, 1984.

7 Patricia Hollis, 'Women in Council', p. 210.

8 Olive Banks, *Faces of Feminism: A Study of Feminism as a Social Movement*, Oxford, Blackwell, 1986, p. 168.

9 Patricia Hollis, 'Women in Council', p. 203.

10 Olive Banks, *Faces of Feminism*.

11 Juliet Mitchell, 'Reflections on Twenty Years of Feminism', in *What is Feminism?*, ed. Juliet Mitchell and Ann Oakley, Oxford, Blackwell, 1986, pp. 34–48.

· 6 ·

The Body of Signification

ELIZABETH GROSS

Kristeva's preoccupation remains the subject's complex and contradictory relation to and in signification. The speaking subject's position in the production and deformation of discourses and representational systems constitutes a broad map of the two axes around which her work is projected: in the one case, a psychoanalytically inspired investigation of the subject's physical development from the time of its most intense dependence on the mother to its location as a speaking subject within the symbolic order; and in the other, an increasingly wide-ranging textual analysis of the ways in which discourses – from the 'cultural' discourses of love and romance to literary, avant-garde, and philosophical texts – position and produce the subject of enunciation. These are not really two distinct interests but are different perspectives on or approaches to one and the same object, the speaking subject. These two perspectives, the psychoanalytic and the textual, the semiotic and the symbolic, are focused at the point of their most intense and contradictory conjunction. This is why Kristeva seems fascinated with physical and textual extremes – states of the infantile, neurotic, and psychotic subject, and poetic, religious, and avant-garde writing and representational practices.

I propose here to examine Kristeva's understanding of the role of the body and corporeality in the constitution of the speaking subject. It is clear that the body must play a crucial role in the subject's psychical formation, given her reliance on the psycho-analytic conceptions of narcissism and corporeal intimacy with the maternal body, infantile sexuality and the unconscious. It is, however, perhaps less commonly recognized within literary or textual analysis and in accounts of language acquisition that the ways in which the body is coded, made meaningful, and rendered representable provide some of the necessary conditions for discursive and cultural representation. In this chapter, I concentrate mainly on *Powers of Horror, An Essay on Abjection* and those other papers in which corporeality is discussed by her. My discussion is divided into three parts: in the first part, I explain in general terms why the notion of the subject's corporeality is a worthy topic of investigation for those interested in questioning prevailing liberal, humanist, masculinist, or naturalist conceptions of subjectivity; in the second, I investigate the ways in which Kristeva understands the role of the body in the constitution (and destabilization) of the speaking subject; and in the third, I critically assess her contributions to an account of the signifying body presumed by and productive of signifying practices.

Corporeality and Subjectivity

For writers as diverse as Lyotard, Irigaray, Deleuze, Derrida, and Foucault, the body is conceived as a fundamentally historical and political object; indeed, for many it is the central object over and through which relations of power and resistance are played out. Although clearly the interests, methods and frameworks of these writers are extremely diverse, each is concerned to challenge the ways in which the body has been relegated to a subordinate or secondary position relative to the primacy of the mind, consciousness or reason. Each is committed to a non-reductive materialism, a materialism which, rather than mere brute physicality, also includes the materiality of discourses, as well as psychical drives and unconscious processes. Each develops a materialism which, while refusing prevailing biologistic, naturalistic and physicalist reductions of the body to the status of brute, given object, nevertheless accepts its irreducible materiality and corporeality as a condition of subjectivity. The subject is produced as such by social and institutional practices and techniques, by the inscriptions of social meanings, and by the attribution of psychical significance to body parts and organs. The interlocking of bodies and signifying systems is the precondition both of an ordered, relatively stable identity for the subject and of the smooth, regulated production of discourses and stable meanings. It also provides the possibility of a disruption and breakdown of the subject's, and discourses', symbolic registration.

In place of the mind/body dichotomy, the fundamental connectedness of the mind to the body, the creation of a psychical 'interior' for the body's object-like status, the mapping of the body's interior on its exterior and its exterior on its interior, all need to be theorized. Kristeva's conception of the body's role in psychical development and in signification provides a major, if undeveloped, contribution to such an understanding. Only if the body's psychical interior is projected outwards, and its material externality is introjected as necessary conditions of subjectivity, can the dualism of our Cartesian heritage be challenged.

Psychoanalytic theory makes a number of conjectures about the ways in which the subject's psychical attitudes and beliefs are bound up with the representation of its body. Freud makes a direct link between the structure of the ego, and the child's libidinal investments in the images of others and in its own corporeality. The ego's identifications with others, particularly the mother, secure it in the illusion of a corporeal coherence which belies the child's own lived experience. This forms the basis of Lacan's understanding of the mirror stage and the mode of imaginary identifications which structures its narcissistic relations with others. Through the fantasy of a cohesive, stable identity, facilitated by its specular identification with its own image, it is able to position itself as a subject within the space of its body.

Freud goes so far as to claim that the outline of the ego, its 'form', is a psychical projection of the erotogenic surface of the body. He indicates an isomorphism between the body's perceived (erotic) cohesion and the ego's limits:

for every change of erotogenicity of the organs, there might be a parallel change in the erotogenicity of the ego.[1]

Freud insists that the ego's form is not purely psychical but is the result of the projection and internalization of the body's erotogenic cathexes. Freud illustrates his claim with the metaphor of the cortical homunculus, the 'little man in the head', an image which he locates in the cerebral cortex. The homunculus is a mirror-image or a map by which the brain is able to control and identify with the body:

The ego is first and foremost a bodily ego; it is not merely a surface entity, but is itself the projection of a surface. If we wish to find an anatomical analogy for it we can best identify it with the 'cortical homunculus' of the anatomists, which stands on its head on the cortex, sticks up its heels, faces backwards and, as we know, has its speech area in the left-hand side.[2]

To reiterate the reliance of the ego and consciousness on a psychical representation of the child's perceived and motor-based corporeality, Freud adds in a footnote to the 1927 English translation of *The Ego and the Id* that:

the ego is ultimately derived from bodily sensations, chiefly those springing from the surface of the body. It may thus be regarded as a mental projection of the surface of the body, besides . . . representing the superficies of the mental apparatus.[3]

While Freud clearly recognizes the ways in which the child's psyche requires the mediation of the image of its own and others' corporeality, he leaves these suggestions undeveloped. Lacan reads the metaphor of the cortical homunculus in terms of the infant's mirror-identification with its own image to provide a more detailed account of the ways in which the representation of the body is necessary for the child's acquisition of an imaginary, and ultimately a symbolic, identity. Where Freud postulates a 'schism between the information provided by visual and by tactile perceptions',[4] Lacan uses the opposition between the perception of tactile and kinaesthetic information (which yields the image of the fragmented body, the body-in-bits-and-pieces) and visual perception (which provides an illusory unity for the body seen from the outside) to explain the genesis of an always alienated identity for the subject. The subject is incapable of adequately integrating the fragmented sense of its corporeality provided by its senses with the completion, cohesion and totalization of the visual image of the body.

For Lacan, the development of the infant's ego is dependent on its ability to identify with an image of its corporeal unity. The alienated mirror-image

will crystallise in the subject's internal conflictual tension, which determines the awakening of his desire for the object of the other's desire: here the primordial coming together (*concours*) is precipitated into aggressive competitiveness (*concurrence*), from which develops the triad of others, the ego and the object, which, spanning the space of specular communion, is inscribed there . . . .[5]

His notion of the imaginary anatomy is derived from his under-standing of the mirror stage. The imaginary anatomy is a psychical map or *image* of the body which is internalized by the subject and lived as real. It is a specular and psychical construct, a representa-tion of the subject's lived experiences of its bodily parts and organs. It is not a photographic or realist representation of the body, nor is it a scientifically valid representation, one capable of accounting for the body's physiological functions. Rather, it is a fantasized image, the complex result of the subject's internalization of its specular image and its acceptance of everyday social and familial beliefs about the body's organic structure – a product, that is, of cultural and libidinal investments in the body:

If the hysterical symptom is a symbolic way of expressing a conflict between different forces . . . to call these symptoms functional is but to confess our ignorance, for they follow a pattern of a certain imaginary Anatomy which has typical forms of its own . . . I would emphasize here that the imaginary anatomy referred to here varies with the ideas (clear or confused) about bodily functions which are prevalent in a given culture. It all happens as if the body-image had an autonomous existence of its own, and by autonomous I mean here independent of objective structure. All the phenomena we've been discussing seem to exhibit the laws of *gestalt*. . . .[6]

Lacan explicitly refers to the formative work of Roger Caillois and Paul Schilder in developing his notion of the imaginary anatomy.[7] Both stress that the subject's acquisition of a sense of self, of continuous identity, is the result of the child's ability to locate itself within a body in space, and thus to have a spatial comportment. Incidentally, the mirror stage not only presents the subject with an image of itself, it also duplicates in representational form the environment, enabling real and virtual space to be directly compared. For Lacan the imaginary anatomy it provides is the 'threshold of the visible world.'[8]

Freud's cortical homunculus is literalized in Lacan's model. Lacan claims that 'the cerebral cortex functions like a mirror' and that 'it is the site where the images are integrated into the libidinal relationship which is hinted at in the theory of narcissism'.[9] This 'cortical mirror' is not however a neuro-physiological but a psychological postulate. Lived in an external, 'natural' space – a space, incidentally, which is acquired and not innate – the body must also gain a conceptual and psychical spatiality in order for it to be lived as the subject's own, for the subject to reside in/as its body.

From these psychoanalytic indications, it seems that the subject is not an unanchored, disembodied psychical entity – whether it is conceived only in terms of consciousness or split between a consciousness and an unconscious. It is a subject, an ego, only with reference to the mapping and signification of its corporeality. Although this occurs through the mediation of the image of the body and the degree of erotogenicity of its surface in the mirror stage and the pre-oedipal period, it is clear that the child's particular mode of corporeality – its sex and concrete corporeality – is also relevant to the kind of symbolic and oedipal identity it comes to acquire. The child is positioned as a symbolic subject with reference to the (patriarchal) meaning of its anatomy: this is what Freud calls the 'oedipus complex' and Lacan defines as the 'Law of the Father'. The body's sexual specificity – or rather, the social meaning of its sexual organs – will position the subject either as having (for men) or being (for women) the phallus, and through its relation to the phallic signifier, positions it as a subject or object in the symbolic.

Psychoanalytic theory, then, may be able to provide one of the ingredients of an account of the necessary embodiment of subjectivity. It may be able, with further research, to account for the ways in which the body must be psychically signified in order for the subject to gain a stable, sexually coded speaking position. Along with the acquisition of a psychical image of its body, the child must also undergo various processes of physical production and transformation, through regimes of diet, exercise, training, processes which physiologically inscribe the body's 'organic' forms, producing it as a body of a determinate type, with socially appropriate skills and form. Kristeva's understanding of the body provides an elaboration and further detail about the body's imaginary and symbolic status. She positions (and accordingly modifies) psychoanalytic postulates in the context of signifying practices. In a broader account of the subject's corporeality, it would thus have to be positioned within a more sociological and historical account of the production of the culturally determinate body.

Abject Bodies

Kristeva's notion of abjection provides a sketch of that period which marks the threshold of the child's acquisition of language and a relatively stable enunciative position. In *Powers of Horror* she argues that it is only through the delimitation of the 'clean and proper' body that the symbolic order, and the acquisition of a sexual and psychical identity within it, becomes possible. Abjection attests to the perilous and provisional nature of the symbolic control over the dispersing impulses of the semiotic drives, which strive to break down and through identity, order, and stability. Through abjection, bodily processes become enmeshed bit by bit in significatory processes in which images, perceptions, and sensations become linked to and represented by 'ideational representatives' or signifiers.

Kristeva explores the ways in which the inside and the outside of the body, the spaces between the subject and object, and the self and other become structured and made meaningful through the child's taking up a position in the symbolic order. These pairs need to be oppositionally coded in order for the child's body to be constituted as a unified whole and for its subjectivity to be definitively tied to the body's form and limits. They are the conditions under which the child may claim the body as its own, and thus also the conditions under which it gains a place as a speaking being and point of enunciation.

Kristeva is fascinated by the ways in which 'proper' sociality and subjectivity are based on the expulsion or exclusion of the improper, the unclean, and the disorderly elements of its corporeal existence that must be separated from its 'clean and proper' self. The ability to take up a symbolic position as a social and speaking subject entail the disavowal of its modes of corporeality, especially those representing what is considered unacceptable, unclean or anti-social. The subject must disavow part of itself in order to gain a stable self, and this form of refusal marks whatever identity it acquires as provisional, and open to breakdown and instability.

Kristeva's claim is not entirely new. It is a variation of Freud's position in *Totem and Taboo* and *Civilization and its Discontents*, where he claims that civilization is founded on the sacrifice or expulsion of pre-oedipal polymorphous pleasures and 'impure' incestual attachments to parental love objects. What is new about

Kristeva's position is her claim that what must be expelled from the subject's corporeal functioning can never be fully obliterated but hovers at the border of the subject's identity, threatening apparent unities and stabilities with disruption and possible dissolution. Her point is that it is impossible to exclude the threatening or anti-social elements with any finality. They recur and threaten the subject not only in those events Freud described as the 'return of the repressed' – that is, in psychical symptoms – they are also a necessary accompaniment of sublimated and socially validated activities, such as the production of art, literature, and knowledges, as well as socially unacceptable forms of sexual drives. Even in the most sacrosanct, purified, and socially sanctioned of activities, the unclean and the improper must be harnessed. The subject's recognition of this impossibility provokes the sensation and attitude that she calls 'abjection'.

The expulsion of the abject is one of the preconditions of the symbolic; and it is also the by-product or excessive residue left untapped by symbolic functioning. It is, as it were, the unspoken of a stable speaking position, an abyss at the very borders of the subject's identity, a hole into which the subject may fall. Psychosis as the dislocation of psychical identity is a possible consequence. The subject must have a certain, if incomplete, mastery of the abject; it must keep it in check and at a distance in order to define itself as a subject.

Lacan argues that the ego and its objects, which are both formed in the mirror phase, are counterparts. If each finds its support in the other, if the stability of the object (paradigmatically, the mirror-image or mother) provides the promise of the subject's (future) stability, the abject is neither subject nor object, neither image nor 'reality'. It is a consequence of recognizing the impossibility of the identity of either subject or object, and yet the necessary dependence of each on the other. If the object is an externalized correlate of the subject, then the abject is with the fading, emersion, or disappearance of the subject and its imaginary hold over the object. The abject is that part of the subject (which cannot be categorized as an object) which it attempts to expel. The abject is the symptom of the object's failure to fill the subject or to define and anchor the subject.

Abjection is a reaction to the recognition of the impossible but necessary transcendence of the subject's corporeality, and the impure, defiling elements of its uncontrollable materiality. It is a response to the various bodily cycles of incorporation, absorption, depletion, expulsion, the cycles of material rejuvenation and consumption necessary to sustain itself yet incapable of social recognition and representation. It is an effect of the child's corporeal boundaries being set through the circulation of (socially unacceptable) drive energies and the rhythms of incorporation and evacuation necessary for existence.

The objects generating abjection – food, faeces, urine, vomit, tears, spit – inscribe the body in those surfaces, hollows, crevices, orifices, which will later become erotogenic zones – mouth, eyes, anus, ears, genitals. All sexual organs and erotogenic zones, Lacan claims, are structured in the form of the *rim*, which is the space between two corporeal surfaces, an interface between the inside and the outside of the body. These corporeal sites provide a boundary or threshold between what is inside the body, and thus part of the subject, and what is outside the body, and thus an object for the subject. This boundary must be traversed by the incorporation and/or expulsion of erotic objects. Objects are, in this sense, neither fully contained within the subject's body nor ever entirely expelled from it. Lacan defines these peculiar objects by the formula *objet petit a*, the 'objects' of the sexual drives. The *objet a* is a part of the subject which is 'detachable' from the body and is thus capable of confronting the subject as alien and external. The *objet a* is typically auto-erotic, a part of the subject that can be treated as if it were an external object.

The erotogenic rim which locates the sexual drive in a particular bodily zone is a hole, a gap or lack seeking an object to satisfy it. Ideally, the processes of incorporating the object into the subject's body through its 'rims' stop up the lack. But, as Lacan stresses, the *objet a* is not the name of a thing, an object, but describes a movement, an activity, the taking in or introjection of the object: it is the locus of the subject's absorption and incorporation of the object. Abjection results when the object does not adequately fill the rim. A gap re-emerges, a hole which imperils the subject's identity, for it threatens to draw the subject rather than objects into it.

Like the broader category of the semiotic itself, the abject is both a necessary condition of the subject, and what must be expelled or repressed by the subject in order to attain identity and a place within the symbolic. Even at times of its strongest cohesion and integration, the subject teeters on the brink of this gaping abyss, which attracts (and also repulses) it. This abyss is the locus of the subject's generation and the place of its potential obliteration. In its various processes of destabilization and breakdown, it is the space inhabited by the death drive or its Hegelian equivalent, negativity.

Abjection is the underside of the symbolic. It is what the symbolic must reject, cover over and contain. The symbolic requires that a border separate or protect the subject from this abyss which beckons and haunts it: the abject entices and attracts the subject ever closer to its edge. It is an insistence on the subject's necessary relation to death, to animality, and to materiality, being the subject's recognition and refusal of its corporeality. The abject demonstrates the impossibility of clear-cut borders, lines of demarcation, divisions between the clean and the unclean, the proper and the improper, order and disorder:

we may call it a border: abjection is above all ambiguity. Because, while releasing a hold, it does not radically cut off the subject from what threatens (sic) it – on the contrary, abjection acknowledges it to be in perpetual danger. But also, abjection itself is a compromise of judgment and affect, of condemnation and yearning, of signs and drives. Abjection preserves what existed in the archaism of pre-objectal relationship, in the immemorial violence with which the body becomes separated from another body in order to be – maintaining that night in which the outline of the signified thing vanishes and where only the imponderable affect is carried out. (Kristeva, *Powers of Horror*, pp. 9–10)

Kristeva distinguishes three broad categories of abjects, against which various social and individual taboos are erected: food, waste, and the signs of sexual difference (roughly corresponding to oral, anal, and genital erotogenic drives). The subject's reaction to these abjects is visceral: it is usually expressed in retching, vomiting, spasms, choking – in brief, in disgust. These reactions signal bodily functions which a 'rational consciousness' cannot accept; yet the subject cannot adequately deny them either. They represent a body in revolt, a body disavowed by consciousness which it is yet unable to ignore.

Although it is highly culturally variable, it seems that all cultures have some corporeal processes which are abjected. Abjection is a by-product of the social and psychical investment in and privileging of certain bodily zones and sensations at the expense of others. It results from those corporeal functions which cannot be readily classified and thus remain ambiguous. The abject is undecidably inside and outside the body (like the skin of milk), dead and alive (like the corpse), autonomous and engulfing (like infection and pollution). It is what disturbs identity, system and order, disrupting the social boundaries demanded by the symbolic. It respects no definite positions, or rules, boundaries, or socially imposed limits.

Abjection is the body's acknowledgement that the boundaries and limits imposed on it are really social projections – effects of desire, not nature. It testifies to the precarious grasp of the subject on its own identity, an assertion that the subject may slide back into the impure chaos out of which it was formed. It is, in other words, an avowal of the death drive, a movement of undoing identity.

Oral disgust is the most archaic form of abjection. Kristeva uses the example of the repulsive skin of milk as an example. This skin makes the subject retch and choke because it also represents the subject's own skin, the boundary dividing itself from the world. In other words, the subject chokes on its own corporeal limits, its own mortality. The expulsion of food and the refusal to accept and incorporate it is a refusal of the very stuff, the very substance, of maternal and parental love. Where a 'spoonful for mummy and a spoonful for daddy' signify their love for the child, the child's spitting out and choking on food is a refusal of their demands, that is, that eating represents the child's reciprocal love of the parents:

'I' want none of that element, sign of their desire. 'I' do not want to listen. 'I' do not assimilate it, 'I' expel it. (Kristeva, *Powers of Horror*, p. 3)

In refusing the (m)other's food, the child is rejecting the mother at the same time as expelling *itself*:

But since the food is not an 'other' for 'me', who am only in their desire, I expel *myself*, I spit *myself* out. I abject myself within the same motion through which I claim to establish myself. (ibid., p. 3)

Oral abjection is a refusal of the corporeal limits of the self. The cultural equivalent of this psychical attitude, Kristeva suggests, is the broad-ranging social taboos surrounding the consumption of food. These taboos are clearly culturally specific; yet a culturally rather than physiologically imposed division between the edible and the inedible, the clean and the unclean, characterizes *every* culture. Kristeva uses Mary Douglas's brilliant analysis of purity and defilement,[10] and her convincing explanations of the prohibitions on food propounded in *Leviticus* to explain these socially necessary restrictions on what can be consumed and what is forbidden.

Leviticus provides a list of abominations and restrictions of dietary codes on which the Judaic notion of *kosher* is based. Basically, those animals are considered unclean and therefore forbidden which are not readily classifiable into clear-cut categories. Only those animals which inhabit their 'proper place', their appropriate environment, may be consumed. Only birds which fly, fish which swim, have fins and gills, and only animals which walk on four legs, chew their cud and have cloven hooves are fit for sanctified consumption. These animals are, as it were, properly matched with their habitat. Animals which cross the boundaries between habitats – especially those whose mode of locomotion is at variance with their 'natural' environment – are considered impure and cannot be eaten. The snake, which slithers indeterminately on land or in the water, birds which cannot fly, creatures of the sea which cannot swim, cross the clear-cut categories of earth, air, and water and are thus forbidden.

Corporeal waste is Kristeva's second category of abjection. Bodily fluids, waste products, refuse – faeces, spit, sperm, etc. – provoke cultural and individual horror and disgust, symptomatic of our cultural inability to accept the body's materiality, its limits, its 'natural' cycles and its mortality. Faeces, for example, in signifying that the opposition between the clean and the unclean draws on the distinction between the body's inside and its outside. Inside the body, it is the condition of the body's ability to regenerate itself; as expelled and external it is unclean, filthy. The subject is implicated in this waste, for it can never be definitively and permanently externalized: it *is* the subject; it *cannot* be completely expelled.

For Kristeva, the most horrifying example of waste is the corpse, which is almost universally surrounded by taboos and rituals to prevent 'contamination' of the living. The corpse is:

the most sickening of wastes, . . . a border that has encroached upon everything. It is no longer 'I' who expels, 'I' is expelled. The border has become object. . . . The corpse seen without God, and outside of science, is the utmost of abjection. It is death infecting life. Abject. It is something rejected from which one does not part, from which one does not protect oneself as from an object. (*Powers of Horror*, pp. 3–4)

The corpse is intolerable; it exists at the very borders of life. It shifts the border into the heart of life itself. The corpse signifies the supervalence of the body, the body's recalcitrance to consciousness, reason or will. It poses a danger to the ego in so far as it questions its stability and its tangible grasp on and control over itself.

Kristeva's third category of abjection is the horror of the signs of sexual difference. If the corpse threatens the ego in its very foundations, probably the most culturally widespread of all forms of abjects is the revulsion of sexual difference, represented in the cultural taboo of incest and the horror of menstrual blood:

Excrement and its equivalents (decay, infection, disease, corpse, etc.) stand for the danger to identity that comes from without; the ego is threatened by the non-ego, society threatened from its outside, life by death. Menstrual blood, on the contrary, stands for the danger issuing from within identity (social or sexual); it threatens the relationship between the sexes within a social aggregate and through internalisation, the identity of each sex in the face of sexual difference. (ibid., p. 71)

The cultural horror of menstruation, however, as Kristeva acknowledges, is not straightforwardly linked to the horror of sexual *difference*. Menstruation does not simply differentiate female from male;[11] rather it marks the differences between men and *mothers* (or potential mothers). The horror of menstruation links women to a (presumed) natural maternity without acknowledging women's sexual specificity.

Menstrual blood is the living matter that helps to sustain and bring forth life. Horror of menstrual blood is a refusal to acknowledge the subject's corporeal link to the mother. It is a border separating one existence, the mother's body, from another, the foetus, which both is and is not distinct from it. It marks the site of an unspeakable and unpayable debt of life, of existence, that the subject (and culture) owes to the maternal body.

Abjection is the expression of both a division (between the subject and its body) and a merging (of self and Other, the social). It is the precondition of castration; castration is an attempt to cover

over and expel it. It derives from a stage preceding binary opposition and distinct categories, before language and naming:

The non-distinctiveness of inside and outside . . . [is] unnamable, a border passable in both directions by pleasure and pain. Naming the latter, hence differentiating them, amounts to introducing language, which, just as it distinguishes pleasure from pain as it does all other oppositions, founds the separation inside/outside. And yet, there would be witnesses to the perviousness of the limit, artisans after a fashion who would try to tap the pre-verbal 'beginnings' within a word that is flush with pleasure and pain. . . . Poetic language would then be, contrary to murder and the univocity of verbal message, a reconciliation with what murder as well as names were separated from. It would be an attempt to symbolize the beginning, an attempt to name the other facet of taboo: pleasure, pain. (ibid., pp 61–2)

An unnamable, pre-oppositional, permeable barrier, the abject requires some mode of control or exclusion to keep it at a safe distance from the symbolic and its orderly proceedings. This is the social function of a number of rituals and religious practices which require a distinction between the sacred and the profane. Kristeva claims that religion wrests the subject away from the abyss of abjection, displacing the abject. By contrast, oedipalization and the acquisition of a symbolic position represses abjection (which, Kristeva claims, is the real 'object' of primal repression (ibid., pp. 10–11). Literature, poetry and the arts are more or less successful attempts to sublimate the abject.

Like her other concepts, the maternal chora and the semiotic, the abject is placed on the side of the feminine in Kristeva's work. It is opposed to the paternal, rule-governed symbolic order. Although incapable of direct expression themselves, these repressed 'feminine' elements can be articulated through the mediation of the symbolic. Kristeva claims that through his anti-semitism Céline retains his precarious connection to the abject, and through an appeal to paternal authority, Dostoievski is able to articulate the abject.[12] By naming or speaking it, they can maintain an imperilled hold on the symbolic and a stable speaking position. Naming it established a distance or space which may keep its dangers at bay. To speak of the object is to protect oneself against it while at the same time relying on its energetic resources.

Maternal, Feminine Bodies

The abject defines a pre-oedipal space and self-conception: it is the space between subject and object, both repulsive and attractive, which threatens to draw the subject and its objects towards it, a space of simultaneous pleasure and danger. This is the space of the body in its pre-oedipal, pre-social organization, not yet ordered in hierarchized or regulated terms. It is the expression of a contradictory self-conception, one in which the subject is unable to reconcile its (imaginary, felt, fragmented) experience of itself with its idealized image. Abjection is the subject's and culture's revolt against the corporeality of subjectivity – its material dependence on others, its mortality and its sexual specificity.

If, however, the subject becomes a gendered subject, masculine or feminine, only in acceding to the symbolic order, nevertheless its forms of corporeality are sexually specific. Whether the child has a basis for comparing its body with that of the other sex or not (this may be the consequence of oedipalization), its very sensations, pleasures, and sexual drives are located, not in a generalized and abstract 'corporeality', but in an always sexually specific form. Bodies are always sexually concrete and specific. It is thus crucial, if one is to explore Kristeva's understanding of the body and its role in the production of discourse, to examine the roles she attributes to the body in her understanding of the differences between the sexes.

It is significant that the sexual couple she focuses on is not man and woman, but mother and child. In accordance with psychoanalytic precepts, femininity and female sexuality are not seen in autonomous terms, but are defined in some relation to the phallus. Thus, the (pre-oedipal, semiotic) mother is the phallic mother, the post-oedipal or symbolic mother is castrated, and the woman who is not a mother and does not desire to be one is suffering from a masculinity complex. This may explain why the one category of love missing from *Tales of Love* is the love of a woman for women. Moreover, here women are the passive receptacles of the masculine activity of romantic love, and not themselves the active lovers of men (or women).

Kristeva's notion of maternity and the maternal body is central in her understanding of sexual specificity. It also provides an index of her concept of female sexual specificity. She uses the concept of the maternal to designate a space and a series of processes. However, the maternal is not to be confused with the position and role of a *subject*, for it is a process without a subject. Pregnancy, for example, does not involve the mother's agency or identity. If anything, it is the abandonment of agency. 'Becoming mother' implies an abrogation of subjective autonomy and conscious control. Pregnancy occurs at the level of the organism, not the subject; it 'happens to' women:

Cells fuse, split, and proliferate; volumes grow, tissues stretch, and body fluids change rhythm, speeding up or slowing down. Within the body, growing as a graft, indomitable, there is an other. And no one is present, within that simultaneously dual and alien space, to signify what is going on. 'It happens, but I'm not there.' 'I cannot realize it, but it goes on' Motherhood's impossible syllogism.[13]

Inhabited neither by one being nor by two, pregnancy is more a filter or cipher than an act or decision. To presume pregnancy is the act of a subject, she claims, is to posit a master (the fantasy of the omnipotent phallic mother) which may produce in the subject a psychotic identification:

if we suppose her to be *master* of a process that is prior to the social-symbolic-linguistic contract of the group, then we acknowledge the risk of losing identity at the same time as we ward it off.[14]

This makes the mother into everything for the child, thus threatening its engulfment. Yet, to deny that there is anything there is to be unable to anchor oneself as a subject anywhere; it is to be unable to take up a position:

every speaker would be led to conceive of its Being in relation to some void, a nothingness asymmetrically opposed to this Being, a permanent threat against, first, its mastery, and ultimately, its stability.[15]

Like abjection, pregnancy is a borderline phenomenon, blurring yet producing one identity and an another:

Frozen placenta, live limb of a skeleton, monstrous graft of life on myself, a living dead. Life . . . death . . . undecidable . . . . My removed marrow, which nevertheless acts as a graft, which wounds but increases me. Paradox: deprivation and benefit of childbirth. But calm finally hovers over pain, over the terror of this dried branch that comes back to life, cut off wounded, deprived of its sparkling bark.[16]

Like the abject, maternity is the splitting, fusing, merging, and fragmenting of a series of bodily processes beyond the will or control of the subject. The woman-mother finds that it is not her identity or value as a woman which maternity affirms, but her position as natural or as a hinge between nature and culture. Pregnancy betrays any tenuous identity she may achieve as a subject and a woman. In pregnancy, she is positioned as space, receptacle, matter; in lactation and nurturing functions, she takes on the position of part-object, complement, and anaclitic prop. In a sense, 'she' is a screen onto which the child's demands are projected and from which images are introjected. 'She' does not exist as such.

Kristeva claims that, on the one hand, maternity positions the woman in a kind of corporeal contiguity with her own mother, satisfying the infantile desire to give/bear her own mother a child: here, maternity functions in a 'maternal-homosexual axis'. The baby comes to represent the mother herself, and she, her own mother, in a vertiginous identification which brings the mother into contact with her own mother's maternity:

> By giving birth, the woman enters into contact with her mother; she becomes, she is her own mother: they are the same continuity differentiating itself. She thus actualizes the homosexual facet of motherhood, through which a woman is simultaneously closer to her instinctual memory, more open to her own psychosis, and consequently, more negatory of the social, symbolic bond.[17]

On the other hand, maternity also positions the mother in a 'symbolic paternal axis', in which her body is marked as phallic or castrated according to masculine criteria. Her long-deferred desire for the father's phallus and/or his child – her oedipal wish – is finally satisfied.

Maternity is both socially productive, in so far as the mother 'produces' the social matter which constitutes social subjectivity; and, on the other hand, maternity is also a breach or rupture in the symbolic, an unspoken residual site of jouissance, whose pleasure is reduced to but never exhausted by the symbolic – except perhaps in art.[18] Maternity is thus the site of the semiotic and the precondition of the symbolic. It is a region which requires territorialization, and marking by the proprietorial name of the father – that is, it must be restricted and contained in order for the father's law to be accepted. She must be positioned as his and thus 'branded' by his name.

Maternity is thus not the function of a *woman* (this is also Kristeva's position regarding femininity): it is an organic, a social, pre-signifying space-time: it is disembodied, a function and not a mode of the corporeal specific to women. It cannot be attributed to woman, for 'woman' is precisely that which does not exist. For Kristeva, 'woman' is an essentialist category. In this respect, although her position is related to Lacan's claim that 'The Woman' does not exist, she distinguishes her position from his. For Lacan, 'The Woman' is in fact man's projection of his own perfection through his fantasy of 'The' woman:

[W]omen cannot *be*: the category woman is even that which does not fit into *being*. From there, women's practice can only be negative, in opposition to what exists. . . . Certain feminist arguments seem to resuscitate a naive romanticism, believing in an identity (the opposite of phallocratism).[19]

It is ironic that she problematizes the concepts of 'man', 'woman' and 'identity', seeing them as forms of a metaphysics of presence, when, at the same time and unlike many other feminists, she concedes the relevance of biological, physiological, genetic and chromosomal structures in her discussion of maternity. She is content to attribute an irreducibly biological basis to pregnancy while refusing an identity or agency to the pregnant woman. While it may be accepted that pregnancy is not the act of an agent but a series of (largely biological) processes the woman is subjected to, she also refuses to designate an agency to acts of nurturance and socialization undertaken by most mothers. In refusing to accord a sex to the maternal body, Kristeva seems to accept an essentialist notion of maternity as a process without a subject:

the childbearing woman . . . cathect[s], immediately and unwittingly, the physiological operations and instinctual drives dividing and multiplying her, first, in a biological, and finally, a social teleology. The maternal body slips away from the discursive hold and immediately conceals a . . . ciphering of the species, however, this pre- and transsymbolic memory make[s] of the maternal body the stakes of a natural and 'objective' control . . .; it inscribes both biological operations and their instinctual echoes into this necessary and hazardous *program* constituting every species. The maternal body is the module of a biosocial program.[20]

If the maternal is the space and time of, in Freud's words, 'phylogenetic inheritance', if it is teleologically directed towards the reproduction of the species, Kristeva's resistance to the idea of an identity for woman is politically problematic. For one thing, it is not clear that women's – or men's – identities must be conceived in *metaphysical* terms: differences between the sexes, like differences between signs, need not imply essentialism. It may be a difference without positive identity, a relative rather than an absolute difference, one which defies logocentrism; a difference modelled on Saussure's understanding of identity rather than Descartes'.

Kristeva claims that maternity is the unspoken foundation of social and signifying relations, the 'origin' of heterogeneity and archaic jouissance, the source of the child's corporeal organization and the object to which its desires are directed. Maternity, however, remains strictly outside symbolization – ideally it is repressed or sublimated in order that unity, stability, identity and a speaking position for the child is possible. Yet, ironically, in Kristeva's work, women have no special link to the maternal body, either as a specifically female child who takes up her position in relation to the maternal body (Kristeva subsumes the girl under an oedipal sameness with the boy: she is, as for Freud, a 'little man'), or in her position as mother. The female is both too close and too distant: too close because she never really resolves her oedipal dilemma; she establishes a woman-to-woman relation with her mother only when she becomes a mother herself, only that is, when she is in a position to replace the mother.

Recovered childhood, dreamed peace restored, in sparks, flash of cells, instants of laughter, smiles in the blackness of dreams, at night, opaque joy that roots me in her bed, my mother's, and protects him, a son, a butterfly soaking up dew from her hand, there nearby in the night. Alone: she, I and he.[21]

She is also, as child, too distant from the maternal body in so far as her relation with the mother is only a pale reflection of the boy's relation. The female is paradoxically precluded from representing or speaking maternity and femininity. Kristeva consistently maintains that only certain men – that is, those who are prepared or able to put their symbolic positions at risk by summoning up the archaic traces of their repressed semiotic and maternal (prehistory) – are able to evoke, to name, to re-inscribe this maternal space-time and pleasure in the production and transgression of textuality. The feminine and the maternal are expressed and articulated most directly in two kinds of discourse: the poetic text and religious discourses. The poetic text materializes the pleasures, rhythms and drives of the semiotic; religious discourse is the site of a privileged symbolic representation of the semiotic, in which the symbolic is able to tolerate the expression of normally unspoken pre-oedipal pleasures.

Yet although poetic and religious texts may represent rare loci for the expression of the feminine and the maternal in culture, there nevertheless remains an unrepresented residue or remainder in maternity that is not evoked, a residue that refuses to conform, as Christianity requires, to masculine, oedipal, phallic representations. This residue is at times touched upon by religious discourses, discourses of the sacred, which may, rarely, evoke the blissful ecstasy of corporeal surrender. Yet, Kristeva makes clear that there are unresolved tensions within religious discourses surrounding the expression of the mother-daughter relation and the 'repudiation of the other sex (the masculine)', which leads to 'an acknowledgement of what is irreducible, of the irreconcilable interest of both sexes in asserting their differences, in the quest of each one – and of women, after all – for an appropriate fulfilment.'[22]

Kristeva's interest in religious discourse is, in a sense, the inverse of her interest in poetic texts. If the poetic challenges and transgresses the present 'bounds of sense' with its open-ended deferral of meaning and its refusal to congeal into a symbolic identity, this is the opposite to the processes revealed in sacred discourses. Where the poetic anticipates a language to come, the sacred attempts to stabilize a situation of decay or breakdown, where the poetic engenders a semiotic breach of the symbolic, the religious represents a semiotic recoded in symbolic terms; where the poetic articulates the unnamable semiotic chora, the religious is its 'revelation', The religious recodes what is becoming uncoded and destabilized in the poetic:

In asserting that 'in the beginning was the Word', Christians must have found such a postulate sufficiently hard to believe and, for whatever it was worth, they added its compensation, its permanent lining: the maternal receptacle, purified as it might be by the virginal fantasy. Archaic maternal love would be the incorporation of my suffering that is unfailing, unlike what happens with the lacunary network of signs. . . . Every God, even including the God of the Word, relies on a mother Goddess.[23]

The child's archaic corporeality requires a complex codification and organization in order that it can become a speaking subject, positioned as an 'I' in the symbolic order. This 'I' is capable of producing regulated, ordered discourses as a consequence of the processes of oedipalization which it undergoes; but it is in a unique position to destabilize and thus transform discursive norms, in so far as the speaking subject continues to draw on the repressed semiotic, maternal, corporeal pleasures. Where these are no longer subordinated to the requirements of meaning, coherence and the presentation of a 'content', where they become ends in themselves, something like the poetic text is produced. This kind of model presupposes that the establishment of a speaking position and the capacity to follow the norms of grammar, syntax, logical argument, narrative structure, owes an unspeakable debt to corporeality, to the corporeality the child must renounce – its own polymorphous pleasures, and the maternal body on which it depends.

Kristeva posits a rift between the maternal body and the child's subjectivity, a split out of which language is born but which language itself can never heal:

there is only one way to go through the religion of the Word, or its counterpart, the more or less discreet cult of the Mother; it is the 'artists' way, those who make up for the vertigo of language weakness with the over saturation of sign systems. By this token, all art is a kind of counter-reformation, an accepted baroqueness . . . [the baroque] renders belief in the Mother useless by overwhelming the symbolic weakness where she takes refuge, withdrawn from history, with an overabundance of discourse.[24]

Bodily movements, processes and energies provide the semiotic impetus and raw materials out of which the symbolic is formed. The pre-oedipal and pre-imaginary body-in-bits-and-pieces are the unsocialized 'elements' which, through their psychical coding, become the 'matter' of phonemes and signifiers, rhythm and intonation. Spasms of infantile laughter are the first anticipations of vocalization. However, it is only if the child's phonemic play is capable of being divided into binary oppositions to form minimal phonemic units, only if its gestures and perceptions are given a meaning (for others) and a form (by the child) that they will, later, form the basis of words and sentences.

With the hierarchical unification of the body posed in thetic 'moments' – the mirror stage and the oedipus complex – the ego becomes identified with the subject's psychical interior, and objects become associated with an opposed externality. The subject is located *in* its body, and its body is positioned within a 'natural' and social space as an object for others. This coding of inside/ outside, self/other and subject/object seems necessary for the binarization of the child's vocal experimentations. However such coding is dependent on the expulsion of the unclean and the improper, for only then can the 'clean and proper' social and civilized body inscribe and reorder the chaotic disorganization of the 'natural' or pre-social body.

In those spaces from which the subject-to-be has expelled the abject through the process of the oedipus complex or the Name of the Father, vocal exchange is inserted. However, the subject's definitive place as an 'I' in discourse occurs only when vocalization substitutes for the pleasures of the maternal body, when the desire of the mother is exchanged for the Father's Name.

If bodies and corporeal pleasures must be organized and ordered in specific ways to facilitate discourse, then the discursive structure and all representational systems are a kind of sublimated cor- poreality which cannot be acknowledged as such. But if corporeality is, as I have claimed, always sexually specific and concrete, in what ways is its specificity discursively registered? In what ways does the fact that there are two kinds of body and thus two kinds of subject affect language? Is discourse itself capable of registering the sexual specificity of bodies? Does the speaking subject occupy a sexually coded position, or does the subject's sexuality become subordinated to the neutrality and sexual indif- ference of the 'I'? These are crucial questions for those concerned with the interrelations between bodies and discourses. Unfor- tunately, Kristeva provides no answers. In her understanding, there can be no specifically female writing, no female text, but only texts about women or evoking a lost, renounced femininity and maternity, as do (patriarchal forms of) religious discourse and poetical textual transgressions. This, it seems to me, is a major problem for Kristeva's work. If the body plays such a major if usually unrecognized role in the production (and deformation) of discourses, the specific contributions of sexually distinguished bodies need to make some difference in the kinds of discourses produced, and in the kinds of debt discourses owe to the corporeal, and particularly to the maternal body.

Notes

1 Sigmund Freud, 'On Narcissism. An Introduction', in *The Standard Edition of the Complete Psychological Works* (hereafter SE), translated by James Strachey, London, Hogarth, 1953–74, vol. XIV, p. 84.
2 Sigmund Freud, 'The Ego and the Id', SE, vol. XIX, p. 26.
3 Ibid., p. 26.
4 See, for example, Freud, ibid., p. 25.
5 Jacques Lacan, 'Aggressivity in Psychoanalysis', in *Ecrits. A Selection*, translated by Alan Sheridan, London, Tavistock, 1977, p. 19.
6 Jacques Lacan, 'Some Reflections on the Ego', *International Journal of Psychoanalysis*, 34, 1953, p. 13.
7 Lacan refers explicitly to Caillois' germinal paper, 'Mimickry and Legendary Psychaesthenia', translated by John Shepley, *October*, 31, 1984. He also refers to Paul Schilder's text, *The Image and Appearance of the Human Body*, New York, International Universities Press Inc., 1978.
8 Jacques Lacan, 'The Mirror Stage as Formative of the Function of the "I" . . .', in *Ecrits. A Selection*, p. 3.
9 Ibid., p. 13.
10 See Mary Douglas, *Purity and Danger. An Analysis of the Concept of Pollution and Taboo*, London, Routledge & Kegan Paul, 1966.
11 Arguably, at any given time, there are more females not menstruating than menstruating: pre-pubertal girls, pregnant and menopausal women, athletes, anorexics, and those with menstrual disorders may well, taken together, represent a majority.
12 Cf. 'By symbolising the abject, through a masterful delivery of the jouissance produced uttering it, Dostoyevsky delivered himself of that ruthless maternal burden.
    But it is with Proust that we find the most immediately erotic, sexual and desiring mainspring of abjection; and it is with Joyce that we shall discover the maternal body in its most unsignifiable aspect, shored up in the individual, the fantasy of the loss in which he is engulfed or becomes inebriated, for want of the ability to name the object of desire' (*Powers of Horror*, p. 20).
13 Julia Kristeva, 'Motherhood According to Giovanni Bellini', in *Desire in Language*, translated by Leon S. Roudiez, New York, Columbia University Press, 1980, p. 237.
14 Ibid., p. 238.
15 Ibid., p. 238.

16 Ibid., p. 239.
17 Ibid., p. 241.
18 *The Kristeva Reader*, ed. Toril Moi, Oxford, Blackwell, 1986, p. 166.
19 Ibid., p. 241.
20 Ibid., p. 241.
21 Julia Kristeva, *Tales of Love*, translated by Leon S. Roudiez, New York, Columbia University Press, 1986, p. 247.
22 Ibid., p. 261.
23 Ibid., pp. 251–2.
24 Ibid., pp. 252–3.

References

Caillois, Roger, 'Mimickry and Legendary Psychaesthenia', translated by John Shepley, *October*, 31, 1984.

Douglas, Mary, *Purity and Danger. An Analysis of the Concept of Pollution and Taboo*, London, Routledge & Kegan Paul, 1966.

Freud, Sigmund, 'On Narcissism. An Introduction', in *The Standard Edition of the Complete Psychological Works*, London, Hogarth, 1953–74, vol. XIV.

Freud, Sigmund, 'Totem and Taboo', in SE, vol. XIII.

Freud, Sigmund, 'The Ego and the Id', in SE, vol. XIX.

Kristeva, Julia, *Desire in Language*, translated by Leon S. Roudiez, New York, Columbia University Press, 1980.

Kristeva, Julia, *Powers of Horror. An Essay on Abjection*, translated by Leon S. Roudiez, New York, Columbia University Press, 1982.

Kristeva, Julia, *Tales of Love*, translated by Leon S. Roudiez, New York, Columbia University Press, 1986.

Kristeva, Julia, 'Julia Kristeva in Conversation with Rosalind Coward', *ICA Documents*, issue on *Desire*, 1984.

Lacan, Jacques, 'Some Reflections on the Ego', *International Journal of Psychoanalysis*, 34, 1953.

Lacan, Jacques, *Ecrits. A Selection*, translated by Alan Sheridan, London, Tavistock, 1977.

Schilder, Paul, *The Image and Appearance of the Human Body*, New York, International Universities Press Inc., 1978.

· 7 ·

Geometry and Abjection

VICTOR BURGIN

simple geometrical opposition becomes tinged with aggressivity[1]

Although it makes no direct reference to Althusser's essay of 1970, 'Ideology and Ideological State Apparatuses',[2] Roland Barthes' essay of 1973, 'Diderot, Brecht, Eisenstein', has the effect of spatializing the Althusserian concept of ideology as representation: 'there will still be representation for so long as a subject (author, reader, spectator or voyeur) casts his gaze towards a horizon on which he cuts out the base of a triangle, his eye (or his mind) form- ing the apex'.[3] Laura Mulvey's essay of 1975, 'Visual Pleasure and Narrative Cinema',[4] subsequently theorized the voyeuristic subject of Barthes' theatrical space in terms of Freudian psycho- analysis. The change across this five-year period is profound. Instead of a contingent set of ideas which might be dissipated by reason, 'ideology' was now conceived of in terms of a space of representations which the subject inhabits, a limitless space which the desiring subject negotiates by predominantly unconscious transactions.

For all these innovations, however, there remained significant ties with tradition. Barthes' optical triangle is, after all, half of the diagram of the camera obscura – a metaphor not unfamiliar to students of Marx. Furthermore, 1975 was also the year of publica- tion, in French, of Foucault's *Discipline and Punish*.[5] Barthes' 'eye at the apex' was therefore easily conflated with that of the jailor, actual or virtual, in the tower at the centre of the panop- ticon. For all that Foucault himself would have opposed it, this further contributed to the survival of that strand of theory accord- ing to which ideology is an instrument of domination wielded by one section of a society and imposed upon another – 'the dominant ideas are the ideas of those who dominate', In this context, then – and given the urgent exigencies of a feminist *Realpolitik* – it is not so surprising that one effect of Laura Mulvey's essay was that all man-made images of women were henceforth viewed, without discrimination, as instruments of sadistic objectification, and were therefore proscribed.

I believe that the metaphor of the 'cone of vision', predominant in theories of representation during the past twelve years, is itself responsible for a reductive and simplistic equation of looking with objectifiction. In so far as this metaphor is drawn from physiological optics, it is inappropriate to the description of psychological functions. In so far as it is drawn from Euclidean geometry, it is inadequate to describe the changed apprehension of space which is an attribute of so-called 'post-modern' culture.

I

Space has a history. In the cosmology of classical Greece, as F.M. Cornford writes, 'the universe of being was finite and spherical, with no endless stretch of emptiness beyond. Space had the form of . . . a sphere with centre and circumference'.[6] This classical space essentially survived the biblically-derived 'flat earth' of early Christian doctrine, to re-emerge in the late Middle Ages. In medieval cosmology, supercelestial and celestial spheres encompassed, but did not touch, a terrestrial sphere – the scene of human action – in which every being, and each thing, had a place pre-ordained by God and was subject to his omnivoyant gaze. Foucault has termed this medieval space the 'space of emplacement'; this space, he observes, was effectively destroyed by Galileo: 'For the real scandal of Galileo's work lay not so much in his discovery, or rediscovery, that the earth revolved around the sun, but in his constitution of an infinite, and infinitely open space. In such a space the place of the Middle Ages turned out to be dissolved . . . starting with Galileo and the seventeenth century, extension was substituted for localisation.'[7]

The vehicle of this changed cosmology was Euclidean geometry. Euclid wrote the *Elements of Geometry* around 300 BC. Husserl, in *The Origin of Geometry*, supposes that this system arose out of practical activities, such as building. However, the classical conception of space seems to have been based upon visual evidence rather than technique – the horizon appears to encircle us, and the heavens appear to be vaulted above us.[8] In the Renaissance this conflict between observation and intellection, between hyperbolic and Euclidean space, was played out during the early stages of the invention of perspective. The absence of a necessary connection between knowledge of Euclidean geometry and the development of perspective is evident from the example of the Islamic world. In the West, the primacy of geometry over perception was stressed by Augustine, who wrote: 'reason advanced to the province of the eyes. . . . It found . . . that nothing which the eyes beheld, could in any way be compared with what the mind discerned. These distinct and separate realities it also reduced to a branch of learning, and called it geometry.'[9]

Although dependent upon Euclid's *Elements*, Renaissance perspective took its most fundamental concept from Euclid's *Optics*. The concept is that of the 'cone of vision'. Some two thousand years after Euclid, Brunelleschi conceives of this same cone as intersected by a plane surface – the picture-plane. By means of this model, something of the pre-modern world-view passes into the Copernican universe – a universe which is no longer geocentric, but which is nevertheless homocentric and egocentric. A basic principle of Euclidean geometry is that space extends infinitely in three dimensions. The effect of monocular perspective, however, is to maintain the idea that this space does nevertheless have a centre – the observer. By degrees the sovereign gaze is transferred from God to Man. With the 'emplacement' of the medieval world now dissolved, this ocular subject of perspective, and of mercantile capitalism, is free to pursue its entrepreneurial ambitions wherever trade winds blow.

Entrepreneurial humanism first took liberties with, then eventually replaced, theocentric determinism according to a model which is implicitly Aristotelian, and in a manner which exemplifies the way in which spatial conceptions are projected into the representation of political relationships. In Aristotle's cosmological physics it was assumed that the preponderance of one or other of the four elements first posited by Empedocles (earth, water, air and fire) would determine the place of that body within a continuum from the centre to the periphery of the universe. This continuum of actual and potential 'places' constituted space. Analogously, the idea that a human being will find his or her 'natural' resting place within the social space of differential privileges according to his or her 'inherent' qualities has remained a cornerstone of humanist-derived political philosophies. Newton disengaged space *per se* from Aristotelian 'place',[10] and Newtonian physics was in turn overtaken by the physics of Einstein, in which, in the words of Minkowski, 'space by itself, and time by itself, are doomed to fade away into mere shadows, and only a kind of union of the two will preserve an independent reality',[11] More recently, the precepts of general relativity have themselves come into question in 'quantum theory'.[12] The cosmology of modern physics has nevertheless had little impact on the commonly held world-view in the West, which is still predominantly an amalgam of Newton and Aristotelianism – 'places in space', a system of centres of human affairs (homes, workplaces, cities) deployed within a uniformly regular and vaguely endless 'space in itself'.

In the modernist avant-garde in art, references to a mutation in the apprehension of space and time brought about by modern physics and mathematics are not unusual. Thus, for example, in 1925 El Lissitsky wrote: 'Perspective bounded and enclosed space, but science has since brought about a fundamental revision. The rigidity of Euclidean space has been annihilated by Lobachevsky, Gauss, and Riemann'.[13] Nevertheless, modernists more commonly ascribed a changed apprehension of space not to scientific concepts *per se*, but rather to technology. Thus Vertov wrote: 'I am the cinema-eye. I am a mechanical eye. I, a machine, can show you the world as only I can see it . . . I ascend with aeroplanes, I fall and rise together with falling and rising bodies'.[14] Constrained by mechanical metaphors, Russian futurism, like cubism, ultimately failed – notwithstanding El Lissitsky's pronouncement – to abandon Euclidian geometry. The mirror of perspectival representation was broken only in order that its fragments, each representing a distinct point of view, be reassembled according to classical geometric principles – to be returned, finally, to the frame and the proscenium arch.[15]

In the modern period, space was predominantly space traversed (by this token we judge that the prisoner has little of it). In the 'post-modern' period, the speed with which space is traversed is no longer governed by the mechanical speed of machines such as aeroplanes, but rather by the electronic speed of machines such as computers and video links, which operate at nearly the speed of light. A mutation in technology therefore has, arguably, brought the technolog*ism* inherited from the spatial perceptions of modernist aesthetics into line with the perceptions of modern physics. Thus, for example, Paul Virilio writes that 'technological space . . . is not a geographical space, but a space of time'.[16] In this space-time of electronic communications, operating at the speed of light, we see things, he observes, 'in a different light' – the 'light of speed'.[17] Moreover, this space seems to be moving, once again, towards self-enclosure. For example, David Bolter, a classics professor writing about computer programming, concludes 'In sum, electronic space has the feel of ancient geometric space'.[18] One of the phenomenological effects of the public applications of new electronic technologies is to cause space to be apprehended as 'folding back' upon itself. Spaces once conceived of as separated, segregated, now overlap: live pictures from Voyager II, as it passes through the rings of Saturn, may appear on television sandwiched between equally 'live' pictures of internal organs, transmitted by surgical probes, and footage from Soweto. A counterpart in the political sphere of the fold-over spaces of information technologies is terrorism. In the economic sphere it is the tendency of multinational capitalism to produce First World irruptions in Third World countries, while creating Second World pockets in the developed nations. To contemplate such phenomena is no longer to inhabit an imaginary space ordered by the subject-object 'standoff' of Euclidean perspective. The analogies which fit best are now to be found in non-Euclidean geometries – the topologist's Möbius strip, for example, where the apparently opposing sides prove to be formed from a single, continuous, surface.

Space, then, has a history. It is not, as Kant would have it, the product of a priori, inherently Euclidean, categories of mind. It is a product of representations. Pre-modern space is bounded; things within it are assigned a place along a predominantly vertical axis – 'heaven-earth-hell', or the 'chain of being', extending from God down to stones. Modern space (inaugurated in the Renaissance) is Euclidean, horizontal, infinitely extensible, and therefore, in principle, boundless. In the early modern period it is the space of the humanist subject in its mercantile entrepreneurial incarnation. In the late modern period it is the space of industrial capitalism, the space of an exponentially increased pace of dispersal, displacement and dissemination, of people and things. In the 'post-modern' period it is the space of financial capitalism – the former space in the process of imploding, or 'infolding' – to appropriate a Derridean term, it is a space in the process of 'intravagination'. Twenty years ago Guy Debord wrote about the unified space of capitalist production, 'which is no longer bounded by external societies', the abstract space of the market which 'had to destroy the autonomy and quality of places', and he commented: 'This society which eliminates geographical distance reproduces distance internally as spectacular separation'.[19] Such 'internal distance' is that of psychical space. Nevertheless, as I have already remarked, psychoanalytically inspired theories of representation have tended in recent years to remain faithful to the Euclidean geometrical-*optical* metaphors of the modern period.

II

At the head of her 1975 exposition of Lacan's concept of 'The Imaginary',[20] Jacqueline Rose places a quotation from Lacan's first seminar (1953–4): 'I cannot urge you too strongly to meditate on the science of optics . . . peculiar in that it attempts by means of instruments to produce that strange phenomenon known as images'.[21] As already observed, 1975 was also the year of publication of Laura Mulvey's essay 'Visual Pleasure and Narrative Cinema', with its own emphasis on, in Mulvey's words, 'the voyeuristic-scopophilic look that is a crucial part of traditional filmic pleasure'. If we re-read these two papers today we should read them in tandem, as the one is an essential, albeit somewhat contradictory, complement of the other.

In terms of theories of visual representation (at least in Britain and the US) Laura Mulvey's essay is, arguably, the single most influential article of the 1970s, and it is worth remembering the context in which it first appeared.[22] The observation that there is a fundamental difference between 'classic' semiology, which reached its apogee in the mid-1960s, and semiotics since about 1970, has become a commonplace. The difference, which in principle affects not only semiotics but all theoretical disciplines, is that the classical subject-object dichotomy has been 'deconstructed' –

the interpreter is no longer outside the act of interpretation; the subject is now part of the object. As I have remarked, the metaphor of the 'cone of vision', inherited from classical perspective, has been used to clarify this insight. If the theme of 'the look' dominated Anglophone theories of film and photography during the 1970s, and entered theories of painting in the 1980s, it is perhaps because, apart from the urgent sexual-political questions it could address, the cone of vision metaphor also functioned as *aide-mémoire* in a crucial epistemological break with Western tradition.

In the 1970s the cone of vision model was often conjoined with Lacan's concept of the 'mirror stage'. In Laura Mulvey's essay, for example, Lacan's early geometric perspective version of 'the imaginary' provides a model of cinematic 'identification' in opposition to identification's own 'mirror-image' – scopophilic objectification. However, as Jacqueline Rose's article on 'the imaginary' is at pains to point out, 'it is precisely at the moment when those drives most relevant to the cinematic experience as such start to take precedence in the Lacanian scheme [she refers to the scopic and invocatory drives] that the notion of an imaginary plenitude, or of an identification with a demand sufficient to be its object, begins to be undermined'.[23] On the one hand, the model of the cone of vision was valuable in reinstating the ideologically elided presence of the observer in the space of representation. On the other hand, it was complicit in preserving what was most central to the ideology it sought to subvert – that punctual ego which Lacan identifies, in his later extended critique of the geometric perspective model of vision, as assuming that it can 'see itself seeing itself'. That much of the point of the Lacanian critique of vision had been lost is nowhere better indicated than in the debates which followed Mulvey's influential paper, which so often revolved around the objection that Mulvey had said nothing about the position of the women in the audience.

We see here precisely what Rose identifies as the, 'confusion at the basis of an "ego psychology"', which is 'to emphasise the relationship of the ego to *the perception-consciousness system* over and against its role as fabricator and fabrication, designed to preserve the subject's precarious pleasure from an impossible and non-compliant real'[24] (my emphasis). The confusion is supported and compounded by the cone of vision model. Certainly, as already noted, the model incorporates the subject as an intrinsic part of the system of representation, in so far as the image projects its sight-lines to an ideal point where that subject is supposed to be; nevertheless, the object in this case is quite clearly maintained as external to the subject, existing in a relation of 'outside' to the subject's 'inside'. The object of psychoanalysis, the lost object, may thus easily be confused with some real object. As Rose indicates, it is precisely for this reason that Lacan subsequently abandons the geometric perspective model.

'The idea of another locality', writes Freud, in a famous phrase. 'The idea of another space', adds Lacan, 'another scene, the *between perception and consciousness*'[25] (my emphasis). Psychoanalysis reveals unconscious wishes – and the fantasies they engender – to be as immutable a force in our lives as any material circumstance. They do not, however, belong to material reality, but to what Freud termed 'psychical reality'. The space where they 'take place' – 'between perception and consciousness' – is not a material space. In so far, therefore, as Freud speaks of 'psychical reality', we are perhaps justified in speaking of 'psychical space'.[26] In the passage I have quoted, Barthes speaks of representation as taking place whenever the subject 'cuts out the base of a triangle, his eye (or his mind) forming the apex'. 'His eye or his mind . . .': clearly, Barthes conflates psychical space with the space of visual perception, which in turn is modelled on Euclid. But why should we suppose that the condensations and displacements of desire show any more regard for Euclidean geometry than they do for Aristotelian logic? Some of the peculiar spatial properties of the theatre of desire are indicated by Freud in his paper 'A Child is Being Beaten'.[27] Here the subject is positioned in the audience *and* on stage – where it is both aggressor *and* aggressed. The spatial qualities of the psychical *mise-en-scène* are clearly non-Euclidean: different objects may occupy the same space at the same (non)instant, as in condensation in dreams; or subject and object may collapse into each other. As Rose observes, what this paper most fundamentally reveals is 'the splitting of subjectivity in the process of being held to a sexual representation (male or female)'.[28]

'Author, reader, spectator or voyeur', writes Barthes, identifying his subject of representation. All of these subjects desire, but none more *visibly* than the voyeur. In the chapter of *Being and Nothingness* which bears the title 'The Look', and to which Lacan refers in his own extended discussion of the look as conceived in terms of geometric perspective, Sartre chooses to describe his 'being-as-object for the Other' from the position of the voyeur:

> Here I am, bent over the keyhole; suddenly I hear a footstep. I shudder as a wave of shame sweeps over me. Somebody has seen me. I straighten up. My eyes run over the deserted corridor. It was a false alarm. I breathe a sigh of relief.

But, Sartre continues, if he now persists in his voyeuristic enterprise,

> I shall feel my heart beat fast, and I shall detect the slightest noise, the slightest creaking of the stairs. Far from disappearing with my first alarm, the Other is present everywhere, below me, above me, in the neighbouring rooms, and I continue to feel profoundly my being-for-others.[29]

As Lacan puts it, 'I am a picture' (just as 'I' was God's picture in the medieval space of emplacement).

If Sartre had been less hostile to the concept of the unconscious he might not have excluded the condition of 'being-for-others' from his relation to the object of his scopophilic interest. Merleau-Ponty's phenomenology moved towards a *rapprochement* with psychoanalysis (in a preface he contributed in 1960 to a book on Freud he spoke of a 'consonance' between the two disciplines). Chapter IV of Merleau-Ponty's final, unfinished, work, *The Visible and the Invisible*, is titled 'The Intertwining – The Chiasm'. (*Chiasm*, an anatomical term for the crossing over of two physiological structures, is derived from a Greek root which means 'to mark with a cross'. A cross usually consists of one line placed 'across' another, but it might also be perceived as two right angles – each the reflection of its inverse other, and only barely touching each other. Appropriately, then, the same Greek root has also given us *chiasmus* – the rhetorical term for the trope of 'mirroring'.) The emphasis upon the alienation of subject and object, so often found in readings of Lacan's paper of 1936 on the mirror stage,[30] is absent from this essay by a man whose work so impressed Lacan (an essay in which we rediscover the 'chiasm' in *chiasmus*). Merleau-Ponty writes:

> since the seer is caught up in what he sees, it is still himself he sees: there is a fundamental narcissism of all vision. And thus, for the same reason, the vision he exercises, he also undergoes from the things, such that, as

many painters have said, I feel myself looked at by the things, my activity is equally passivity – which is the second and more profound sense of the narcissism: not to see in the outside, as the others see it, the contour of a body one inhabits, but especially to be seen by the outside, to exist within it, to emigrate into it, to be seduced, captivated, alienated by the phantom, so that the seer and the visible reciprocate one another and we no longer know which sees and which is seen.[31]

Fenichel begins his paper of 1935, 'The Scopophilic Instinct and Identification', by remarking on the ubiquity of references to the incorporative aspects of looking – for example folk tales in which 'the eye plays a double part. It is not only actively sadistic (the person gazing puts a spell on his victim) but also passively receptive (the person who looks is fascinated by that which he sees)'.[32] He adds to this observation a reference to a book by G. Roheim on 'looking-glass magic'; the mirror, Fenichel observes, by confronting the subject with its own ego in external bodily form, obliterates 'the dividing-line between ego and non-ego'. We should remember that Lacan's paper on the mirror stage concerns a *dialectic* between alienation and identification, an identification not only with the self, but also, by extension, with other beings of whom the reflected image is a simulacrum – as in the early phenomenon of transitivism. Fenichel writes:

one looks at an object in order to *share in* its experience . . . . Anyone who desires to witness the sexual activities of a man and woman really always desires to share their experience by a process of empathy, generally in a homosexual sense, i.e. *by empathy in the experience of the partner of the opposite sex* (my emphasis).[33]

As I have remarked, as far as is known, it never ocurred to Euclid to intersect his cone of vision with a plane surface. This idea, which gave birth to perspective, is attributed to Brunelleschi, who gave a famous practical demonstration of his invention. Using his perspective system, Brunelleschi painted a picture of a church upon a panel. In order that the viewer see the image from the correct position – the true apex of the cone of vision – Brunelleschi made a small hole in the panel. The viewer, from a position behind the panel, looked through the hole into a mirror. What the viewer then saw was not him or herself, nor the reversed image of the screen behind which he or she was concealed. What they saw was the church of Santo Giovanni de Firenze, and the Piazza del

Duomo.[34] In the description of a contemporary:

> he had made a hole in the panel on which there was this painting . . .
> which hole was as small as a lentil on the side of the painting, and on
> the back it opens out pyramidally, like a woman's straw hat, to the size
> of a ducat or a little more. And he wished the eye to be placed at the
> back, where it was large, by whoever had it to see . . . it seemed as if
> the real thing was seen: and I have had it in my hand, and I can give
> testimony.[35]

To my knowledge, and surprise, Lacan never spoke of
Brunelleschi's experiment. But this hole in the panel, 'like a
woman's straw hat', is the same hole through which Norman Bates
peers in Hitchcock's *Psycho*. Had we been able, there and then, to
arrest this eye in the name of a moral certainty, we might have
saved Janet Leigh. In reality there would have been no choice. We
should not, however, confuse police-work with psychoanalysis, or
with art criticism, or with art. It is a mistake to believe that the
truth of psychological states may be derived from observable
behaviour. The cone of vision model, however, encourages
precisely such misrecognitions. As Sarah Kofman writes in her
book on the model of the camera obscura, 'All these specular
metaphors imply the same postulate: the existence of an originary
sense . . . the "real" and the "true" pre-exist our knowledge of
them'.[36]

The model of the cone of vision in 1970s theory has both a
positive and a negative aspect. On the positive side, it reinstates
the subject in the space of representation; on the negative side, it
maintains a subject-object dichotomy as a relation of inside/
outside, underwriting that familiar confusion in which the
psychical becomes a mere annexe to the space of the social. Thanks
to such positivism, certain critics pay lip service to psychoanalytic
theory while speaking of scopophilia as if there were nothing more
to say about it than that it is a morally reprehensible form of
behaviour by men.

Catherine Clément has described Lacan's 'era of models' as falling into two distinct periods. The first was a time of points, lines,
arrows and symbols – two-dimensional representations. The
second 'began when he realised that two dimensions were not
enough to make his audience understand the theory of the
unconscious as he conceived of it: specifically, he wanted to show

that the unconscious is a structure with neither an outside nor an inside'.[37] To this second period belong the topological models – the torus, the Möbius strip, the Klein bottle – which 'gave him the means to represent forms without insides or outsides, forms without boundaries or simple separations, forms of which a hole is a constitutive part'.[38] Clément concludes that such geometrical models 'merely complicated the exposition of his ideas'. However, in the special case of the application of psychoanalytic theory to 'visual' art, I believe this metamorphosis of models provides a necessary corrective to a too-easy confluence of psychoanalytic concepts with some familiar prejudices of positivist-intuitionist art theory and criticism – a discourse too ready to collapse sexuality into gender, psychology into sociology, and too ready to take for granted precisely that sexual *difference* which psychoanalysis puts into question.

III

No space of representation without a subject, and no subject without a space it is not. No subject, therefore, without a boundary. This, of course, is precisely the import of the mirror stage: the founding *Gestalt*, the matrix within which the ego will take place. For Kristeva, however, there is a necessary gesture anterior to this first formation of an uncertain frontier in the mirror stage, a prior demarcation of space. In so far as geometry is a science of boundaries, and in a certain interpretation of Kristeva, we might say that the origin of geometry is in *abjection*.[39]

As a concept, the 'abject' might fall into the gap between 'subject' and 'object'. The abject, however, is in the history of the subject, prior to this dichotomy; it is the means by which the subject is first impelled towards the possibility of constituting itself as such – in an act of revulsion, of expulsion of that which can no longer be contained. Significantly, the first object of abjection is the pre-oedipal mother – prefiguring that positioning of the woman in society which Kristeva locates, in the patriarchal scheme, as perpetually at the boundary, the borderline, the edge, the 'outer limit' – the place where order shades into chaos, light into darkness. This peripheral and ambivalent position allocated to woman, says Kristeva, has led to that familiar division of the field of representations in which women are viewed as either saintly or demonic – according to whether they are seen as bringing the darkness, or as keeping it out. Certainly, in Kristeva's work, the 'feminine' – in the wider sense she has given this term – is seen as marginalized by the symbolic, patriarchal, order; but it is biological woman – the procreative body – that this order abjects. In *The Revolution of Poetic Language*, Kristeva writes:

It is not the 'woman' in general who is refused all symbolic activity and all social representativity . . . . That which is . . . under the sign of interdiction is the reproductive woman, through whom the species does not stop at the imaginative producer and his mother, but continues beyond, according to a natural and social law.[40]

The woman's body, that is to say, reminds men of their own mortality. When Narcissus looks into this abjected pool of milk and blood, he sees the pale form at the feet of Holbein's ambassadors. Thus in *Powers of Horror* Kristeva reiterates: 'Fear of the archaic mother proves essentially to be a fear of her generative power. It is this power, dreaded, that patrilineal filiation is charged with subduing'.[41] Thus, in the rites with which certain tribal peoples surround menstruation, Kristeva identifies a fear of what she calls the 'power of pollution'.[42]

There is an extraordinary passage in Plotinus[43] in which this particular apparition of the abject is allowed to reveal itself in a discourse created precisely to conceal it. Plotinus has been speaking of beauty; he continues:

But let us leave the arts and consider those works produced by Nature and admitted to be naturally beautiful which the creations of art are charged with imitating, all reasoning life and unreasoning things alike, but especially the consummate among them, where the moulder and maker has subdued the material and given the form he desired. Now what is the beauty here? *It has nothing to do with the blood or the menstrual process*: either there is also a colour and form apart from all this or there is nothing unless sheer ugliness or (at best) a bare recipient, as it were the mere Matter of beauty [my emphasis] . . . .

Whence shone forth the beauty of Helen, battle-sought; or of all those women like in loveliness to Aphrodite; or of Aphrodite herself; or of any human being that has been perfect in beauty; or of any of these gods manifest to sight, or unseen but carrying what would be beauty if we saw?[44]

Plotinus' Platonic answer to his own question is, of course, the 'Idea'. What is abjected here – distanced by that trope of *accumulation*, that wave of perfect beings which carries the speaker away – is the body itself, as the mere 'matter' of beauty. The abjected matter of which Kristeva speaks, from fingernail clippings to faeces – all that which we must shed, and from which we must distance ourselves, in order to be (in order, as we say, to 'clear a space for ourselves'). 'It has nothing to do with . . .', writes Plotinus, using a device similar to that which classical rhetoric named 'preterition', but which must wait another fifteen hundred years for Freud to conceptualize as 'negation' – for, of course, it has everything to do with Plotinus' desire. We have only to view the abject from a certain angle to see a category which might have been known to Plotinus, from a text by Longinus – the 'sublime'. Thus, in its eighteenth-century incarnation, at the edge of Romanticism, in Shaftesbury: 'the rude rocks, the mossy caverns, the irregular unwrought grottos and broken falls of waters, with all the horrid graces of the wilderness itself . . . these solitary places . . . beauties which strike a sort of melancholy'.[45] For all the discussions recently devoted to the sublime, I still see in it a simple displacement, a banal metaphorical transference of affect from the woman's body to these caverns and chasms, falls and oceans, which inspire such fervant ambivalence, such a swooning of identity, in these Romantic men.

'Beauties which strike a sort of melancholy' – in *Soleil noir*, Julia Kristeva shows me the path which leads from beauty to an object I have lost, or which has abandoned me;[46] I also know that depression may be the mask which anger wears – the concept of the sublime may be the sublimation of a more violent fear. Adopting the voice of the fascism he describes, here is Klaus Theweleit in *Male Fantasies*:

If that stream reaches me, touches me, spills over me, then I will dissolve, sink, explode with nausea, disintegrate in fear, turn horrified into slime that will suffocate me, a pulp that will swallow me like quicksand. *I'll be in a state where everything is the same, inextricably mixed together.* (my emphasis)[47]

It proves, finally, to be not woman *as such* who is abjected, but rather woman as privileged signifier of that which man both fears and desires: the extinction of identity itself. In the terms of the thermodynamic model which informs Freud's concept of the death drive, what is feared is the 'entropy' at work at the heart of all organization, all differentiation. In religious terms, it is the indifferent 'dust' to which we must all return. The transient matter of the woman's body however is doubly abjected, in that it is chronically organized to remind us of our common condition as brief events in the life of the species. By this same token, however, the woman also signifies precisely that desired 'state where everything is the same': the pre-oedipal bliss of the fusion of bodies in which infant and mother are 'inextricably mixed', that absence of the pain of differing, condition of identity and meaning, whose extinction is deferred until death.

IV

Apropos of looking, Sartre writes: 'it appears that the world has a sort of drain hole in the middle of its being and that it is perpetually flowing off through this hole'.[48] It is perhaps this same intimation of loss in the register of the visual which the quattrocento defended itself against by fetishistically turning the intuition into a system, 'perspective' – built not only upon founding subject, the 'point of view', but also upon the diappearance of all things in the 'vanishing point'. Previously, there was no *sign* of absence – the *horror vacui* was central to Aristotelianism. In classical cosmologies, space was a plenum. Similarly, in the medieval world, God's creation was a fullness without gap. In quattrocento perspective the subject first confronts an absence in the field of vision, but an absence disavowed: the vanishing point is not an integral part of the space of representation; situated on the horizon, it is perpetually pushed ahead as the subject expands its own boundary. The void remains abjected. In later, non-Euclidean, geometry we find the spherical plenum of classical cosmologies collapsed upon itself to enfold a central void. For Lacan, this figure, the 'torus', can represent a psychical space in which the subject repetitively comes into being, in a procession which circumscribes a central void – locus of the lost object, and of the subject's death.

Much has been made of the insecurity of the 'post-modern condition', and of its attendant 'crisis of representation'. There is nothing new in insecurity; it is the very condition of subjectivity, just as it is the condition of representation to be in crisis. This is not to say, however, that nothing changes. I have argued that our space has changed, and that our optical models for negotiating it are now out of their time. In 'Women's Time' Kristeva describes a mutation of space, a new 'generation' of 'corporeal and desiring mental space', in which 'the very dichotomy man/woman as an opposition between two rival entities may be understood as belonging to metaphysics'. She asks, 'What can "identity", even "sexual identity", mean in a new theoretical and scientific space where the very notion of identity is challenged?'[49]

In this changed space, this new geometry, the abject can no longer be banished beyond some charmed, perfectly Euclidean circle. The post-modern space of our 'changing places' can now barely accommodate the old ghettos, which are going the way of the walled city-state. Perhaps we are again at a moment in history when we need to define the changing geometries of our changing places. I do not believe that it is a time when an art theory which thinks of itself as 'political' should admonish, or exhort, or proffer 'solutions'. I believe it is a time when it should simply describe. Perhaps it is again, in this time of post-industrial revolution, the moment for a realist project. It cannot, of course, be what it was at the time of Courbet, or even of Brecht. Attention to psychical reality calls for a *psychical realism* – impossible, but nevertheless . . .

Notes

1 G Bachelard, *The Poetics of Space*, New York, Harper & Row.
2 L. Althusser, 'Ideology and Ideological State Apparatuses (Notes Towards an Investigation)', in *Lenin and Philosophy and Other Essays*, London, New Left Books, 1971.
3 R. Barthes, 'Diderot, Brecht, Eisenstein', in *Image-Music-Text*, New York, Hill & Wang, 1977, p. 69.
4 L. Mulvey, 'Visual Pleasure and Narrative Cinema', *Screen*, vol. 16, no. 3, Autumn 1975.
5 M. Foucault, *Discipline and Punish*, Harmondsworth, Penguin, 1977.
6 F.M. Cornford, *Plato's Cosmology*, New York, Harcourt, Brace, 1937.
7 M. Foucault, 'Of Other Spaces', *Diacritics*, vol. 16, no. 1.
8 This remark is prompted by Panofsky's essay, 'Die Perspektive als "symbolische Form"' – today an unpopular article. For a summary of

the debates, see Samuel Y. Edgerton, Jr, *The Renaissance Rediscovery of Linear Perspective*, New York, Harper & Row, 1976, pp. 153ff.

9 Augustine, *De Ordine*, Ch. 15, 42 in A. Hofstadter and R. Kuhns, *Philosophies of Art and Beauty*, Chicago, University of Chicago Press, 1976, p. 180.

10 'Absolute space in its own nature, without relation to anything external, remains always similar and immovable. Relative space is some movable dimension or measure of the absolute spaces; which our senses determine by its position to bodies; and which is commonly taken for immovable space' (Newton, *Mathematical Principles of Natural Philosophy*, quoted in F. Durham and R. Purrington, *Frame of the Universe*, New York, Columbia University Press, 1983, p. 156).

11 H. Minkowski, 'Space and Time', in *The Principle of Relativity*, ed. A. Sommerfeld, London, Dodd, Mead & Co., 1923.

12 'For example, at extremely short distances, on the order of 10^{-33}cm, the geometry of space is subject to *quantum fluctuations*, and even the concepts of space and space-time have only approximate validity' (F. Durham and R. Purrington, op. cit., p. 191).

13 E. Lissitsky, 'K. und Pangeometrie', quoted in P. Descargues, *Perspective: History, Evolution, Techniques*, Van Nostrand Reinhold, 1982, p. 9. It is necessary to distinguish between 'Non-Euclidean geometry' (*or metageometry*), and 'n-dimensional geometry' (or *hypergeometry*). The former, initiated in the nineteenth century by Gauss and Lobachevsky, and developed by Riemann, is a geometry of curved surfaces – spaces which are boundless and yet finite; the latter, also developed in the nineteenth century, is the geometry of 'hyperspace' – a hypothetical space of more than three dimensions. The idea of a fourth dimension as a *literal* fact gained much popularity from the close of the nineteenth century and into the 1930s, and exerted some considerable influence on the early modern movement in painting, not least in its more mystical formulations (the fourth dimension as 'higher reality' – for example, in the Theosophism of Kandinsky and Mondrian). Beyond the 1920s, however, after the popular dissemination of the ideas of Einstein and Minkowski, the idea of a fourth dimension of space largely gave way to the idea of a four-dimensional spatio-temporal continuum – with *time* as the fourth dimension. See L.D. Henderson, *The Fourth Dimension and Non-Euclidean Geometry in Modern Art*, Princeton, NJ, Princeton University Press, 1983.

14 D. Vertov, 'Film directors, A Revolution', *Lef*, vol. 3, in *Screen Reader 1*, London Society for Education in Film and Television, 1977, p. 286.

15 At this point, the necessary simplicity of my outline risks an injustice to Vertov. The industrial-materialist emphasis of some Russian Formalism was asserted against the mysticism which had entered early Russian Futurist art, primarily from the philosophy of P.D. Ouspensky. In *Tertium Organum* (1911), Ouspensky identifies the 'fourth dimension' (see note 12) as that of the Kantian 'noumena', and

allocates to the artist the function of revealing that 'higher' world, 'beyond' phenomena. When, in 1913, the Futurist Matyushin translated extracts from Gleizes and Metzinger's *Du Cubism* (1912) for the journal *Union of Youth*, he accompanied them with passages from *Tertium Organum*. In the same year, Mayakovsky published 'The "New Art" and the "Fourth Dimension"', in which he counters the notion of a higher, non-material, reality with the assertion that the 'fourth dimension' is simply that of *time*: 'There is in every three-dimensional object the possibility of numberless positions in space. But to perceive this series of positions ad infinitum the artist can only conform to the various moments of time (for example, going around an object or setting it in motion)' (quoted in C. Douglas, *Swans of Other Worlds: Kazimir Malevich and the Origins of Abstraction in Russia*, Ann Arbor, UMI Research Press, 1980, p. 31). Mayakovsky's observations adequately describe the programme of French Cubism (which, in today's terms, we might say 'shatters the object', rather than deconstructs the subject-object dichotomy); further, his observations are in agreement with Eisenstein's subsequent thought: 'the fourth dimension (time added to the three dimensions)' ('The Filmic Fourth Dimension' (1929), in *Film Form: Essays on Film Theory*, ed. J. Leyda, New York, Harcourt, Brace, 1949, p. 69). Vertov's 'unmotivated camera mischief' (Eisenstein), on the other hand, often seems to point outside such accommodation of ideas from 'n-dimensional geometry', and towards 'wrap-around' spaces of Non-Euclidean geometry. [Information in this note derived from L.D. Henderson, *The Fourth Dimension and Non-Euclidean Geometry in Modern Art*, Princeton, NJ, Princeton University Press, 1983.]

16 P. Virilio, *L'Espace Critique*, Paris, Christian Bourgeois, 1984.

17 P. Virilio, *Speed and Politics*, New York, Semiotext(e), 1986.

18 D. Bolter, *Turing's Man*, North Carolina, University of North Carolina Press, 1984, p. 98.

19 G. Debord, *Society of the Spectacle*, London, Black & Red, 1983, paragraph 167.

20 J. Rose, 'The Imaginary', in *Sexuality in the Field of Vision*, London, Verso, 1986.

21 J. Lacan, *Le Séminaire, livre I: Les écrits techniques de Freud*, Paris, Seuil, 1975, p. 90.

22 We should also, incidentally, bear in mind that Mulvey herself has continually denounced the widespread attempt to freeze her evolving argument – an argument to be traced through her film-making, as well as through her writing – at that particular, 1975, frame.

23 J. Rose, op. cit., p. 182.

24 Ibid., p. 171.

25 J. Lacan, *The Four Fundamental Concepts of Psycho-Analysis*, London, Hogarth, 1977, p. 56.

26 Since writing this paper, I have come across the following notes by Freud: 'Space may be the projection of the extension of the psychical apparatus. No other derivation is probable. Instead of Kant's *a priori*

determinants of our psychical apparatus. Psyche is extended; knows nothing about it' (*The Standard Edition of the Complete Psychological Works of Sigmund Freud*, London, Hogarth, 1953–74, vol. XXIII, p. 300).

27 S. Freud, '"A Child is Being Beaten": A Contribution to the Study of the Origin of Sexual Perversions', in *The Standard Edition of the Complete Psychological Works of Sigmund Freud*, vol. XVII, pp. 175–204.

28 J. Rose, op. cit., p. 210.

29 J.-P. Sartre, *Being and Nothingness*, New York, Washington Square Press, 1966, pp. 369–70.

30 Laura Mulvey's article is clear in its insistence on the narcissistic, identificatory, aspect of looking (see section II.B). However, in this article, identification is seen uniquely as 'that of the spectator fascinated with the image of his like . . ., and through him gaining control and possession of the woman within the diegesis' (op. cit., p. 13).

31 M. Merleau-Ponty, *The Visible and the Invisible*, Evanston, Northwestern University Press, 1968, p. 139.

32 O. Fenichel, 'The Scopophilic Instinct and Identification', in *The Collected Papers of Otto Fenichel*, First Series, ed. H. Fenichel and D. Rapaport, New York, Norton, 1953, p. 375.

33 Ibid., p. 377.

34 It has been proposed that the purpose of this experiment was to demonstrate that the vanishing point is equal in distance 'behind' the picture-place to the distance of the point of view in front of it. A little 'reflection' will reveal that the viewer of Brunelleschi's panel was, in effect, positioned 'looking back at herself' from the 'other' building at which she was looking.

35 A. Manetti, *Vita di Filippo di Ser Brunellesco*, ed. Elana Tosca, Roma, 1927, pp. 11ff (quoted in J. White, *The Birth and Rebirth of Pictorial Space*, London, Faber, 1972, p. 116).

36 S. Kofman, *Camera Obscura de L'Idéologie*, Paris, Galilée, 1973.

37 C. Clément, *The Lives and Legends of Jacques Lacan*, New York, Columbia University Press, 1973, p. 160.

38 Ibid., p. 161.

39 In a response to this paper (at a conference at the University of Warwick, May, 1987) Julia Kristeva said she would 'more cautiously' prefer the word 'precondition', rather than 'origin', here; she referred to abjection as the 'degree zero of spatialization', adding: 'abjection is to geometry what intonation is to speech'.

40 J. Kristeva, *La Révolution du langage poétique*, Paris, Seuil, 1974, p. 453.

41 J. Kristeva, *Pouvoirs de l'horreur*, Paris, Seuil, 1980, p. 92.

42 Ibid., p. 93.

43 My thanks to Francette Pacteau for having shown this passage to me.

44 Plotinus, *Ennead I*, Eighth Tractate, Beauty (quoted in A. Hofstadter and R. Kuhns, *Philosophies of Art and Beauty*, Chicago, University of Chicago Press, 1964, p. 152).

45 Shaftesbury, The Moralists, Part III, Section II, in A. Hofstadter and R. Kuhns, op. cit., pp. 245–6.
46 J. Kristeva, *Soleil noir: dépression et mélancolie*, Paris, Gallimard, 1987, pp. 107ff.
47 K. Theweleit, *Male Fantasies*, Oxford, Polity, 1987.
48 J.-P. Sartre, *Being and Nothingness*, p. 343.
49 J. Kristeva, 'Women's Time', in *The Kristeva Reader*, ed. Toril Moi, Oxford, Blackwell, 1986, p. 209.

· 8 ·

Primary Narcissism and the Giving of Figure
Kristeva with Hertz and de Man

CYNTHIA CHASE

In Neil Hertz's essay on the writing of Paul de Man, entitled 'Lurid Figures', the concept of primary narcissism takes on a peculiar privilege: that of mediating between psychoanalytic and non-psychoanalytic interpretive discourse, between the discourse to which the concept of primary narcissism would seem to belong, and a practice of rhetorical theory that denies that discourse explanatory authority. The specular relation of primary narcissism becomes the inevitably recurrent instance of the 'uncertain agency' (Hertz's key phrase) of language.[1] How does this particular structure take on such singular power to occur and to explain? It is Kristeva's work on narcissism and melancholia that makes this comprehensible, and it was her 1982 essay 'L'Abjet d'Amour' which reinterpreted primary narcissism in the terms that made it crucial for Hertz's reading of de Man and for the re-reading of Romantic texts (or one could call it the elaboration of Romantic theory) in which that reading remarkably intervenes. In this elaboration, the specular relation between mother and infant becomes a figure for the specular relation between figure and grammar, or between the cognitive and performative dimensions of language. Hertz's essay explains why 'a drama of subjectivity' – submerged but recurrent figures of seduction, of the 'shelter' and 'threat' of a specular relation – must occur 'within a discourse, de Man's, which is committed to questioning its privilege as an interpretive category' ('Lurid Figures', p. 6). De Man's discourse thereby performs, rather than simply asserts, the irreducibility of language to a single order of agency. The 'lurid figures' of seduction, matricide, defacement, while they assert the severance of language from the figured, cognized phenomenal world, *perform* the figural, cognitive dimension of language.

That primary narcissism can serve as a figure, not simply an instance, of the uncertain agency of language, of the disjunction between cognition and performance, is a function of the structure of primary narcissism as it is analysed by Kristeva. 'Primary' structure, not primary state, it is not the earliest state of existence, the mergedness of mother and infant, but rather their first differentiation. It is a specular structure that is triadic: not simply the dyad of mother and infant, but its complication by a third instance. 'L'Abjet d'Amour' returns to Freud's definitions of primary narcissism in the discussion of the origin of the ego-ideal in Chapter 3 of *The Ego and the Id* and in 'On Narcissism', where it is defined as a triadic structure composed when 'a new psychical action' impinges on the auto-erotism of the mother-infant dyad. This action consists in the 'individual's first and most important identification', one that is 'immediate, direct, and anterior to any object-cathexis', 'his identification with the father of his personal prehistory'.[2] Kristeva brings to Freud's definitions an emphasis on the gap, or emptiness, that identification implies and conceals: 'ce *vide* constitutif du psyche humain'.[3] She identifies 'the primal separation or blank or emptiness experienced by the infant', and 'the bar or gap separating signifier and signified' in Saussurean linguistic theory.[4] The identification with the Imaginary Father, Kristeva maintains, sustains the gap constitutive of the structure of signification. Kristeva's interpretation of primary narcissism thus makes an identification, or as she says, a transference, constitutive of the structure of the sign. This is to describe how the sign is a trope – and to place figural language, *Dichtung*, poetry, at the origin of signification. More exactly, it is to describe how an act of figuration, a performative of a sort, is the condition of the emergence of signs or figures. Prior to the sign is a figuration *producing* that structure. A performative dimension of language exceeds its cognitive function.

That Kristeva works with a performative model of language is no news, and can hardly be offered as surprising. But the *way* it emerges in the reinterpretation of primary narcissism reveals a great deal about the implications of the performative model. I want to show this by aligning Kristeva's description of that structure with Paul de Man's account of the conditions of the possibility of signification. The salience of Kristeva's description comes out in its similarity with the leading rhetorical terms or structures in the recent writing of de Man and Hertz: prosopopoeia, the making or giving of a face or a figure, and the 'end of the line' or 'T on its side structure', as Hertz sometimes calls it, a form of asymmetrical chiasmus.[5] The giving of a face is involved, unmistakably, in the 'new psychical action' of the infant's 'immediate identification' with the Imaginary Father, which constitutes the first identity. To align the giving of face in de Man's sense with a specific 'psychical action' is to risk an unwarranted phenomenalization and an erroneous literalization; still, it is by comparing the two accounts that we will be able to address that problem, which is also the problem of performative models of signification.

Kristeva's analysis of the infant's 'immediate identification' with the Imaginary Father draws near de Man's considerations as it becomes the analysis of an act of *reading*. It does so as a differentiation between two modalities of the primal parent – primary narcissism being a phase or mode in which sexual difference is yet unknown – comes into play. For that the first identification is 'immediate' does not mean that it takes place by itself – only that it cannot be mediated, that this moment is not part of a dialectic. In what sense it can take place, then, how it occurs, becomes the burden of the analysis. It occurs via the 'relay' of the mother, according to Kristeva; by 'the father of the individual's prehistory', Freud means the 'father' indicated to the infant by the mother's desire. Freud's footnote to the phrase amends, 'Perhaps it would be safer to say [an identification] "with the parents"; for before a child arrives at a definite knowledge of the difference between the sexes, the lack of a penis, it does not distinguish in value between its father and its mother'.[6] It distinguishes in value between the penis and its lack. This 'distinguishing' is simply the action of identifying with the phallic instance, with an ungendered phallic parent. Prior to gender difference is a sexual difference within an act of reading.

Here is how this comes out. The 'immediate identification' with the Imaginary Father takes place, Kristeva writes, 'thanks to the relay by the so-called pre-oedipal mother, insofar as she is able to signify herself to her infant as having a desire other than that of responding to the demand of her offspring (*son rejeton*), (or simply to refuse it)'.[7] In so far, that is, as the infant receives the mother's care as an indication, as a sign of something other. The gestures of maternal care are at once, and indeterminably, the satisfaction of the mother's and infant's needs, and the indication of the mother's desire or love. The instance of the Imaginary Father is elaborated, the first identity or *form* is constituted, as the infant *reads* those indeterminably significative marks. Whether it should be said that it is the infant that *confers* on them the status of signs, or the mother who confers on them the possibility of being so received, is as undecidable as the marks' perceptual and semantic status. To read, the implied catachresis for the infant's action, is precisely not to know, but nor is it assertably an action, which may have, which has to have, previously taken place.

The first identity or form is constituted as the infant *gives a face* to the indeterminably significative marks of maternal care: the face of the sign. Kristeva's analysis of this moment draws near de Man's reflection on prosopopoeia or the giving of figure, even in deploying concepts alien to de Man's discourse, as she comes to describe the dual implications of this gesture. It brings into being not a subject and an object, but the Phallus and an 'abject'. For in reading the marks of maternal care, the infant rejects taking them as fulfilment of the need that merges mother and infant; rejects taking them as non-significative, accepts them as indicative, as signifying, indicating, something other than that mergedness. The first identity is the infant's identification with this other, this instance set apart from the conglomeration of fulfilling mother and fulfilling infant, of marking and marked. That instance, that which is received as the desire of the mother, is the Phallus. The Phallus is the sign of signifying. Kristeva intervenes, in this more or less familiar account, to affirm that simultaneously with the identification with this instance there takes place 'a process of rejection vis-à-vis what could have been a chaos and which begins to become an . . . *abject*. The place of the mother does not emerge as such, before becoming an object correlative with the desire of the ego, except as an *abject*'.[8] The rejection of the abject is the rejection of what is not received as a sign. The rejection of the mother as abject, which Kristeva sees at the origin of all the various misogynistic affects and rituals of culture, is the repudiation of the uncertainty about those marks that may or may not be significative, that are significative only in so far as they are read.

My purpose in recasting this analysis as an account of reading is to bring the complications that emerge in Kristeva's description into proximity with an analysis that I think clarifies and accounts for them, de Man's analysis of the intervention of reading in the construction of the predicative function or deixis. We have seen it said that the instance of the Imaginary Father – which is the structure of the sign – is set up in so far as maternal care is able to signify, to indicate, something other than itself. This is not a tautology, but the articulation of an enigma. How are the signifying and the sign held together, and held apart? Both Hertz (with his 'end of the line' structure, found out in poems of Wordsworth and novels of George Eliot and Flaubert) and de Man (juxtaposing Hegel and Hugo) draw their answers from literature; doesn't Kristeva, as well, if from more distant reading? – Mallarmé and Lautréamont, before Céline, or Ovid. The critical texts on the Romantic texts provide an interpretation of the effects in Kristeva's essay, of how as it differentiates the indicating from the indication, the difference blurs. In 'L'Abjet d'Amour', that which is identified with or transferred onto and that which is rejected are distinguished in the following way: as a 'unity', on the one hand, 'the most archaic unit . . . that of the Phallus desired by the mother: . . . the unity of the Imaginary Father, a *coagulation* of the mother and her desire'; and on the other, 'that which could have been a chaos', the conglomeration of fulfilling mother and fulfilling infant. The 'coagulation' of the mother and her desire, the conglomeration of the mother and her need: what blurs here is the distinction between what is read and what is read from or not read. I want to turn in a moment to de Man's description of why and how that is necessarily the case. Kristeva's work on 'abjection' and melancholia I take to be an exploration of the consequences of the failure of this distinction, of the fact that the differentiation of the sign and the other fails to take place. The phrasings in 'L'Abjet d'Amour' certainly suggest that the primary identification does not simply give a face to one instance and deprive of face another one. Rather the instance identified with is indistinguishable from, though it is not identifiable with, the instance repudiated. For the repudiation of indeterminably significative marks – the rejection of the 'abject' – is in another sense a repudiation of language, of the moment and the material without which no such thing as language could come into being.[9] The 'process of rejection of an abject' alluded to in 'L'Abjet d'amour' separates and rejects, but this rejection fails, inasmuch as it can in no way be separated from the identification with the sign. Hence Kristeva comes to write in *Pouvoirs de l'horreur* not simply of the 'rejection' of the abject, but of *abjection*, a recurrent condition of the speaking subject.

In describing the gestures of maternal care as indeterminably significative marks, I am drawing together psychoanalytic characterizations of sexuality and textuality as 'propped on' the fulfillment of needs, and de Man's characterization of the anagrammatic patterns in Latin and Vedic poetry traced by Saussure, in the aborted work known as the *Anagrammes* that is also a key reference for Kristeva.[10] De Man dwells on Saussure's abandonment of his project as he discovered that no evidence whatever, including mathematical analysis, could be adduced determining whether the assonantal patterns he had identified were deliberate or random, encoded or simply the effect of probability or chance. The impossibility of determining this undid the premise with which Saussure began and invalidated a particular term for his object: he had called what he was finding, at one point, 'hypograms', and noted the etymology, 'to underline by means of make-up the features of a face'.[11] Saussure discovered the impossibility of perceiving the semiotic process without *conferring* on some patterns of recurrence, and not on others, the status of meaningful articulations: only by means of make-up is a face there. (This camp version of the discovery that Saussure drew back from is straight from de Man.)[12] How that conferring is carried out is the subject of de Man's essay 'Hypogram and Inscription', which identifies the *giving* of face, prosopopoeia, as the move that enables the predicative and demonstrative function of language to take place. De Man retraces in Hegel's analysis of deixes (Chapter One of the *Phenomenology*, the distinction between perception and sense-certainty) the interplay of prosopopoeia and inscription elaborated in a so-called 'descriptive' poem by Hugo, entitled 'Ecrit sur la vitre d'une fenêtre flamande' ('Written' – inscribed – 'on the pane of a Flemish window'). The 'immediate identification' in primary narcissism, as interpreted by Kristeva, turns on the very issue addressed by Hegel and Hugo: what are the conditions of indicating, what is involved in the emergence of a sign which points.

What is involved, according to de Man, is an identification of the materiality of an *inscription*, such as the word 'Written' written in Hugo's and Hegel's texts, with the phenomenality of a *signified*, with its accessibility to cognition as a meaningful form. 'If there is to be consciousness (or experience, mind, subject, or face)' de Man writes, 'it has to be susceptible of phenomenalization. But since the phenomenality of experience cannot be established *a priori*, it can only occur by a process of signification'.[13] De Man adduces a text of Hugo categorized as 'descriptive' poetry by Riffaterre as an instance of how description or perception is conditioned by a figuration that links it with a process of signification. In Hugo's poem praising the sound of the *carillon* that chimes from the bell towers of Flemish cities, the ringing of the bells, the carillon, functions as 'the material sign of an event (the passage of time) of which the phenomenality lacks certainty'. 'The phenomenal and sensory properties of the signifier have to serve as guarantors for the certain existence of the signified', writes de Man.[14] This takes place via a figure. The opening of the poem is, 'J'aime le carillon de tes cités antiques,/[. . .]/Noble Flandres'. The underlying figure or matrix of the poem, de Man establishes, is the prosopopoeia 'I love time'. That figure, writes de Man, 'accomplishes the trick [of] arbitrarily linking the mind to the semiotic relationship that connects the bells to the temporal motion they signify'. The phenomenality of the mind or cognition can seem to be ensured by the phenomenality of the signifier because the mind and time are linked by the prosopopoeia. De Man: 'The senses become the signs of the mind as the sound of the bells is the sign of time, because time and mind are linked, in the figure, as in the embrace of a couple'.[15] The chime is apprehensible as a sign of time, which in turn makes consciousness apprehensible, because signifier and signified have been united in a *form* by the giving of face to the chime, by means of the figure linking time and its sign to the mind and its senses. Thus the phenomenalization of consciousness occurs, the apprehension of the *indicating* of something occurs, through an act of reading, the *giving* of figure, the prosopopoeia that gives a face to the sound of the bells.

The resonances between de Man's and Kristeva's accounts of the conditions of cognition are apparent, I hope. Once again: in the Hugo poem, perception and cognition (ego-functions) are constituted – 'the senses become the signs of the mind as the sound of the bells is the sign of time' – 'because time and mind are linked, in the figure, as in the embrace of a couple'. So the ego-ideal originates, in primary narcissism, as the mother and the phallus, signifying marks and sign, are linked in the figure of the phallic parent or Imaginary Father. If the matrix of the Hugo poem is the prosopopoeia 'J'aime le temps', the matrix of the *Ego and the Id* passage read by Kristeva is – the matrix: the mother *cum* her desire, the mother with the phallus.[16] De Man's reading of the *Hegel* text likewise identifies a 'coagulation' that is the matrix of all acts of perception. It is the confusion of the undeniable existence of inscription, evoked by Hegel's sudden allusion to 'this piece of paper on which I am writing', (or in the case of Saussure, by the demonstrable existence of a sequence of letters in a text that can be assembled to form a proper name), with the phenomenal reality of the signified. It is that confusion, on which 'perception' depends, that blurs the distinction between the sign and its other, between what is read and what is not readable. Not readable – yet read – are the indeterminably significative gestures of maternal care. Not readable is the inscription of the word 'written' in Hugo's and in Hegel's texts, marking a fact which 'is undeniable', de Man writes, 'but totally blank'[17] – as blank as the marks of maternal care, unless they be read as signs of desire. In the wake of all the other demonstratives and deictics, all the 'this's and 'here's and 'now's in Hegel's first chapter, its closing pages confront us with another one: '"this" bit of paper on which I am writing – or rather have written – "this"'.[18] This 'this', as de Man points out (in a prosopopoeia of his own I wish I could reproduce here), is unlike those others, in that it is pointing, if it is at all, only to itself. Writing and referent, marking and marked, merge, and this coagulation, which indicates nothing, and signifies nothing, is the matrix of all future acts of reference, which take it as the guarantee of their validity.

What merges is the positing of the significative status of the marks, and the signification thereby composed. Neil Hertz, in his book *The End of the Line*, maps Kristeva's definition of primary narcissism onto the structure he describes as 'a T on its side'.[19] It gives us a good way of conceiving the confusion I have been discussing: the identification of the performative with the cognitive dimension of language, brought about in the *giving* of figure, or prosopopoeia. The long horizontal part of the T would represent the 'giving', and the short vertical part (the joining of two points) the 'face'. (Although, in fact, 'face', in de Man, would mean the entire figure; and not mean one's face, the face one thinks one has.) The long part would represent the performative dimension of language, and the short part the cognitive. What happens as this figure comes into play is that the long part gets identified with the short part, performance with cognition. The long side of the T is misconstrued as being made on the model of the short side, as the matching and joining of two poles, an object and its subject, or a signified and its signifier. Reconstructing the figure represents an attempt to reconstrue the short side of the T as modelled and produced by the long side; to construe the signifier, say, as Kristeva would, not simply as a pole in a cognitive structure (a sign) but as a drive or a motion or performance. Or to construe 'face', as de Man in fact does, as the giving of face – which disfigures, in so far as it inscribes the *lack* of an existing face or figure. Such gestures go against the grain of our infantile narcissism. In *that* primary and unsurpassable gesture, structure, the long side of the figure (of the T, of the face), gets identified with the short, the happy side: that is, the indeterminably significative marks and the arbitrary positing of their significativeness gets identified with the determinate relation of signification, the structure of the sign as a symbol. The fact of occurrence, of arbitrary marks, is apprehended as the power to mean.

This is the *specular* relation between cognition and performance I alluded to at the start: their incommensurability, but by the same token, the impossibility of maintaining the distinction between them. Otherwise there would be no disparity, but the *cognition* of a performance. Instead we are faced with the *performance*, the production, of the disjunction between performance and cognition. We are faced by a giving of face that de-faces.

Figures such as 'defacement' recur disconcertingly in de Man's theoretical writing, Hertz observes, and in Hertz's essay on de Man one of them – one that is singularly pertinent to the scenario of primary narcissism – becomes a means of explaining why. Remarking de Man's 'lurid figures' for the disjunction between performance and cognition – 'the wound of a fracture that lies hidden within all texts'[20] – Hertz cites de Man writing on Benjamin's 'The Task of the Translator' (I quote de Man quoted by Hertz):

All these activities – critical philosophy, literary theory, history – resemble each other in the fact that they do not resemble that from which they derive. But they are all intralinguistic: they relate to what in the original belongs to language, and not to meaning as an extralinguistic correlate susceptible of paraphrase and imitation. They disarticulate, they undo the original, they reveal that the original was always already disarticulated. They reveal that their failure, which seems to be due to the fact that they are secondary in relation to the original, reveals an essential failure, an essential disarticulation which was already there in the original. They kill the original by discovering that the original was already dead.[21]

Hertz comments: something is added here to the familiar deconstructive notion that a decanonization 'discovers a disarticulation that was always already there'.

What these lines add to that is the discomfiting, because seemingly gratuitous violence of construing 'disarticulation' as murder and murder as paradoxically, 'discovering that the original was already dead' . . . what they add is, fleetingly, the pathos of uncertain agency. A subject is conjured up . . . who can serve as a locus of vacillation: did I do it? or had it already been done?[22]

Such 'pathos of uncertain agency', I suggest, inheres in Kristeva's concept of 'abjection'. As Jacqueline Rose has observed, Kristeva's writing about the primary role of abjection raises an uncertainty posed as Hertz suggests by the lurid figures of de Man's: if 'matricide' is imported – as it is in de Man's reading of a poem of Yeats ('Those Dancing Days are Gone') that Hertz dwells on later in his essay – if a term such as 'matricide' or 'abjection' is imported into an account precisely *not* of specific cultural manifestations but of universal linguistic structures or of intralinguistic activities, the question arises as to whether the writer is not *enforcing* the misogynistic gesture – is not killing the mother by finding her already dead. Such writing may *enact* the performative gesture on which it seeks to comment. It thereby confronts the reader with a problem of *ethical* as well as critical judgement. To sustain that confrontation unrelentingly is the strength, I would contend, of Romantic theory, by which I mean the rhetorical practice of those Romantic texts, Rousseau and Wordsworth, in which these figures of specular violence find their originals.

One original for the 'murder' evoked by de Man that I have too rapidly conflated with matricide is the 'blessed babe' of Book II of *The Prelude*, who '*claims* manifest kindred with an earthly soul' as he 'drinks in passion from his mother's eye'.[23] This is the contradictory self-cancelling gesture of *positing* meaningful form or determinate relationship that we saw was at stake in the infant's 'immediate identification' with the phallic parent analysed by Kristeva. That the blessed babe's 'verbal deed'[24] is murderous in the ambiguous sense expressed by de Man is shown in a reading of the poem that uncovers in Wordsworth's story of the loss of his mother the account of her non-phenomenal existence as sheer device for the production of meaning; thus Wordsworth writes of his mother's death, oddly, 'the *props* of my affections were removed' (II. 294). The congruence of Wordsworth's props and Freud's – via, appropriately enough, a *translation* of Freud's term 'Anlehnung' – is brilliantly worked out in an essay by Catherine Caruth on 'Narrative Origins in Freud and Wordsworth'.[25] Kristeva's account of the mother's abjection comes close to this sense of killing the mother by discovering her to be already dead: the mother is rejected as abject in so far as the gestures of maternal care are encountered as insignificative marks, material inscription.

I want to return to the significance of de Man's calling this intralinguistic encounter '*killing* the original by finding it already dead'. Taken alone, 'finding it already dead' would mean *recognizing* the material, performative status of the original. That would be a *cognition* of the performative – a move the delusive nature of which we have already examined. It is the ethical, as well as epistemological, dubiousness of such a claim that I now wish to stress. To recognize the original as dead is to accept that death as a given, to receive it as pre-established in the nature of things. It is to take the materiality of indeterminably significative marks as matter: as determinably and definitively mere device, mere material – lifeless, without meaning. It is to return, in short, to the metaphysical categories of matter and spirit. This has meant, always, accepting *the mother* as already dead. It has meant 'recognizing' the merely natural nature of maternal care, and its supersession by the child's identification with an Imaginary Father, or a patriarchal Imagination.

When de Man writes 'to *kill* the original by discovering that the original was already dead', he insists on the violence of this gesture of 'recognition', which legitimates the authority, as 'life', of the spirit alone. He fleetingly evokes the life, 'killed', of language, of the materiality of indeterminably significative signs. The materialness of such gestures is part of the case de Man brings against acts of reading, including his own. The case one could *not* make is that his readings perform the ambiguous murder, the matricide, that would consist in employing the term 'matricide' as mere device, dead metaphor, 'mere' figure.

The coming to life, in a text, of such ambiguous figures as 'abjection' or 'killing by discovering dead' would be the primary condition not of cognition or consciousness, but of history. In preserving the question, 'did I do it?', the figure reserves the possibility of an action. In coupling it with the reserve, 'or had it already been done?', it gives a shape to the imperative of linking an ethical or political project with a critical epistemology. I 'could wish' that to be the significance of Kristeva's reconfiguration of primary narcissism.[26]

Notes

1 Neil Hertz, 'Lurid Figures', in *Reading de Man Reading*, ed. Wlad Godzich and Lindsay Waters, Minneapolis, University of Minnesota Press, 1988.
2 *The Standard Edition of the Complete Psychological Works of Sigmund Freud*, ed. James Strachey, London, Hogarth, 1953–74, vol. XIV, p. 77; vol. XIX, p. 31.
3 Julia Kristeva, 'L'Abjet d'Amour', *Tel Quel*, 1982, p. 19. This text reappears as part of Chapter One of *Histoires d'amour*, Paris, Denoel, 1983, recently translated by Leon S. Roudiez as *Tales of Love*, New York, Columbia University Press, 1987.
4 Neil Hertz, *The End of the Line, Essays on Psychoanalysis and the Sublime*, New York, Columbia University Press, 1985, p. 231.
5 Paul de Man, *The Rhetoric of Romanticism*, New York, Columbia University Press, 1984, pp. 75–6, 89–90; Neil Hertz, *The End of the Line*, p. 218.
6 Freud, *Complete Psychological Works*, vol. XIX, p. 31.
7 Kristeva, 'L'Abjet d'Amour', pp. 21–2.
8 Ibid., cited by Hertz, p. 231.
9 Cf. Paul de Man, *Allegories of Reading*, New Haven, Yale University Press, 1979, p. 293.
10 See, for instance, Kristeva, 'The Speaking Subject', in *On Signs*, ed. Marshall Blonsky, Baltimore, The Johns Hopkins University Press, 1985, p. 210.
11 Paul de Man, *The Resistance to Theory*, Minneapolis, University of Minnesota Press, 1986, pp. 44, 37.
12 The status of 'camp' in psychoanalytic theory and interpretation is

identified by Phil Barrish, 'Rehearsing a Reading', *Diacritics*, 16, 4, Winter 1986.

13 De Man, ibid., p. 48.

14 Ibid.

15 Ibid., pp. 48–9.

16 Neil Hertz alerted me to the potential significance of the term 'matrix', querying whether 'the close proximity in "Hypogram and Inscription" of [de Man's] use of the word "material" to Riffaterre's use of "matrix" might indicate a possible connection to be made between them'.

17 De Man, *The Resistance to Theory*, p. 42.

18 G.F.W. Hegel, *Phenomenology of Spirit*, translated by A.V. Miller, Oxford, Oxford University Press, 1977, p. 66.

19 Hertz, *The End of the Line*, pp. 218, 231.

20 De Man, *The Rhetoric of Romanticism*, p. 120 (cited by Hertz, 'Lurid Figures').

21 De Man, *The Resistance to Theory*, p. 84.

22 Hertz, 'Lurid Figures'.

23 *William Wordsworth*, ed. Stephen Gill, London, Oxford University Press, 1974.

24 De Man, *The Rhetoric of Romanticism*, p. 91.

25 Cathy Caruth, 'Past Recognition, Narrative Origins in Wordsworth and Freud', 100, 5, Dec. 1985, pp. 935–48.

26 Cf. Wordsworth, 'My heart leaps up when I behold', ed. Stephen Gill, p. 246: 'The Child is Father of the Man;/And I could wish my days to be/Bound each to each in natural piety.'

· 9 ·

Julia Kristeva
Theorizing the Avant-Garde?

LESLIE HILL

The association between Julia Kristeva and the Paris literary and theoretical journal *Tel Quel* was a close one. After Kristeva's arrival in France in 1966, *Tel Quel* became an important outlet for much of her early work. In 1969 the *Tel Quel* book series, published by the Editions du Seuil, brought out her first collection of essays, *Séméiotiké*, which was followed, over the next ten years or so, by five further titles in the series.[1] By 1970, Kristeva had become a member of the journal's editorial board and *Tel Quel* continued to provide her with her major theoretical platform until 1983, when the journal was discontinued, and renamed and reformulated under the title *L'Infini*. Now published by Gallimard, after an initial period with its subsidiary, Denoël, the new journal, having adopted a more catholic editorial policy than its predecessor, has remained under the direction of *Tel Quel*'s other leading figure, the novel writer, polemicist and essayist, Philippe Sollers.

Throughout the period of Kristeva's involvement with *Tel Quel*, the journal's theoretical position underwent a number of radical shifts. In 1971, still in the wake of the events of May 1968, amidst numerous divisions and with a resulting change of personnel, the journal abandoned its policy of theoretical dialogue with the French Communist Party, which had given rise, for instance, to the group's involvement in the 1970 Cluny Conference organized by the Communist monthly, *La Nouvelle Critique*, on the theme of 'Littérature et Idéologies' ('Literature and Ideologies'). In the summer of 1971, *Tel Quel* broke with official Marxism and declared its support for the Chinese Cultural Revolution. This new turn was consolidated at *Tel Quel*'s own conference at Cerisy in 1972, which was devoted to the writings of Antonin Artaud and Georges Bataille and prefixed with the title, 'Vers une révolution culturelle' ('Towards a Cultural Revolution').[2]

In 1977, however, after the death of Mao Zedong and the disillusioning experience of the visit to China which some of the prominent members of the group had undertaken in 1974, the journal brought out a triple issue on the theme 'Pourquoi les États-Unis?' ('Why the United States?'), which detailed its enthusiasm for the post-European melting-pot of American culture. In American society, as Kristeva argued in a round-table discussion which first appeared in the issue, the place of culture was admittedly marginal, but that marginality had a 'polyvalent' dimension which seemed to be lacking in Europe. In the United States, there appeared to be more scope and latitude for experimental artistic practices, notably in the domain of non-verbal expression or the realm of performance. Thus, by 1977, it seemed to Kristeva and her *Tel Quel* colleagues that the lofts and studios of New York offered a more sustaining idea of the aims and possibilities of the avant-garde enterprise than the communes of the now bureaucratically normalized regime of post-Maoist China.[3]

Arguably what was most importantly at issue in these changing enthusiasms, first for communist China, then for post-modern America, was not so much the concrete reality of those countries, however it was construed, as the way they could be made to work as possible models for the avant-garde project to which *Tel Quel* was committed. To this extent, China and America remained images, images not of cultural identity but of cultural difference. The logic of how they were produced as images by *Tel Quel* was, of course, set out in Barthes's self-consciously Utopian account of Japan, *L'Empire des signes*, which was published in 1970. Between 1971 and 1977, what changed, then, was not so much China or the United States (though much did change in those countries over that period) as the emphasis and internal dynamic of *Tel Quel*'s own avant-garde enterprise. Indeed, it was most likely because of its various shifts in position rather than in spite of them that *Tel Quel* remained, throughout the 1970s, as far as Paris intellectuals were concerned, the major focus for the elaboration of a theoretical, political, and literary avant-garde project. By the same token, *Tel Quel* also became the major forum for the internal conflicts and differences that arose within the avant-garde. During this period Kristeva had the role of *Tel Quel*'s principal theoretical voice, and what I want to do here, briefly, is to examine some aspects of Kristeva's theoretical work in relation to the changing context of the avant-garde in France.

At the Cerisy conference in 1972, Kristeva presented two papers, on Artaud and on Bataille. These were later collected in the volume, *Polylogue*, which borrows its title from Kristeva's review of Sollers's novel *H* (1973). This bringing together of her essays under a heading provided by Sollers's novel was important in a tactical sense, for it indicated the convergence of both the theory and the practice of the avant-garde within *Tel Quel* as an intellectual venture. The novel had begun with an evocation of the funeral of Pierre Overney, the Maoist activist killed in 1972 by a factory security guard, and continued without visible punctuation or sentence breaks for nearly 200 pages. The novel, Sollers put it, worked not as a variation on the idea of the 'internal monologue' but as an 'external polylogue'. In the place of one voice came the babble of many, instead of subjectivity as inner space came the explosion of the subject as a dynamic struggle of languages. Mixing levels of discourse, shifting abruptly from one topic to another, the novel was a roving inquiry into the different possibilities of writing and, both formally as well as thematically, sought to challenge and transgress all available limits or boundaries in an operation that identified writing both with polyphonic musicality and with the possibility of harnessing that verbal energy to stage and to analyse the world at large in its languages, its discontinuities and mobile contradictions.[4]

One of the strengths of *Tel Quel* as a journal, Kristeva argued in 1983, lay in this close relationship within the group between theory and literary practice.[5] As Kristeva points out, most of the editorial team were practising writers engaged in their own artistic projects, and it was in tandem or in parallel with that experimental textual activity that Kristeva, in her account of Artaud and Bataille, developed a theory of the avant-garde which explored the links between subjectivity, language and transgression. In that work Kristeva began to lay the foundations of her doctoral thesis, *La Révolution du langage poétique*. When it appeared, in 1974, the book was received as an authoritative statement of the current theoretical position of *Tel Quel* and an important reassessment of the history and future possibilities of the literary avant-garde in France. To this extent it was not an academic piece interested only, in the words of the subtitle, in 'the avant-garde at the end of the nineteenth century', but represented a concerted attempt to articulate the theoretical base of avant-garde literary practice in France in the early 1970s. Its closing allusion to the work of *'une nouvelle taupe'* ('a new mole') (p. 620), gnawing away at the thetic (as well as the thesis itself) was a reference to revolutionary Marxism that few readers at the time were likely to miss.

La Révolution du langage poétique draws together a wide range of different theoretical traditions and methods of analysis, from linguistics and semiotics to Marxism, phenomenology, psychoanalysis, and Russian formalism. At all stages of her work, Kristeva has never been less than a systematic theorist with a remarkable appetite for intellectual synthesis and much of the impact of *La Révolution du langage poétique*, at least within Kristeva's own immediate circle, derived from this twin commitment both to the explanatory power of theory and to the possibility of saturating the object of theory – here, poetic language – by deploying a number of different, seemingly contradictory types of analysis. In *La Révolution du langage poétique*, the aim was to articulate a comprehensive theory which would grasp the heterogeneous character of poetic language and remain attentive to the risks and challenges of avant-garde literary practice. To this end, Kristeva adopted an encyclopaedic approach with the ambition of assimilating within one body of theory a large number of the various disciplines, which, in the France of the 1960s and 1970s, notably in the case of anthropology and psychoanalysis, were all in process of being redefined with regard to the central problematic of the analysis of language.

In the late 1960s in France the theory of the avant-garde literary text, which had only recently thrown off the charge of bourgeois frivolity levelled at it by the moralistic theory of Sartrean 'engagement', still remained largely dominated by conventionalist approaches. These were in part inherited from Russian Formalism, but were also much influenced by current structuralist readings of Saussure. As far as the avant-garde was concerned, there were, so to speak, two different versions of structuralism, the one largely conservative and the other potentially much more radical. On the one hand, structuralist literary theory claimed to sever the direct, so-called referential link between the literary text and the concrete world. The literary text, it was argued, needed first to be understood as an autonomous object, independent of context, before it could be related (if at all) to the historical, social or political world within which it had been produced and might be interpreted. On this reading, the literary text, within structuralism, was an object defined by its own formal regularities and norms, the source of which, in so far as cause or origin were at issue at all, lay in the symbolic infrastructure of human language and cultural forms.

There was, of course, a more radical version of structuralism, most clearly represented, as far as the avant-garde was concerned, by the work of Roland Barthes, whose defence of the novels of Alain Robbe-Grillet and, subsequently, those of Sollers, was an important moment in the re-emergence of the avant-garde in the 1960s.[6] Barthes argued, for example, that since the link between the literary text and the concrete world was a conventional, discursive one, the text came into direct contact with that world not in any referential, and already empirically meaningful, way, but because reality too, like the literary text, was itself inseparable from the language and discourse which shaped it. The link between text and world was not direct, but it was mediated and that mediation between text and real, for Barthes, was provided by the discourses making up what, in an Aristotelian move, he called the doxa. The doxa, for Barthes, was the sum of those oppressively self-evident, ready-made discourses which form and inform reality, making it familiar and recognizable. In the case of the literary text the term adopted was that of the '*vraisemblable*'. This was a term borrowed from the literary rhetoric of the seventeenth century and became used as a translation of Aristotle's *eikos*, meaning plausibility, or likelihood. What it encapsulated was the notion that a literary text became acceptable only by tacitly endorsing that which seemed to be the case for the greatest number. In the 1960s it became an essential way of maintaining continuity between the avant-garde and contemporary mass culture, while simultaneously legitimating the avant-garde's refusal of that culture.

This criterion of correspondence to the doxa became a key consideration for Barthes. A work could be called realist (or, as Barthes rephrased it in *S/Z*, 'classically readable') only because it failed to question the assumptions behind this ready-made construction of reality. By the same token, a text which refused to comply with the 'already-said' could have a critical function by undermining the hegemony of classic modes of reading or understanding. To challenge narrative form, then, was ultimately to challenge the social doxa and thus to subvert social norms. Paradoxically, the extent to which a text intervened in reality could almost be measured by the degree of its failure to correspond to prior, existing discourse. The crucial issue was the homology that was claimed to exist between literary and extra-literary discourse. Nevertheless, little attention was paid to the way the doxa worked in detail or how literary texts related to the doxa in pragmatic terms. (In Barthes's later work this antagonism is thematized in terms of a conflict between the disruptive thrills of writing ['écriture'] and the nauseous weight of cultural stereotype. His most provocative formulation of the position was given in his inaugural lecture of the Collège de France, where Barthes spoke of the struggle between the 'fascistic' nature of language and the disruptive energy of literature.[7] Though the phrase was a startling one, it also proved to be largely self-defeating, but that contradiction itself followed from Barthes's use of the idea of the doxa as conforming to pre-established authority.)

Writing about Robbe-Grillet in 1955, in an essay reprinted in 1964, Barthes defended the author's novel *Le Voyeur*, with the words that it 'perhaps prepares the way, without really completing the task, for a *deconditioning* of the reader with respect to the essentialist art of the bourgeois novel'.[8] The formulation, though hedged with an ironic disclaimer (Barthes refers, in the same sentence, to 'the constitutionally reactionary status of literature at the present time'), was a symptomatic and influential one, and though the mention of essentialism owed something to Sartre, the claim was taken up as a convincing defence of avant-garde innovation. As a result, structuralist literary theory began to legitimate and promote a large number of different types of literary experiments. In particular, the 'nouveau roman' of authors like Robbe-Grillet became most adept at expanding the notion of the underlying homology between established cultural discourse and traditional literary narrative. The argument was put most consistently, if most reductively, by Jean Ricardou (who was a member of the *Tel Quel* editorial board till the schism of 1971), who claimed that the task of the avant-garde lay in liberating the 'productive' potential of writing (mainly identified with its degree of linguistic self-awareness) from the repressive, essentialist doctrines of 'representation'. For Ricardou, to comply with the doxa of reference or representation meant accepting the order of things as they were in the world.[9]

In this broad perspective, changing the novel seemed to be much the same thing as changing the world. The position rested, of course, on the assertion, firstly, that the conventions regulating the traditional novel were the same as those maintaining the political and social status quo; second, that one could therefore identify a central legislative norm, common both to literary texts and to the social whole, which could be breached by an act of textual disobedience. As a result, at the beginning of the 1970s, the avant-garde – and this stood for *Tel Quel* as well as for the writers of the 'nouveau roman' – could take comfort in the belief that by challenging conventional, legislative norms in one domain it was challenging them in all other domains as well.

Kristeva's first intervention into this debate had taken place some years earlier with her early development of the work of Bakhtin, whom she was one of the first to introduce into France. For Kristeva, within the context of second-generation Russian Formalism, Bakhtin was important for elaborating a far more dynamic model of literary texts than his predecessors. For Bakhtin, texts were not just engaged in dialogue with all earlier texts, for this is what Formalism in its first state had argued, as part of its attempt to isolate the autonomy or 'literarity' of literature. For Bakhtin, the principle of dialogue was posed in more radical ways and the texts of, say, Rabelais and Dostoievski were seen to be engaged in unresolved, open dialogue with themselves. Texts were not anthologies of ironic or inverted quotations from earlier works, but carnivalesque riots.[10]

This emphasis Kristeva took up and developed further, within the theoretical frame of psychoanalysis, to arrive at the concept of the subject in process. Though the term, initially, was an ironically critical response to Althusser's concept of history as a process without a subject, it became a crucial means for Kristeva of integrating within literary theory the dynamic energy and structural complexity of the Freudian subject while, at the same time, elaborating a theory of the subject in literature that was designed to be non-reductive. Formalist or conventionalist approaches to literature relied on a fundamentally contemplative view of the reading subject, one that is able to acknowledge, as though from a distance, the playful ironies of self-conscious artifice and the toying with convention.[11] By reintroducing Freud into the theory of the avant-garde, Kristeva shifted the whole emphasis of the debate away from conventionalism towards the question of meaning and subjectivity.

Most theories of modern art, as well as, probably, most modern theories of art, are theories of negativity. This is certainly true of theories of the avant-garde, which, for the most part, attribute the existence of the avant-garde to the negativity of historical change or class division. For some, the avant-garde is a sign of the inevitable break-up of bourgeois cultural hegemony; for others it is more a symptom of cultural alienation; some argue that the avant-garde is a fundamentally self-indulgent enterprise, allowing its interests to stray from the real world to engage in petty-bourgeois literary antics; while others see the avant-garde as having the somewhat dubious function of a safety valve of protest. In this way, accounts of the avant-garde are often never very far from being a pretext for the moral grinding of axes, and as a result many theories of the avant-garde remain ultimately dependent on an acceptance or description of those artistic norms which, for good or for ill, are seen to be under attack.

La Révolution du langage poétique innovates by doing none of these things. It does not, for instance, base its analysis of the work of Lautréamont and Mallarmé on the notion of the avant-garde text as an infringement of pre-established conventional norms. Much of the originality of the book as a work of literary theory comes rather from its elaboration of the concept of negativity. Negativity is seen as the driving force within the pre- and trans-linguistic medium of the semiotic, which corresponds roughly to the moment of Freud's primary processes, condensation and displacement. The symbolic dimension, which is the realm of the speaking subject as such, where statements are made and positions taken up, functions as an interruption within the semiotic, a pause and thus a posing of thematic sense, intention and positivity. By relating these two concepts in dialectic fashion Kristeva is able, she argues, both to analyse the practice of writing as the articulation of specific themes and ideas and to account for the release of a variety of non-semantic energies, which surface in literary texts (and did so particularly in the Symbolist and post-Symbolist era) as musicality, linguistic self-consciousness, punning, and the other aspects which used to be referred to by the notion of the play of the signifier.

Kristeva moves the concept of the avant-garde text away from a conventionalist view of writing as an activity devoted to replacing old norms with new ones. She similarly abandons a narrow sociological explanation of the avant-garde by articulating negativity within a much broader socio-cultural, subjective context. Kristeva's recourse to the logic of negativity in her account of the avant-garde process is a characteristic of all her writing through all its various phases. In *La Révolution du langage poétique*, importantly, it is employed to make sense of the literary avant-garde not as an object of contemplation but as a dynamic process. The avant-garde begins to represent a crisis, the ingredients of which are inherent in all literature and which is fundamental to the economy of the speaking subject in post-Christian Europe. The avant-garde is no longer a state of exception. It stands at the centre of the literary as such, at the crossing point of the relationships Kristeva brings into dialectical focus in *La Révolution du langage poétique*. These embrace subjectivity, language, sexuality, religion, history, the theory of the state, and much else besides, in a complex and exhaustive web of relations.

Though Kristeva's work constitutes a sustained critique of formalist literary theory, it shares with formalism and structuralism a reliance on the absolute centrality of language. It is true that the point behind Kristeva's concept of the semiotic, by denoting all that escapes meaning and intention in the literary text, is to avoid the trap of a reductive, rationalist view of writing which would take the process of its production for granted. But nonetheless, the dialectic relationship that Kristeva posits between the semiotic and the symbolic means that it is the symbolic order which, by intervening into the semiotic process as a moment of stasis, gives the semiotic body (or 'chora') the means of entering into a set of social and subjective relations, without which it would remain purely in the service of the negativity of the Freudian death drive. The order of language has the role of enabling as well as holding in place that which both threatens it and makes it possible. Language functions therefore, in Kristeva's work, as a legislative order which mediates and thus constitutes the signifying process. In the same way, in the web of relations that Kristeva plots between the speaking subject and the larger structures within which that subject is articulated, it is language as a symbolic activity that provides the mediating link. Seeking to establish the political dimension of language as the constitutive medium of any society or community, Kristeva argues for the position of language as a fundamental common denominator. 'La commune mesure de base', Kristeva writes in *Polylogue*, 'c'est le langage' ('the fundamental common measure is language') (p. 13).

If the avant-garde is disruptive, Kristeva maintains, it is not because it transgresses one or other of the conventions attendant on writing as a social practice, but because it transgresses the closed rationality of the thetic, of that symbolic moment or instance which corresponds to positionality, to acts of judgement or intention. At the same time, that relationship is construed as a dialectical one and the thetic is seen as a crucial moment in the movement by which avant-garde writings are able to harness their own disruptive negativity. Without disruptiveness there is no avant-garde, but without the thetic moment, Kristeva suggests, there can be no writing as such, except for echolalia or other semiotic gestures, and thus no transgression of the thetic.

In terms of the theory of the avant-garde, this emphasis on the role of the thetic function is an important one. It represents a powerful critique of those theories which take the avant-garde to be solely an anarchic force. Kristeva rejects the argument that the theory of the avant-garde can be based solely on the idea of art as an assault on rationality, meaning, social values, or audiences. In placing the thetic at the heart of the avant-garde enterprise, Kristeva makes it possible to argue that avant-garde texts produce statements which have their own truth value and can therefore serve as a means of analysing the symbolic structure of the culture or society within which those texts were produced. For Kristeva, unlike most analysts of the avant-garde, the experimental text has something to say, and that something, for Kristeva, goes beyond the oppositional challenge to prevailing values.

The concept of transgression, as has often been pointed out, is a double-edged weapon.[12] Though it provides for the possibility of going beyond established structures or practices in a generalized infringement of the law, it also, inevitably, serves to acknowledge the existence of the law and ascribe to it a central, mediatory function. In the early 1970s in France, particularly in relation to the work of Georges Bataille, there was much debate on this topic, which ended with some writers, like Kristeva, redefining and maintaining the concept of transgression with regard to the avant-garde, while others, such as Deleuze and Guattari in the *L'Anti-Œdipe* (1972), or Michael Foucault in *Surveiller et Punir* (1975) or in the first volume of his *Histoire de la sexualité* (1976), embarked on a fundamental critique of the concept of transgression and the dialectic of repression and subversion which it implied. It is worth recalling that *La Révolution du langage poétique* was contemporary with Derrida's *Glas*, which also appeared in 1974 and with which Kristeva's book shared some common references. Some years earlier, Derrida himself had published a group of essays in *Tel Quel*, notably on Mallarmé, Artaud and Bataille. It seems not to be by coincidence that (in addition to many other things) *Glas* took shape as a deconstructive reading of Hegelian dialectics together, or in dialogue, with an encounter with France's arch-transgressor, Jean Genet, who had till then been largely interpreted (as a result of Sartre's efforts in his *Saint Genet*) as an instance of dialectical thought made flesh. Where Kristeva posited the existence of the thetic in avant-garde writing as theoretically indispensable, Derrida opened up the question of whether a text such as Genet's (a text such as Genet) was at all compatible with (or reducible to) anything as single-minded as a thesis.

Kristeva's account of negativity, the corner-stone of *La Révolution du langage poétique* as well as much of her subsequent work, is derived from a presentation of Hegel. In the context of the avant-garde text she reformulates Hegelian negativity as the concept of 'rejection' (*rejet*) and locates it in the rhythmic movement of expulsion which drives the semiotic *chora* and traverses the moment of the thetic. The negativity of the *rejet*, she argues, is the fourth term of Hegelian dialectic, and it is Hegel's logic that allows Kristeva to think through the complex interconnections between the semiotic and the symbolic as well as the various levels of representation and identification which run back and forth between the speaking subject and language, the unconscious, religion and politics. The issue of Kristeva's reading of Hegel is a question which I cannot deal with here in any detail. But nobody, it would seem, enlists Hegelian dialectics with impunity. (The converse is also true, no doubt, as Derrida is at pains to point out in *Glas*, and no one quite ignores Hegel, it would seem, without paying the price somewhere or other.) In the context of Kristeva's theory of the avant-garde, however, it seems that a number of almost canonic difficulties or problems arise which, in the last resort, can all be traced back to the use Kristeva makes of Hegelian dialectics in her account of the relationship between the symbolic and the semiotic.

These almost canonic questions concern a number of crucial emphases in *La Révolution du langage poétique*. The first has to do with the status of the semiotic in Kristeva's readings of poems by Mallarmé and Lautréamont. To argue that the semiotic traverses the symbolic is to imply that the trace of the semiotic can be read off from the written text, and Kristeva suggests various ways (both in *La Révolution du langage poétique* and in more recent work) in which the semiotic can be made accessible to analysis in this way. These include having recourse to methods such as Ivan Fonágy's psychoanalytic phonetics, in which certain phonemes are matched with specific unconscious drives, the application of statistical parameters to literary texts to measure recurrent sounds or syntactic forms, the use of audiometric techniques in analysing vocal production, and, more broadly, exploring the pre-oedipal within the context of the psychoanalytic dialogue itself.

In *La Révolution du langage poétique*, Kristeva offers a phonetic reading of Mallarmé's famous poem, 'Prose pour des Esseintes'. The aim is to follow the movement of the semiotic across the sound structure of the poem and its elliptical syntactic relations. What Kristeva attempts is therefore an interpretation of the non-signifying dimensions of the text. But what the reading reveals is how the phonetic patterns of the poem dialectically reinforce the symbolic or thematic meanings of the text. Kristeva remarks that

it is possible to note a semiotic patterning, a rhythm, which fills in the syntactic elisions of the text and not only confirms, but displays and specifies the meaning and the function of 'prose' within Mallarmé's practice.[13]

What seems clear here is how the analysis of the semiotic seems almost to have been anticipated by the thematic or thetic. The semiotic is taken to supplement and confirm the symbolic reading rather than to displace or transform it. The problem is that, since the semiotic, in Kristeva's account, is defined as being prior or transversal to meaning, the only role the semiotic is left to fill in Kristeva's reading of the poem is for it to replicate what is already apparent at the thematic level. The objection is not that an alternative or better interpretation of the semiotic patterning of the text might be produced. Indeed, the semiotic has no semantic function of its own, and its articulation can at best be surmised or described. Its impact on the meaning of the poem as such becomes essentially indeterminate, variable according to the type of reading attempted and, no doubt, the subject attempting the reading.

Yet if one takes the view, following Kristeva, that the relation between the semiotic and the symbolic is a dialectical one, it seems almost inevitable for the semiotic to be colonized by the symbolic as a confirmation and extension of the thematic meanings of the text. In other words, following the uncontrollable logic of the speculative dialectic, an interpretative privilege necessarily accrues to the pole of the symbolic. The semiotic begins to play second fiddle to that meaning which has always preceded it as the ground on which it operates. In Kristeva's work, as a result, it is arguable that rather than displacing the symbolic and the possibility of an unproblematic thematic reading, the semiotic is in fact continually aligned with the symbolic, which it serves ultimately to redouble, indeed to reinforce as though it were no more than its internalized other. Arguably what takes place, as a result, in a number of readings of specific texts in Kristeva's work, (for instance, in *Polylogue*, or the more recent *Histoires d'amour*, or *Soleil noir*) is that the thematic dimension is privileged and comes, increasingly, to predominate. However brilliantly executed, Kristeva's method of reading literary texts becomes, as her work proceeds, less and less easy to distinguish from the psychoanalytic interpretation of themes.

While the thetic is taken, in Kristeva's work, to refer to acts of judgment and the process of linguistic signification, the semiotic is usually described in terms of musicality, gesture, rhythm, or colour. Though there may be good empirical reasons for drawing the contrast in this way, it is clear that the distinction between musicality and signification is far from innocent. Since at least the beginnings of the last century, the theme of music as the exotic, though sometimes troublesome, other of discourse, somehow truer and closer to the origins of language, has been an enduring one in literary discourse and while it would be crude to suggest that Kristeva's argument in *La Révolution du langage poétique* subscribes to that tradition in a naive or unproblematic way, it is difficult to maintain that the book is entirely divorced from the effects of that tradition. Whatever its theoretical sophistication, by thematizing the semiotic primarily as music, what the book risks is simply reproducing or updating the Symbolist poetics of Mallarmé.

One of Kristeva's aims in embarking on this account of the avant-garde at the end of the nineteenth century was to intervene, as I have noted, in the theoretical debate on the subject of the development of the avant-garde in France in the 1970s. When Kristeva began work on *La Révolution du langage poétique*, the choice of Mallarmé and Lautréamont was not an arbitrary one. Indeed, as part of the debate on the future direction of experimental writing, a series of names regularly used to appear in the pages of *Tel Quel*, and in the essays of Kristeva, as forming the basis for an alternative pantheon of the avant-garde. The names included Sade, Mallarmé, Lautréamont, Artaud, and Bataille. Later, Joyce was sometimes added to the list. What these writers had in common was that each of them seemed to practise a mode of writing that was fundamentally transgressive of philosophical, political, social and sexual taboos. Each of them (and they were all male) enjoyed what one could term an incestuous relationship with language where language is treated as a metaphor for the maternal body (and incest occurs as a theme or motif in the work of all six authors).

Promoting such writers as these as an alternative tradition implied, as far as both *Tel Quel* and Kristeva were concerned, drawing up a particular agenda for the avant-garde in the 1970s. That agenda, today, seems as interesting for what it leaves out as for what it says. The abiding metaphor on which the concept of the avant-garde depends is a military one, and though Kristeva often distances herself from the word by putting quotation marks around it, her work still privileges the transgressive style of avant-garde innovation and seems to place particular stress on the specific kinds of innovation embodied in the *Tel Quel* alternative canon. Indeed, to the extent that Kristeva's strategy for the defence and promotion of the avant-garde is wedded to such a pantheon, there is an inevitable slippage from the descriptive to the prescriptive, and the theory begins to impose its options rather than deduce them.

There is, in Kristeva's text, a constant mentioning of writers in typological lists (as though in dispatches), with the implication that certain writers can be made to function as paradigms, as models, even, for the aims and possibilities of the avant-garde. After about 1976, there is perhaps some partial recognition of the inherent teleology brought about by this reliance on canonic models, the result of which is to establish a norm – potentially of dogmatic character – for the genuine avant-garde text. After the publication of *La Révolution du langage poétique*, one finds Kristeva beginning to extend the range of reference of her work to include the work of other experimental writers, notably Beckett and Céline (and later the list grows to take in others, including, in 1987, the novels of Marguerite Duras). In 1977, the surprise expressed at the many different avant-garde possibilities America could offer would seem to denote a growing awareness that the transgressive model might not be the only valid one. In the United States, she notes 'il y a une polyvalence qui effrite la loi mais ne la prend pas de front' ('there is a polyvalent opposition which erodes the law but does not attack it head-on').[14]

At stake here is the central issue of the whole avant-garde project. This might be described as a search for cultural difference or as the desire for some relationship, within a culture, with the other of that culture. Both literary and political concerns come together in this ethical questioning. The commitment of Kristeva's work to the thetic moment of sense-making cuts off any escape route she otherwise might envisage into a literary relativism which treats all texts, whether avant-garde or not, as being fundamentally the same, or into any kind of political scepticism or nihilism that would relinquish the need for involvement in the public sphere. It is, Kristeva might argue, no reflection on the position of the theorist if the political solution first envisaged turns out not to correspond to the initial aspirations or if the literary model of the avant-garde has within it the possibility of a text which espouses fascism rather than the revolution.

For readers of avant-garde texts in English, Wyndham Lewis, say, or Ezra Pound, the problem of the links between literary innovation and the politics of the extreme right is a familiar one. For the French in the 1960s and 1970s, still deeply influenced by the right-thinking (or, rather, left-thinking) assumptions of the post-war Left Bank, the possible relationship between the avant-garde and right-wing politics was less keenly advertised than in Britain. In the mid-1970s, Céline was still viewed with suspicion and ambivalence by literary critics for his troubled but clearly anti-semitic, pro-Fascist opinions, which it was difficult, if not impossible, to detach from his literary texts. The interest in Céline, then, was part of re-orientation in Kristeva's view of the avant-garde project, especially with regard to its presumed transgressive political implications. And it is worth noting that one of Kristeva's first essays on Céline to appear (entitled 'Actualité de Céline' ('Céline's Relevance Today')) did so in the America issue of *Tel Quel*.

Céline's picture of himself in his novels was less as the heroic transgressor than the martyr or scapegoat. In Sartre's *Réflexions sur la question juive*, Céline was the sacrificial victim on the altar of 'engagement': if Céline wrote in support of the Fascists, Sartre alleged, it was because he was paid to do so, since literature was only ever thinkable within the context of the free exchange of ideas between reader and writer. The notion of a fascist writer, for Sartre, was a contradiction in terms.[15] But if it was possible for Sartre to discard Céline in this way, the same was not the case for Kristeva, who, in *Pouvoirs de l'horreur*, approached Céline's case with a sense that in Céline the transgressive coherence of the whole avant-garde project was under threat. The fact that *Tel Quel's* own avant-garde project was in crisis, as the turn from Maoist China to America revealed, was an even better reason for examining the political impasse into which Céline's writing had led him.

Céline, then, was not only important in his own right as a writer of a different avant-garde from that of the Left Bank, but he was also valuable as a pretext or occasion for Kristeva's reassessment of the direction in which her own work, as well as *Tel Quel*, was moving. In the 1970s generally in France, intellectuals were being increasingly detached from their traditional function and denied, as Sartre conceded, their 'classic' role as spokespersons for universal values. But if it had become impossible to endorse political systems in a way which seemed indispensable only ten years before, the role of the intellectual could at least be that of a dissident. It was in those terms, to the dismay of a number of traditional radicals (especially in Britain), that Kristeva also analysed the situation, and in 1977 she was writing, in *Tel Quel*, of 'a new type of intellectual: the dissident'.[16]

In Kristeva's writing in the late 1970s, Céline was used as a means of articulating this crisis in the realm of the political. Rather than political discourse being a method of explanation, it was political discourse itself, or, more pertinently, the impasse of political discourse, that needed to be explained, and Kristeva claimed that the only theory adequate to provide that explanation was Freudian psychoanalysis. In Céline's writing, therefore, political themes were analysed as symptomatic. They were a manifestation of Céline's own family drama, but they also represented the fall-out from the crisis of the end of Christianity. The decline of the Holy Family as well as the contradictions visible within Céline's own account of the family in novels like *Mort à crédit* (*Death on the Instalment Plan*) were aspects of the same cultural moment. They were signs of a profound dislocation which found expression in Céline's text in paranoid fashion. The negativity of what, in *La Révolution du langage poétique*, Kristeva had termed 'rejection', in Céline's case, became the horror of 'abjection'. Céline's writing allowed the reader, or theorist, to understand some of the underlying symbolic causes and satisfactions of Fascism not because Céline wanted to unmask them with the insight of a transgressor, but because he revealed them, as a symptom, within the body of his own writing. The political vision that haunted Céline's writing was a literary delirium. What this suggested to Kristeva, in response to the crisis of the avant-garde in the 1970s, was that it was in the nature of political discourse to be a delirium, a closed system excluding all non-conformist singularity on the part of the speaking subject.

There was a second reason why Céline became an important area of concern to Kristeva. In a number of important respects, as Kristeva herself confesses, Céline comes close to offering Kristeva a mirror-image of her own theory. Céline made much, for instance, of the logical and chronological primacy of emotion or affect. He returned insistently to the figure of his mother, who worked repairing old lace, and the identification between himself handling the delicate gossamer of the written text and the woman whose name he adopted as a pseudonym was a central element in his literary self-image. Céline, too, said that literature was primarily an affair of style and music rather than communication. In the light of this strange degree of overlap between the theory of the text and Céline's own working image of himself, it became essential, for Kristeva, if her theory was not to be defeated by such a wayward figure as Céline, for some part of the text to be rescued for the analysis of Céline's fascism. Failing this, Kristeva's stress on the importance of the thetic moment would appear simply irrelevant when confronted with the avant-garde writer as proto-Fascist apologist rather than as rebel or revolutionary.

Kristeva analyses the case of Céline as representing a risk inherent in all avant-garde literary practice, should the negativity of rejection turn into abjection and give rise to a paranoid delirium rather than ethically responsible fictional production. It is worth remembering, in this connexion, that, for Kristeva, while it is true that the literary text has irreplaceable value as a symptom, it is the psychoanalyst rather than the author of the text who is in the position of knowledge.[17] That knowledge, increasingly in Kristeva's work, takes the form of an insight into the implications for the speaking subject of the historical end of Christianity. The backdrop for Kristeva's account of Céline, as of other writers to whom she has recently turned her attention, is the symbolic fabric of monotheism and the Judaeo-Christian tradition.

Here again Kristeva displays her fundamental concern with the symbolic, religious order within which the relations between language and subjectivity are articulated, and from this point on, the major interlocutor, the major addressee of Kristeva's work, is no longer semiotics or literary theory but a version of Freudian psychoanalysis suitably expanded to assimilate them. For Kristeva, psychoanalysis gives privileged access not only to the singular speaking subject but also to the macro-symbolic level of the cultural, the religious, the sacred, even the ecclesiastical. In this perspective, Kristeva suggests, writing, within modernity, is to engage in an endless dialogue with Judaeo-Christian monotheism. Both Kristeva's reading of Céline and her brief essay on Beckett (who, like Céline, is unavailable for any scenario of textual transgression, preferring to transform the world, through writing, into a sinister farce where no single law remains) bear this out: both are variations on the homologies between the authors' fictional versions of the Freudian family romance and the Holy Family of Judaeo-Christian culture.

In a paradoxical but circular fashion, Kristeva takes us back here to a ground some no doubt thought they had left: the idea of the Christian substratum of all modern art. As this happens, the privileged notion of the avant-garde gives way, in Kristeva's work, to the argument that literature corresponds to a general crisis in the speaking subject and it is in order to transform and sublimate that crisis that literature exists. At the end of *Soleil noir*, Kristeva mentions, in passing, the 'challenge of the post-modern'.[18] For Kristeva, the 'post-modern' seems mainly to raise the question of the possibility of new narrative synthesis, perhaps resembling one of Philippe Sollers's more recent novels (*Femmes*, say, or *Le Coeur absolu*), which might be able to carry the cultural process forwards, through sublimation, towards a new human comedy of enjoyment, parody, and love. If that is true, it probably means that the epoch of the avant-garde will have finally come to an end.

Notes

1 Julia Kristeva, *Séméiotiké, recherches pour une sémanalyse*, Paris, Seuil, 1970; *La Révolution du langage poétique*, Paris, Seuil, 1974; *Polylogue*, Paris, Seuil, 1977; *Pouvoirs de l'horreur*, Paris, Seuil, 1980. Two volumes of papers from Kristeva's seminars were also published in the series: *La Traversée des signes*, 1975, and *Folle vérité*, 1979. All references to Kristeva's work will be to these editions and will be given directly in the body of the text.

2 The papers from the Cluny conference were published in a special issue of *La Nouvelle Critique*, 39, 1971. *Tel Quel* explained its endorsement of Maoism in an editorial in *Tel Quel*, 47, 1971. The papers from the Cerisy colloquium were published in two volumes, *Artaud*, and *Bataille*, ed. Philippe Sollers, Paris, Union Générale d'Editions, 1973.

3 See the discussion 'Pourquoi les États-Unis?' in *Tel Quel*, 71–3, 1977, and in *The Kristeva Reader*, ed. Toril Moi, translated by Harry Blake, Thomas Gora, Seán Hand, Alice Jardine, Leon S. Roudiez, and Margaret Waller, Oxford, Blackwell, 1986, pp. 291–2.

4 Kristeva's review of *H* is published in *Polylogue*, pp. 173–222, and in *Desire in Language*, ed. Leon S. Roudiez, translated by Thomas Gora, Alice Jardine, and Leon S. Roudiez, Oxford, Blackwell, 1980, pp. 159–209.

5 See Julia Kristeva, 'Mémoire', *L'Infini*, 1, 1983, pp. 39–54.

6 See R. Barthes's essays on Robbe-Grillet in *Essais critiques*, Paris, Seuil, 1964; *Critical Essays*, translated by Richard Howard, Evanston, Northwestern University Press, 1972. The articles on Sollers are collected in *Sollers écrivain*, Paris, Seuil, 1979.

7 See R. Barthes, *Leçon*, Paris, Seuil, 1978; *A Barthes Reader*, ed. Susan Sontag, translated by Richard Howard, London, 1982, pp. 457–78.

8 Barthes, *Essais critiques*, p. 70. '*Le Voyeur*,' writes Barthes, 'ne peut se séparer du statut, pour l'heure, constitutivement réactionnaire de la littérature, mais en tentant d'aseptiser la forme même du récit, il prépare peut-être, sans l'accomplir encore, un *déconditionnement* du lecteur par rapport à l'art essentialiste du roman bourgeois.'

9 See Jean Ricardou, *Pour une théorie du nouveau roman*, Paris, Seuil, 1971, and *Le Nouveau Roman*, Paris, Seuil, 1973.

10 See Kristeva, *Séméiotiké*, pp. 143–73; *The Kristeva Reader*, pp. 34–61.

11 For more detail, see Leslie Hill, 'Formalism and its Discontents', *Paragraph*, 3, 1984, pp. 1–24.

12 On the whole issue of transgression, see Peter Stallybrass and Allon White, *The Politics and Poetics of Transgression*, London, Methuen, 1986.

13 *La Révolution du langage poétique*, p. 259: 'nous avons pu constater un dispositif sémiotique, un rythme, qui supplée les élisions syntaxiques du texte et qui non seulement confirme, mais déploie et spécifie la signification et la fonction de "Prose" dans la pratique de Mallarmé.'

14 *Tel Quel*, 71–3, p. 4; *The Kristeva Reader*, p. 274, translation modified.

15 J.-P. Sartre, *Réflexions sur la question juive*, Paris, Gallimard, 1954; *Portrait of the Anti-Semite*, translated by Eric de Mauny, London, 1949. Sartre wrote that 'si Céline a pu soutenir les thèses socialistes des nazis, c'est qu'il était payé' ('If Céline was able to support the socialist ideas of the Nazis, it was because he was paid to do so') (p. 49).

16 See J.-P. Sartre, *Situations VIII*, Paris, Gallimard, 1972, pp. 456–76; *Between Existentialism and Marxism*, translated by John Matthews, London, New Left Books, 1974. Kristeva's essay, 'Un nouveau type d'intellectuel: le dissident', was published in *Tel Quel*, 74, 1977, and is reproduced in *The Kristeva Reader*, pp. 292–300. For a more contemporary account, see Jean-François Lyotard, *Tombeau de l'intellectuel et autres papiers*, Paris, Galilée, 1984.

17 See Kristeva, *Polylogue*, p. 16.

18 Julia Kristeva, *Soleil noir: dépression et mélancolie*, Paris, Gallimard, 1987, pp. 264–5.

· *10* ·

Virginia Woolf
'Seen from a Foreign Land'

MAKIKO MINOW-PINKNEY

I must begin by disowning the apparent exoticism of my subtitle: this is in fact *not* going to be an 'oriental' reading of Virginia Woolf, first thought up in the mysterious Empire of Signs. Roland Barthes once complained that when a photograph of him appeared in a Japanese newspaper it was subtly 'japanized' – his hair made darker, his eyes becoming slanted rather than round. I hope that by the end of this paper Julia Kristeva doesn't feel that she has suffered a similar fate, her eyes elongating and narrowing as I proceed. If she is 'japanized' in this presentation, I can only apologize and say it was unconsciously done.

For the 'foreign land' of my subtitle is Kristeva's phrase rather than mine, her theoretical concept rather than my ethnic origin. She writes: 'in women's writing, language seems to be seen from a foreign land; is it seen from the point of view of an asymbolic, spastic body?'. In similar vein, Virginia Woolf in *A Room of One's Own* evokes 'a sudden splitting off of consciousness . . . when from being the natural inheritor of that civilization, [woman] becomes, on the contrary, outside of it, alien and critical'.[1] My topic will be a heterogeneity of this kind operating in both the subject and the language of Woolf's writing.

Kristeva's 'foreign land' crops up in an interview in which she discusses the question of 'feminine writing'. For her, of course, the 'feminine' has nothing to do with biological gender, but is 'the moment of rupture and negativity which conditions and underlies the novelty of any praxis', involving a psychical position rather than an essence.[2] And Kristeva has traced in the texts of the literary avant-garde the force of negativity unleashed by heterogeneity, as it renovates and infinitizes signification. Modern writing is thus bound up from the start with the very question of feminine writing as a challenge to the dominant phallic position of the speaking subject. The dialectic between the heterogeneous modalities of semiotic and symbolic, this dynamism which constantly pushes to and beyond the limit, which constantly shatters the established and again brings forth synthesis, is, I think, the crux of Kristeva's theorization of signifying process and of her new notion of subjectivity. Though she valorizes the irruption of the semiotic, she also stresses the necessity of the thetic. The breach made by the semiotic is necessarily relative, especially in literary practice. A text requires a 'completion', 'a kind of totalization of semiotic mobility' (Kristeva's phrases), in order to *be* a text;[3] otherwise it would be merely neurotic or psychotic discourse. Again we can shift across to Virginia Woolf's writings to find a relevant parallel, since this necessary dialectic of semiotic impulses and thetic control is figured in a powerful metaphorical passage in *Jacob's Room*:

> What can be more violent than the fling of boughs in a gale, the tree yielding itself all up the trunk, to the very tip of the branch, streaming and shuddering the way the wind blows, yet never flying in dishevelment away?
> The corn squirms and abases itself as if preparing to tug itself free from the roots, and yet is tied down. (JR, p. 119)

The emphasis on dialectic is especially important to the question of feminine writing: how to hold a position against the 'phallic' position, how to inscribe the repressed and unspeakable in language, without simply collapsing into silence or even psychosis. As Kristeva writes in *About Chinese Women*, 'an ostensibly masculine, paternal . . . identification is necessary in order to have some voice in the record of politics and history'. She has also spoken about women's tendency towards 'oscillation between power and denial',[4] about a utopian existence which lives at once desire and repression, which summons *jouissance* and yet has voice in the socio-symbolic order: 'An impossible dialectic: a permanent alternation: never the one without the other'.[5] In Kristeva's view, this dialectic is partially attained in the texts of the literary avant-garde, and among such women writers Virginia Woolf is one of the few women she occasionally mentions.

Human beings, Woolf once wrote, are composed of 'instincts and desires which are utterly at variance with their main being, so that we are all streaked, variegated, all of a mixture'. But, she adds, 'circumstances compel unity: for convenience sake a man must be a whole. The good citizen when he opens his door in the evening must be banker, golfer, husband, father . . .' (CE 4, p. 161). For Woolf, reading the texts of the French avant-garde was rather like being ill: illness and the avant-garde, the avant-garde *as* illness, both foreground that which the transcendental subject had repressed – the body and the materiality of language. Reading in illness makes us 'grasp what is beyond their surface meaning, gathering instinctively this, that, and the other – a sound, a colour, here a stress, there a pause':

In health meaning has encroached upon sound. Our intelligence dominates over our senses. But in illness, with the police off duty, we creep beneath some obscure poem by Mallarmé or Donne. . . . And the words give out their scent and distil their flavour, and then, if at last we grasp the mean-ing, it is all the richer for having come to us sensually first. Foreigners, to whom the tongue is strange, have us at a disadvantage. The Chinese must know the sound of *Anthony and Cleopatra* better than we do. (CE 4, p. 200)

(And perhaps, the present author ventures to hope, the Japanese might too!) To be avant-garde is to be ill, is to be foreign – or, in Woolf's term, is to be an 'outlaw' and to escape 'paternal govern-ment'. The unitary self is then pluralized, infinitized. There return 'embryo lives which attend us in early youth until "I" suppressed them'; for 'with the responsibility shelved and reason in abeyance . . . other tastes assert themselves; sudden, fitful, intense' (CE 4, p. 199). A curious equation is forged between symptoms and semiosis – the pain of the body being also the pleasure of the text.

In Woolf's writings, the policeman is a familiar and recurrent image for the thetic position of the subject. Spokesman for the symbolic, he urges us 'straight on the continuity of our way', shepherding us away from the 'chasms' of our being (JR, pp. 94–5). Once we have slipped the leash of the police and the polite, a feminine writing might be possible. In *The Waves* Bernard's desire to reach the realm beneath what he terms 'Roman roads' leads to a deep scepticism about the classical canons of linear narrative which cannot, however, simply be repudiated, 'since they compel

us to walk in step like civilized people with the slow and measured
tread of policemen, though one may be humming any nonsense
under one's breath at the same time – "Hark, hark, the dogs do
bark", "Come away, come away, death"' (W, p. 184). Though
she wants to liberate such phonic, somatic pleasures, Woolf – like
Bernard but with more reason – has no desire to flagrantly violate
the laws of the symbolic. Kristeva is right to point out that Woolf
does not 'dissect' language as Joyce does; but this is more a condition of her literary enterprise than a criticism of it. As a woman,
estranged from language like a foreigner, she *cannot* do so: in a
foreign land, one is naturally more cautious about infractions of the
law, because of the danger of expulsion. Grammatical anomaly
would then just be dismissed as error, as simple nonsense, rather
than as the adventure of defamiliarization. Yet at the same time
Woolf cannot but be a trespasser, as when the narrator is turned
off the turf of an Oxbridge college by the Beadle in *A Room of
One's Own*. Woolf's project thus becomes a subtle and elegant
infraction of the laws of writing, undermining its protocols from
within, 'fluctuating' rather than drastically demolishing the fixed
positionality of the subject in language. Natural descriptions in her
texts often emit a lateral message about the work's own construction, as in the London cloudscape of *Mrs Dalloway*:

Fixed though they seemed at their posts, at rest in perfect unanimity,
nothing could be fresher, freer, more sensitive superficially than the snow-
white or gold-kindled surface; to change, to go, to dismantle the solemn
assemblage was immediately possible; and in spite of the grave fixity, the
accumulated robustness and solidity, now they struck light to the earth,
now darkness. (MD, p. 153)

One major technique for such dismantling is free indirect
speech. In developing his notion of 'dialogism', Mikhail Bakhtin
has already drawn attention to devices (of which free indirect
speech would be one) by which narrative discourse can set up a
dynamic interaction between two or more voices. Since it shares
the conventional form of third-person past tense, such indirect
speech sustains the seamless appearance of the sentence. But just
as Bakhtin's 'polyphonic' novel is founded on the breach of the 'I'
within such an apparently homogeneous medium, so too is the
narrative voice of Woolf's novels fractured and wavering. The
location of the subject is hazily suspended between character and

author. Even as the laws of grammar are maintained, the subject shifts constantly among multiple voices; 'fluid' and 'chameleon-like' are the terms usually applied to this style in conventional Woolf criticism. Normative syntactic structures remain in place, but are now, paradoxically, the support of a radically heterogeneous subjectivity which – like Mrs Ramsey at her dinner party – 'hangs suspended' rather than 'urging herself forward' (TL, p. 166).

The list of technical devices could be extended. It includes the excessive use of present participles, whereby sentences acquire a sprawling autonomous energy; excessive use of the conjunction 'for' in slippery, only 'half-logical' ways; making writing 'porous' by mining the present into the 'caves' of the past by means of what Woolf called her 'tunnelling process' (WD, pp. 60–1), creating an indeterminacy of time-scales; the intrusion of lengthy phrases between subject and predicate, disorientating conventional reading expectations; the break up of syntax into parataxis, of syntactical relations into a mere listing of nouns. All such devices serve to 'fluctuate' the unified, fixed positionality, to create effects of non-linearity and multi-dimensionality. Woolf thereby seeks to adumbrate the realm anterior to the logical, integrating subjectivity, to allow the body to intervene, introducing *jouissance* into the order of representation. The semiotic irrupts as the domain of rhythm, sounds, intonation, colour, shape. Sensory intensities have their origin in utilitarian objects, but then detach and foreground themselves, becoming objects of textual pleasure in their own right, as in such curious intense sketches as 'Blue and Green' and 'Kew Gardens':

Yellow and black, pink and snow white, shapes of all these colours, men, women, and children were spotted for a second upon the horizon, and then, seeing the breadth of yellow that lay upon the grass, they wavered and sought shade beneath the trees, dissolving like drops of water in the yellow and green atmosphere, staining it faintly with red and blue. ('Kew Gardens' in HH, p. 39)

One point where the semiotic breaks through with unusual explicitness is those troubled pages in *Orlando* which deal with Orlando's pregnancy, labour, and childbirth. What rescues the embarrassed 'biographer' here is the intervention of the barrel-organ; for music, coming closest to pure semiotic 'discourse', effects what Kristeva terms 'a breakthrough of "primary" process, those dominated by intonation and rhythm', in conjunction with (but not below) the limits of sentence, meaning, significance. It 'leads us directly to the otherwise silent place of its subject'.[6] The text takes this opportunity to 'allow it [the barrel-organ], with all its gaps and groans, to fill this page with sound', to 'transport us on thought, which is no more than a little boat, when music sounds, tossing on the waves' (O, p. 263). Under the naturalizing pretext of this passing barrel-organ, there takes place what Kristeva calls 'the semiotization of the symbolic', which represents the flow of *jouissance* into language.[7] The narrative now privileges the phonic, semiotic elements of rhyme and rhythm, with the narrator 'flinging a cloak under (as the rhyme requires) a cloak' (O, p. 264). 'For dark flows the stream – would it were true, as the rhyme hints, "like a dream"'. Or again, 'we rise, and our eyes (for how handy a rhyme is to pass us safe over the awkward transition from death to life) fall on . . .' (O, pp. 265–6). The text becomes whimsical and intimate in tone, nonchalant about its signifieds – 'Well, Kew will do . . .'. And narrative caprice leads on to more radical disorientations: landscape and dream, fact and fantasy, blur and blend (after all, whose dream, memory or fantasy is at issue here? or, to ask Roland Barthes's well-known question about Balzac's *Sarrasaine*, who is speaking thus?). Time is also loosened from its irrevocable linearity: to walk through the flowers in Kew Gardens is 'to be thinking bulbs, hairy and red; thrust into the earth in October; flowering now'. It is to 'be dreaming of more than can rightly be said', embracing semiotic realms beyond the symbolic order (O, p. 264). Nor is it accidental that this release of the semiotic takes place in Kew. Parks, gardens, parties and dinners are privileged symbols for Woolf; they are places of a libidinal indulgence that must be repressed elsewhere by the social ego – the recurrent 'policeman' of Woolf's symbology. Liberated from thetic control, the mind 'slops . . . all over the saucer', takes 'silly hops and jumps' (O, p. 264). Desire and *Jouissance* now threaten the very principle of the symbolic order:

Hail! Natural desire! Hail! happiness! divine happiness! and pleasure of all sorts . . . anything that interrupts and confounds the tapping of typewriters and filing of letters and forging of links and chains, binding the Empire together. . . . Hail, happiness! kingfisher flashing from bank to bank, and all fulfilment of natural desire, whether it is what the male novelist says it is; or prayer; or denial; hail! in whatever form it comes, and may there be more forms, and stranger. (O, pp. 264–5)

After this brief effloresence of pleasure, this mini-carnival of polymorphous perversity, the symbolic order again rivets down the flow of *jouissance*. The banks across which the kingfisher once flashed now assert themselves as a solid limit to the flow: as the trees on the bank efface the blue of the vanishing bird, so meaning effaces music. The sequences of both narrative and life resume after this moment of rupture, as the Thames did earlier after the carnivalesque interruption of the Great Frost. 'The barrel-organ stops playing abruptly', and at the end of this semiotic interlude the test announces the birth of Orlando's son – the child being, Kristeva argues, the 'sole evidence, for the symbolic order, of *jouissance*'.[8]

As I have noted, Kristeva emphasizes the dialectic operation of symbolic and semiotic in signifying practice. As her neologism subject in process/on trial [*sujet en procès*] suggests, this is because poetic language *puts* the subject in process or on trial, dissolving its meanings and unity. For Virginia Woolf too, dissemination is the precondition of the literary. She aspires, she tells us, to write as a 'mere sensibility, not having to draw upon the scattered parts of one's character' (WD, p. 48); and this is, clearly, the mode of being ('non-being' might be more appropriate) that her novels present. *Mrs Dalloway* has been called by one critic 'the most schizophrenic of English novels'.[9] As Mrs Dalloway walks through London (thereby perhaps enacting Deleuze and Guattari's dictum that 'a schizophrenic out for a walk is a better model than a neurotic lying on the analyst's couch'),[10] her dispersed self momentarily fuses with the objects that she sees; she is dispersed across the cityscape. On other occasions, the focused centre of self dissolves gradually in the rhythm of her manual occupation; she becomes mere empty stage or register for physical sensations, as when she mends her silk dress:

Quiet descended on her. . . . So on a summer's day waves collect, over-balance, and fall; collect and fall. . . . Fear no more, says the heart, committing its burden to some sea, which sighs collectively for all sorrows, and renews, begins, collects, lets fall. (MD, pp. 44–5)

With the ego thus disseminated, there remains only the body blissfully immersed in some great semiotic ocean. As another of

Woolf's recurrent images, the sea is a kind of anti-policeman, especially in *Mrs Dalloway*; it figures as a vast semiotic *chora*, traversed by natural pulses, rhythms and currents in which one can lapse out into libidinal gratification.

But the true 'site' of the subject is the very dialectic between dissemination and reconstruction; and this is also the case in *Mrs Dalloway*. To become a social actor, Clarissa must put back together the broken jigsaw of herself. As the novel puts it, she collects 'the whole of her at one point (as she looked into the glass). . . . That was herself – pointed, dart-like, definite. That was her self when some effort, some call on her to be her self, drew parts together' (MD, p. 42). The body 'turns to wax in the warmth of June, hardens to tallow in the month of February' (CE 4, p. 193); and as with the body, so with the self, since, as Woolf argues in her essay on illness, mental processes can never be absolutely independent of the body. Or in Kristeva's terms, the semiotic never ceases to trouble and disrupt the symbolic. The dualism of June and February recurs in the dirge from *Cymbeline* which the novel cites repeatedly: 'Fear no more the heat o' the sun/Nor the furious winter's rages'. I take it as a song sung to the kind of subjectivity that the book adumbrates, the *sujet en procès*, constantly making, unmaking and remaking it, through semiotic dissolution and thetic consolidation.

If we take the opposition feminine/masculine as a matter of positionality in relation to the symbolic order, then Woolf's dialectic of semiotic and symbolic can also be taken as a dialectic between feminine and masculine, as a continuous crossing of the boundary between the two positions. In Kristeva's terms, some avant-garde writings confront the 'phallic position either to traverse it or deny it'. It is the former option which concerns me in relation to Woolf. Kristeva elaborates: '"traverse" implies that the subject experiences sexual difference, not as a fixed opposition ("man"/ "woman"), but as a process of differentiation. . . . Only the truly great "literary" achievements bear witness to a traversal, and therefore to sexual differentiation'. Thus the subject of writing makes it clear that 'all speaking subjects have within themselves a certain bisexuality which is precisely the possibility to explore all the sources of signification, that which posits a meaning as well as that which multiplies, pulverizes, and finally revives it'.[11] Woolfean androgyny is just such a bisexuality. Poetry ought,

Woolf writes, 'to have a father as well as a mother', 'one must be woman-manly or man-womanly' (RO, pp. 98–9). And I agree with Mary Jacobus in reading Woolfian androgyny as 'a simultaneous enactment of desire and repression', as heterogeneous and open to the play of difference, rather than with Elaine Showalter's interpretation of it as a flight into asexuality or eunuchism.[12] In *Orlando*, too, androgyny is a bisexuality of this kind, a traversal, a constant alternation of positions; it dramatizes as narrative the *formal* principle of Woolf's writing, that 'impossible dialectic' of which Kristeva wrote. 'She was man; she was woman. . . . It was a most bewildering and whirligig state to be in' (O, p. 145). Androgyny here should not be seen as utopian resolution or fusion of opposed terms, not as Hegelian *Aufhebung* which could be represented by symbol or metaphor. The novel thus takes the form of the *fantastic*, whose principle is metonymical displacement and the transgression of boundaries – for only this genre (or anti-genre) can embody such a permanent alternation.

In *The Waves* (to follow the novels through chronologically), effects of rhythm pulse, pass, and recur throughout the book. Rhythmic patterns or images of in/out, up/down, rise/fall, appear innumerably: 'lifts rise and fall; trains stop, trains start as regularly as the waves of the sea' (W, p. 139). Bernard argues that 'the rhythm is the main thing in writing', and in 'A Letter to a Young Poet' Woolf agrees. She calls rhythm 'the most profound and primitive of instincts', and advises the poet to 'let your rhythmical sense open and shut, open and shut, boldly and freely, until one thing melts in another' (CE 2, p. 191). As rhythm is central to Kristeva's semiotic, so too is it in *The Waves*, breaking through the thetic, subduing all the elements conventionally expected in a novel. Repetition and tautology, multiplied for the sake of rhythmical wave-effect, persistently hinder linear narrative development: '"What is lost? What is over?" and "Over and done with". I muttered, "over and done with", solacing myself with words' (W, p. 131). The conventional concept of character is also eroded: the same rhythms and tautologies traverse all six figures, dissolving particularity. If rhythm is the most primitive of all instincts, the repetition which is used to effect it is hardly less so. 'The compulsion to repeat is an ungovernable process in the unconscious', and in the theory of *Wiederholungszwang* Freud finally sees repetition 'as the expression of the most general character of the instincts'.[13] *The Waves* gives the reins to the 'discourse' of the unconscious, allowing the semiotic to play dissolvingly across meaning.

But Woolf also worries about a possible excess of fragmentation for she believes that 'writing must be formal. The art must be respected' (WD, p. 69), that 'everything in a work of art should be mastered and ordered' (CE 2, p. 228). She would thus concur with Julia Kristeva that 'a text, in order to hold together as a text . . . requires a completion [finition], a structuration, a kind of totalization of semiotic mobility. This completion constitutes a synthesis that requires the thesis of language to come about, and the semiotic pulverizes it only to make it a new device'.[14] Thus the more Woolf destroys the thesis, the more rigid control she in another sense requires; Septimus Smith in *Mrs Dalloway* and Rhoda in *The Waves* are eloquent warnings of the dangers of psychosis and powerlessness that threaten here. If Woolf dissolves the sequentiality of classical narrative, she must also introduce a more rigid, almost rebarbative formal sequence. Hence *The Waves* is structured by temporally progressive interludes, which effect a rough parallelism between the sun's position and the phase of the characters' lives. But this sclerotic framework can also be seen as an opportunistic concession to the disabilities of contemporary readers. Woolf wrote: 'my difficulty is that I am writing to a rhythm and not to a plot', 'the rhythmical . . . is completely opposed to the tradition of fiction and I am casting about all the time for some rope to throw to the reader'.[15] Though it was precisely rhythm that had fragmented the thetic in the first place, Woolf comes to rely on rhythm to weld the book into unity. 'What it wants is presumably unity . . . Suppose I could run all the scenes together more? – by rhythm chiefly' (WD, p. 163). The result, notoriously, is a monotonous uniformity in contrast to the flowing richness of Woolf's earlier novels; the meandering here becomes the monumental. *The Waves* abounds with short sentences, organized in an often simple syntax. Though syntax is subordinated to phonic and semantic repetition, creating an extreme effect of anti-linearity, its laws are never shattered. What the novel is left with is what Donald Davie, in his book on syntax in poetry, calls 'pseudo-syntax, a play of empty forms'.[16] The forms are not grossly fractured as, say, with Joyce, but they are subtly emptied of any real articulatory function; they are, rather, structured according to the 'principles' of sound, rhythm, and imagery. By reintroducing words and phrases, or by redeploying a simple, emphatic syntactic structure, repetition and tautology activate the paradigmatic axis of language, which is usually excluded by the developmental urgency of the syntagmatic chain, and in so doing they begin to dissolve the syntagma. *The Waves* shows a consistent reluctance to give up the paradigmatic substitutions which in practice have to be repressed as the 'Other' in that meaning may be produced along the signifying chain. The novel explores the vertical axis, playing associational variations on a single signifier which, as Saussure argues, 'will unconsciously call to mind a host of other words' from the paradigm.[17] Lacan contends that 'strict coherence in the syntagmatic chain provides a position for the transcendental ego';[18] and thus to unleash the paradigm, to juxtapose rather than subordinate signifiers, threatens that security. *The Waves*, with its discrete clusters of words in isolated images, with its aesthetic 'substitutionalism', takes one back behind the patriarchal, releasing a language of and for the mother's presence. Or, in Bernard's terms, 'words of one syllable such as children speak when they come into the room and find their mother sewing' (W, p. 209).

The arrangement of the monologues also contributes to the book's effect of broken stasis. They are not addressed to each other, achieve no dramatic interaction, do not establish local links of logic or sequence; whether the units are sentences or monologues, *The Waves* forgoes syntagmatic relations of implication, causality or subordination. Parataxis is once more the order of the day, again depriving the reader of the fixed subject position of Kristevan thesis. Similarly, the 'hard', external linguistic mode of the monologues denies the reader the pleasure of 'inwardness', of that ultimate access to subjectivity which the stream of consciousness or interior monologue affords. Even the dislocation of syntax may be recuperated as the transcription of a disordered but still basically homogeneous – even lyrical – subjectivity (Pound's *Pisan Cantos*). But Woolf avoids this danger of recuperation into homogeneous identity, first by emptying rather than fracturing syntax, and second by a rhetoric of externality which rebuffs the reader's empathy.

Earlier in her career Woolf meditated on the fictional 'image of oneself' created in solitude:

As we face each other in omnibuses and underground railways we are looking into the mirror . . . and the novelists of the future will realise more and more the importance of those reflections, for of course there is not one reflection but an almost infinite number; those are the depths they will explore, those the phantoms they will pursue. ('The Mark on the Wall' in HH, p. 43)

We could translate the passage out in terms of the Lacanian theory of the mirror stage: the narrator seeks identity in a single specular image only to find an unnerving process of splintering and fission take place. That *The Waves* is precisely an exploration of these specular depths and phantoms is confirmed when we examine the development of the structure of the book. Initially Woolf took as the narrative basis for her novel a 'man and a woman' talking at a table; then a woman talking or thinking, with the man left dim or silent; then 'a mind thinking', a mere 'she' without a name, unlocated in particular place or time; 'all sorts of characters' to be called forth by the unidentified figure at the table to tell a story. Finally, the third-person description of the narrative subject was dissolved into a series of first-person dramatic soliloquies.[19] These monologues are an exteriorization of the diversity of the 'mind' or the writing 'I', rather than true interior monologues of a stream of consciousness; *The Waves*, like the Bakhtinian 'polyphonic' novel, is built upon the breach of the 'I', and the 'characters' are nothing more than discursive points of view.

As a would-be novelist, Bernard is acutely aware that subject-identity can never be a pure immanence or simple homogeneity; it is, rather, a continuous intermixture and intermittence, a dispersal and reassembly of diverse elements, Kristeva's subject in process. Though Woolf's work is often a quest for the essence of a character, Woolfean 'personality' is never essentialist; the quest always involves a sense of the impossibility of fixing the sought-after essence. Bernard ponders: 'What am I? . . . We are forever mixing ourselves with unknown quantities'; he is 'made and remade continually . . . there is something that comes from outside and not from within' (W, pp. 84, 96). The separation of oneself, as subject, from the environment coincides with the acquisition of language. Subjectivity is achieved through acceptance of the third term (the Name-of-the-Father), through the comprehension of mediation, the separation of the word from the thing itself: 'it steals in through some crack in the structure – one's identity. I am not part of the street – no, I describe the street. One splits off, therefore' (W, p. 82). And this ability to erect himself as subject against object makes language possible for Bernard, that 'natural coiner of words' – 'striking off these observations spontaneously, I elaborate myself: differentiate myself' (W, pp. 82–3). Bernard's potential as writer resides in his precarious poise or alternation between identity and its dissolution, since 'at the moment when I am most disparate, I am also integrated' (W, p. 55). We might say that for him, as for Julia Kristeva, 'without the completion of the thetic phase . . . no signifying practice is possible', art must 'not relinquish the thetic even while pulverizing it'; in short, an 'unstable yet forceful positing of the thetic' is crucial for poetic practice.[20] Perhaps more than any other character in *The Waves*, Louis has an acute sense of the self as disparate, multiple: 'I am not single and entire as you are' (W, p. 97). But he must accordingly strive all the more to shore up a unitary selfhood, to the point where 'all the furled and close-packed leaves of my many-folded life are summed up in my name' (W, p. 119). For as poet, Louis has a near manic investment in integration and fixity: 'if I do not nail these impressions to the board and out of the many men in me make one . . . then I shall fall like snow and be wasted' (W, p. 121).

'Broken into separate pieces', Rhoda is the most negative and tormented of the six figures. She can neither judge, name, nor be logical; untruth, she finds, is not just a contingent linguistic stratagem but structural to discourse. 'I am not composed enough . . . to make even one sentence. What I say is perpetually contradicted' (W, pp. 96–7). This sense of psychic breakdown then produces hallucinations of corporeal disintegration – not surprisingly, since for Lacanian theory it is the body which founds the unitary identity of the human subject. When the transcendental ego is threatened, the mirror phase is reversed in fantasies of bodily fragmentation, a terror not peculiar to Rhoda; 'little bits of ourselves are crumbling', remarks Bernard (W, p. 166). Louis describes the others at the dinner party in more lurid but analogous terms, as 'the flames leap over . . . the bleeding limbs which they have torn from the living body' (W, p. 100). Neville, who had been haunted as a child by a vision of the dead man with his throat cut, conceives the descent into the Tube as a matter of being 'dissevered by all those faces' (W, p. 127). The very intensity with which the characters seek to compose unity among themselves testifies to their obsession with the disintegration of the body. It is no accident that their brief experiences of successful communion occur at collective meals, which then take on the resonances of a fantasy return to primitive oral fusion at the breast.

Fragmentation of the self entails the disintegration of time. For Rhoda, 'blown for ever outside the loop of time' (W, p. 15), 'one moment does not lead to another': 'they are all violent, all separate; and if I fall under the shock of the leap of the moment you will be on me, tearing me to pieces. I have no end in view' (W, p. 93). Maturation and teleology are thus impossible; she cannot believe that she will 'grow old in pursuit and change' (ibid.). And fragmentariness, clearly, is as characteristic of the time of the book as it is of Rhoda herself. Time in this novel will not conform to the canons of constructive development; it is discrete rather than continuous, cyclical rather than linear. Bernard summarizes its nature in the image of the falling drop, whose forming represents habitual behaviour with its complacement routines. 'As a drop falls from a glass heavy with some sediment, time falls. These are the true cycles, these are the true events' (W, p. 131). The rough parallelism between the sun's position and the phases of the characters' lives sufficiently bespeaks the cyclical temporality of the book; it makes Bernard, at the novel's close, wearily regard dawn as 'some sort of renewal', 'another general awaking' (W, pp. 210–11). With almost no evidence of development or history, the time of the book is either the detached moment or a 'substance made of repeated moments' contained within no religious or humanist framework. Agnostic to the last, Woolfean time constantly confronts 'the whirling abysses of infinite space' (W, p. 161).

Kristeva argues that the dialectic of the two heterogeneous modes operates not only in the subject and language but also in *time* – between 'time as *rhythmic* agency', 'spatialized, volume rather than line', and 'time as evolutive *duration*', namely 'repression – or history' which achieves its goals as the fulfilment of a socio-cultural contract.[21] *The Waves* is dominated by rhythm and moment; for as Woolf herself wrote, 'waste, deadness comes from the inclusion of things that don't belong to the moment; this appalling narrative business of the realist: getting on from lunch to dinner: it is false, unreal, merely conventional' (WD, p. 139). This doctrine of the 'moment' is also explicated in 'A Sketch of the Past', where 'exceptional moments' rupture the 'sealed vessels' of being in a 'sudden violent shock', tearing one out of the ruck of the mundane non-being which, in Woolf's view, the realist novel tends to reproduce.[22] Hence the issue of temporality is necessarily implicated with that of narrativity. Both time and narrative are sustained by the logical subjectivity that is constituted by repression of 'the senses of sight, of sound, of touch – above all the sense of human being, his depth, and the variety of his perceptions, his complexity, himself in short' (CE 2, pp. 158–9). That which refuses this oppressive 'general sequence' is evoked in terms of a central Woolfean image that I have already touched upon – 'a combination of thought; sensation; voice of the sea' (WD, p. 139).

However, Woolf remains anxious about total dissolution. As with syntax at the microstructural level, so with time at the macrostructural: temporality is emptied rather than shattered, with duration being just sustained by the sclerotic framework of the interludes and with the sun/life parallelisms. In *The Waves* lines and continuity come to exist merely from repeated dots and moments, without logical necessity or meaning:

> observe how dots and dashes are beginning, as I walk, to run themselves into continuous lines, how things are losing the bald, the separate identity that they had as I walked up those steps . . . . The world is beginning to move past me like the banks of a hedge when the train starts, like the waves of the sea when the steamer moves. I am moving too, am becoming involved in the general sequence when one thing follows another and it seems inevitable that the tree should come, then the telegraph pole, then the break in the hedge. And as I move, included and taking part, the usual phrases begin to bubble up. (W, p. 134)

Bernard's attitude to the formation of such continuous lines is ambivalent, simultaneously celebratory and protesting.

Woolf's scepticism towards the sequentiality of time, narrative, life, is, in short, a protest against the symbolic order. Bernard comes to dismiss classical narrative, with its 'extreme precision, this orderly and military progress', as 'a convenience, a lie'; for 'there is always deep below it . . . a rushing stream of broken dreams, nursery rhymes, street cries, half-finished sentences and sights – elm trees, willow trees, gardeners sweeping, women writing' (W, p. 181). He calls for music (to which of course the narrator of *Orlando* had already had recourse in her predicament), a music primitively close to the body – 'guttural, visceral' – but also rhythmical and joyous – 'soaring, lark-like, pealing song' – to replace the 'flagging, foolish transcripts' (W, p. 177). Woolf's frustration with the symbolic and her desire for a 'beyond' was already expressed in her very first novel, *The Voyage Out*, in which Terence aspires to write a 'novel about Silence', and Rachel prefers music to the detours of the written signifier, since 'music goes straight for things' (VO, pp. 262, 251).

Yet despite his distrust of 'logical story' and ordered 'biographical style' (W, p. 84), Bernard remains ambivalent about general sequences and continuous lines. Sustaining us within civilization and sanity, they are paradoxically enabling *and* disabling. 'Laid down like Roman roads across the tumult of our lives', they 'compel us to walk in step like civilized people with the slow and measured tread of policemen though one may be humming any nonsense under one's breath at the same time – "Hark, hark, the dogs do bark", "Come away, come away, death"' (W, p. 184). The social system's regulation of wanton, vagrant desire is both repressive and *im*pressive. In *The Waves* a polemic is constantly fought out between music and meaning, moment and sequence, infinity and individuality, or the social and all that precedes or exceeds it. Woolf's aim is, we might say, 'aporetic'; she seeks to forge a discourse which thinks language against itself, which speaks that which the symbolic order represses but without thereby simply consigning itself to psychosis and silence. The Woolfean work thus situates itself precisely in the Kristevan dialectic, in that 'constant alternation between time and its "truth", identity and its loss, history and the timeless'.[23]

This precarious dialectic has its counterpart at the level of character in Bernard, for however 'pulverized' and fused with the other, subject identity or the 'self' always returns to him; he 'has been so mysteriously and with sudden accretions of being built up . . . has collected himself in moments of emergency' (W, p. 201). Only in this way can dissemination emerge into language; only thus can schizophrenic fragmentation find its way back to a common code. 'Forceful, yet unstable': Kristeva's epithets for the positing of the thetic in poetic practice apply precisely to Bernard. He enacts that process of what she terms 'rebound, whereby the violence of rejection, in extravagant rhythm, finds its way into a multiplied signifier'.[24] Incessantly traversing positions, in wildly veering moods of exhilaration and anxiety, Bernard is appropriately described as androgynous. *The Waves*, unlike *Orlando*, has no more than a banal, conventional language for this: 'joined to the sensibility of a woman . . . Bernard possessed the logical sobriety of a man' (W, p. 55). But androgyny must here be seen as formally *enacted*, rather than merely thematically reflected, in a continuous traversal of limits, a process of sexual differentiation, a simultaneous enactment of desire and its repression, of feminine and masculine conceived as the positionality of the subject. For Bernard, it is a 'perpetual warfare, it is the shattering and piecing together' (W, p. 191); and the rhythm of the sea as the rhythm of the semiotic chora – its patterns and pulses of one/two, in/out, rise/fall – mercilessly cuts across the syntax of sentences and plot throughout the text to the very last, yet without dissolving them completely. In the end, the ocean (or the 'oceanic', we might say with Freud in mind) itself becomes the metaphor for this endless, unsublatable alternation – 'the eternal renewal, the incessant rise and fall and fall and rise again' (W, p. 211).

Woolf's literary manifestos valorize the process of rupture, but the symbolic and thetic remained essential, as a framework to work against. But when writing *Between the Acts* during the Second World War, she lamented that 'the writing "I" has disappeared', that 'the protecting and reflecting walls' which 'thickened [her] identity' had crumbled (WD, pp. 337–9). With one of the two terms of the Woolfean dialectic disintegrating, hope has to be invested solely in its counterpart, in the fertile ocean of the semiotic. But within Woolfean symbology, the primeval swamp replaces the sea. For in *Between the Acts* semiotic drives manifest themselves as a primeval force underlying the present, working through and across it, as when Miss La Trobe is saved during the pageant by the bellowing of the cows. 'It was the primeval voice sounding loud in the ear of the present moment. . . . The cows annihilated the gap; bridged the distance; filled the emptiness and continued the emotion' (BA, pp. 165–6). And this archaic voice turns out, as we should expect, to be the voice of the mother – 'one of the cows calling for her lost calf' – since the semiotic reaches back into the primitive pre-oedipal relation to the mother.

The socio-symbolic and its thetic subject are on the point of ruin, their firm ligatures disappearing, as when during the pageant 'the wind blew away the connecting words of the chant' (BA,

p. 98). Its repressions are lifted, and hence there comes about a certain libertarian euphoria in the novel – 'the airy world', as Woolf herself termed it (WD, p. 292). The values of meaningful linear plot and organicity are swept away. The text is a litter of word-plays, of recollected fragments of poems, snatches of nursery rhymes which, like the rhythms and refrains which run through Isa's mind, cannot shape themselves into any kind of elegant whole. Prose, poetry and drama, the categories of human/nature, artifice/reality, physical/psychological, are mixed or abruptly juxtaposed, as in a collage. The symbolic function of language is subordinated to the semiotic, to a more primitive play and pleasure of the signifier. In the pageant itself, the book tells us, 'it didn't matter what the words were; or who sang what. Round they whirled, intoxicated by the music' (BA, p. 113). Surcharged with an excess of either signifier or signified, words stray from their mundane communicational functions. Characters articulate their inner thoughts in scraps of rhyme, and a powerful rhythmic drive turns conversations into recurring tunes. Dislodged from any unitary position, Isa is dominated by the more archaic drives of the semiotic – 'Love and hate – how they tore her asunder!' (BA, p. 252). She can make nothing of the pageant, which represents literary history, and longs for a 'new plot' to be invented. Semiotic drives thus appear both in such characteristic dualisms and as a primordial force in the novel. For the semiotic activity, Kristeva argues,

is from a synchronic point of view, a mark of the workings of drives (appropriation/rejection, orality/anality, love/hate, life/death, and, from a diachronic point of view, stems from the archaisms of the semiotic body.[25]

Or, in the by now familiar Woolfean oceanic aesthetics, '"Yes", Isa answered, "No", she added. It was Yes, No. Yes, yes, yes, the tide rushed out embracing. No, no, no, it contracted' (BA, p. 251). Isa's yes/no answers Streatfield's remark that 'we act different parts but are the same' (BA, p. 257). And the text similarly oscillates between such dual drives: sameness/difference, continuity/disruption, or what it terms 'Unity-Dispersity' (BA, p. 235). Such dualisms, appropriating and rejecting by turns, are the bearers of fundamental oral and anal drives which are structured around the maternal body, the ordering principle of the semiotic chora. For the novel, the apocalyptic question of communal survival hinges on these dual drives. In the primeval matrix of the chora, there doesn't yet fully exist an identity or subject, though from the interplay of assimilative and destructive drives a subject will finally emerge. Formally and thematically, then, *Between the Acts* is situated in such a semiotic chora. It ends implying the possibility of the birth of 'another life' from the prehistoric darkness, a hope for the emergence of a *new* subject out of the mass destruction of war. Now the emphasis is more on the potentiality of the semiotic or the prehistoric for transformation rather than for disruptive 'negativity', for the unity of the symbolic has, grimly enough, crumbled of its own accord. The archaic realms are invested with the energy to form a new, different subjectivity – a subjectivity *of* difference – which will paradoxically guarantee continuity by the transformation.

I have been emphasizing the dialectic between challenge and unity, rupture and 'completion', in Woolf's writings; I have stressed the necessity for *both* terms, which for me is the crux of Kristeva's theory. But this is not to stress Woolf's apparent conformism, not to imply some critical evaluation of her in relation to male modernist writers, but rather to recognize her *strategy* (both conscious and unconscious) as a woman, to whom language is seen from a foreign land. If the problem is how to inscribe the repressed, the body, *jouissance*, in language without collapsing into silence or psychosis, then her response is not a violent, conspicuous demolition, but rather an elegant, subtle infraction of the laws of writing. This aesthetic elegance meets ideological expectations about women's writing precisely in order ultimately to elude their censorship. But this cleaving to the symbolic is also, in Kristeva's view, of psychoanalytical import. For women, insertion into the symbolic order by paternal identification is difficult and precarious; it needs a special defence. As Kristeva writes, 'a woman has nothing to laugh about when the paternal order falls',[26] and hence women's tendency to oscillate 'between power and denial'. Here lies the difficulty for women writers who try to situate their work across the interplay of symbolic and semiotic. But here too, perhaps, lies their privilege, their possibility of being in touch with a utopian existence which lives Kristeva's impossible dialectic, as she herself cautiously suggests in *About Chinese Women*. Woolf's lament over the mass destructiveness of the

Second World War was tempered by a resigned aloofness; for her it was a *man*-made mess.[27] She hopes for the emergence of a new 'I', plunging into the semiotic. The notes for the book she was planning in her last days read: 'The song . . . the call to our primitive instincts./Rhythm – Sound. Sight'.[28]

Notes

1 Julia Kristeva, 'Oscillation between Power and Denial', translated by Marilyn A. August, in *New French Feminism*, ed. Elaine Marks and Isabelle de Courtivron, Amherst, The University of Massachusetts Press, 1980, p. 166; Virginia Woolf, *A Room of One's Own*, London, Hogarth, 1967, p. 146.

   In this chapter the following abbreviations will be used for Woolf's works (all works are published by the Hogarth Press; the date of first publication is given in brackets):

   BA   *Between the Acts* (1941), London, 1965.
   CE   *Collected Essays*, 4 volumes, ed. Leonard Woolf, London, 1966–7.
   HH   *A Haunted House and Other Stories* (1944), London, 1962.
   JR   *Jacob's Room* (1922), London, 1980.
   MD   *Mrs Dalloway* (1925), London, 1980.
   O   *Orlando* (1928), London, 1978.
   RO   *A Room of One's Own* (1929), London, 1967.
   TL   *To the Lighthouse* (1927), London, 1977.
   VO   *The Voyage Out* (1915), London, 1965.
   W   *The Waves* (1931), London, 1976.
   WD   *A Writer's Diary*, ed. Leonard Woolf (1953), London, 1969.
2 Kristeva, 'Oscillation between Power and Denial', p. 167.
3 Julia Kristeva, *Revolution in Poetic Language*, translated by Margaret Waller, New York, Columbia University Press, 1984, p. 51.
4 Julia Kristeva, *About Chinese Women*, translated by Anita Barrows, London, Marion Boyars, 1977, pp. 37–8; Kristeva, 'Oscillation between Power and Denial', p. 166.
5 Kristeva, *About Chinese Women*, p. 38.
6 Julia Kristeva, 'The Novel as Polylogue', in *Desire in Language: A Semiotic Approach to Literature and Art*, ed. Leon S. Roudiez, translated by Thomas Gora, Alice Jardine, and Leon S. Roudiez, Oxford, Blackwell, 1980, p. 167.
7 Kristeva, *Revolution in Poetic Language*, p. 79.
8 Kristeva, *About Chinese Women*, p. 34.
9 Phyllis Rose, *Women of Letters: A Life of Virginia Woolf*, London and Henley, Routledge & Kegan Paul, 1978, p. 125.
10 Gilles Deleuze and Félix Guattari, *Anti-Oedipus: Capitalism and Schizophrenia*, New York, The Viking Press, p. 2.

176

11 Kristeva, 'Oscillation between Power and Denial', p. 165.

12 Mary Jacobus, 'The Difference of View', in *Women Writing and Writing about Women*, ed. Mary Jacobus, London/New York, Croom Helm/Barnes & Noble Books, 1979, p. 20; Elaine Showalter, *A Literature of their Own: British Women Novelists from Brontë to Lessing*, London, Virago, 1978, pp. 289, 296, 318.

13 See J. Laplanche and J.-B. Pontalis, *The Language of Psycho-Analysis*, translated by Donald Nicholson-Smith, London, Hogarth and The Institute of Psycho-Analysis, 1973, pp. 78–80.

14 Kristeva, *Revolution in Poetic Language*, p. 51.

15 Virginia Woolf, *A Reflection of the Other Person: The Letters of Virginia Woolf*, vol. 4: 1929–1931, ed. Nigel Nicolson, London, Hogarth, 1978, p. 204.

16 Donald Davie, *Articulate Energy: An Inquiry into the Syntax of English Poetry*, London, Henley and Boston, Routledge & Kegan Paul, 1976, p. 10.

17 Ferdinand de Saussure, *Course in General Linguistics*, ed. Charles Rally and Albert Sechehaye in collaboration with Albert Reidlinger, translated by Wade Baskin, Glasgow, Fontana/Collings, 1974, p. 123.

18 Cited in Anthony Easthope, *Poetry as Discourse*, London, Methuen, 1983, p. 142.

19 See WD, pp. 108, 142–6 and 159, and also the early part of *The Waves: The two holograph drafts* transcribed and edited by J.W. Graham, London, Hogarth, 1976.

20 Kristeva, *Revolution in Poetic Language*, pp. 63, 69, 62.

21 Kristeva, 'The Novel as Polylogue', pp. 204–5.

22 Virginia Woolf, 'A Sketch of the Past', in *Moments of Being*, ed. Jeanne Schulkind, London, Hogarth, 1978, pp. 70–1, 122.

23 Kristeva, *About Chinese Women*, p. 38.

24 Kristeva, 'The Novel as Polylogue', p. 187.

25 Kristeva, 'From One Identity to an Other', in *Desire in Language*, p. 136.

26 Kristeva, *About Chinese Women*, p. 30.

27 See WD, p. 361, and E.M. Forster, *Virginia Woolf* (The Rede Lecture, 1941), Cambridge, Cambridge University Press, 1942, p. 8.

28 '"Anon" and "The Reader": Virginia Woolf's Last Essays', ed. Brenda R. Silver, in *Twentieth Century Literature: Virginia Woolf Issue*, vol. 25, no. 3/4, 1979, p. 374.

· 11 ·

Eliot's Abjection

MAUD ELLMAN

In a story of Oscar Wilde's, Gerald, the narrator, runs into his old friend Lord Murchison and finds him so anxious and confused that he urges him to unburden his mind. Murchison confesses that he fell in love some time ago with the mysterious Lady Alroy, whose life was so entrenched in secrecy that every move she made was surreptitious, every word she spoke conspiratorial. Fascinated, he resolved to marry her. But on the day he planned for his proposal, he caught sight of her hurrying down the street, 'deeply veiled', and sneaking into a lodging-house with her own key. Suspecting a secret lover, he abandoned her in rage and stormed off the Continent to forget her. Soon afterwards, however, he learnt that she was dead, having caught pneumonia in the theatre (as if in retribution for her masquerades). Still tormented by her mystery, however, he returned to London to continue his investigations. He cross-examined the landlady of the lodging-house, but she insisted that Lady Alroy always visited her rooms alone, took tea, and left as blamelessly as she had come. '"Now, what do you think it all meant?"' Murchison demands. For Gerald, the answer is quite simple: the lady was '"a sphinx without a secret"'.[1]

Now, *The Waste Land* is a sphinx without a secret, too, and to force it to expose its hidden depths may be a way of killing it, as the heroine of Wilde's fable was destroyed.[2] It is interesting that Hegel saw the sphinx as the symbol of the symbolizing faculty itself, because it did not know the answer to its own question: and *The Waste Land*, too, remains a secret to itself.[3] Eliot's poem, which has been so thoroughly *explained*, is rarely *read* at all, and one can scarcely see the 'waste' beneath the redevelopments. Most commentators have been so busy tracking its allusions down that they have overlooked its broken images in search of the totality it might have been. The poem has been read as a pilgrimage, a homosexual love song, a Grail romance, or an elegy to Western culture devastated by the carnage of the First World War.[4] Eliot mocked these readings rather possumishly in his later years, dismissing his most famous poem as 'a personal . . . grouse against life', a mere 'piece of rhythmical grumbling' (WL Fac, p. 1). Yet despite their differences, these readings all attempt to reinstate a hidden meaning which the text has systematically reduced to hints and guesses. Even Eliot is really trying to reclaim the poem as the allegory of his personal despair.

Freud and Breuer argue in a famous formulation that 'hysterics suffer mainly from reminiscences': and by this definition, *The Waste Land* is the most hysterical of texts.[5] However, the hysteric represses these reminiscences so that they surface on her body in the form of symptoms. Similarly, *The Waste Land*, I shall argue, is compelled to re-enact the conflicts that it cannot bring to consciousness. Now, just as many critics of *The Waste Land* think that they can solve its contradiction by digging up its sources and allusions, Freud at first believed that he could cure hysterical symptoms by deciphering their secret history. The illness would dissolve if he could speak the magic words which would erase the written sorrows from the body. These archaeologies, however, left his patients cold: and he gradually realized that their illness lay in their resistance to interpretation more than in the memories that they were trying to withhold. For this reason, he shifted his attention from the past to the present, from reminiscence to resistance, from the secrets to the silences themselves (SE, XVIII, p. 18). Likewise, the meaning of *The Waste Land* lies in its resistance to interpretation, in its ravaged memories and jumbled codes. Only a scrupulously superficial reading can detect the ways in which the poem struggles to forget its history and to stifle its unbearable realities. Indeed, written in the aftermath of the First World War, and in the midst of a disastrous marriage, the poem has so much to forget: madness, feminism, sexuality, the slaughtered millions, and the rattle of its own exhausted idioms. Yet this essay argues that *The Waste Land* works like an obsessive ceremonial, because it re-inscribes the horrors it is trying to repress. For Freud argues that obsessive rituals repeat the very acts that they are thought to neutralize: the ritual, he says, is ostensibly a protection against the prohibited act; but *actually* . . . a repetition of it' (SE, XII, p. 50). In *The Waste Land*, the very effort to deny its motives lays the poem open to be wracked by the nightmare of its history.

Throbbing between Two Lives

The Waste Land is a poem about waste. In a ceremonial purgation, Eliot inventories all the 'stony rubbish' that he strives to exorcize (20). It was his fascination with cathartic ritual that drew him towards poetic drama in his later work, but *The Waste Land* is already struggling towards incantation. For the poem is a crazed dramatic monologue, and more specifically a violent rewriting of the fevered narrative of *Maud*, although it fails in its attempt to exorcize the ghost of Tennyson. The 'waste *land*' could be seen as the thunderous desert where the hooded hordes are swarming towards apocalypse. But it also means 'waste ground' or urban waste where life has been and gone, like vacant lots where ancient women gather the wreckage of Europe. Indeed, it is the desolation of the city that the poem fears, rather than the purifying desert: 'Jerusalem Athens Alexandria/Vienna London/Unreal' (374–6). These ruined cities suggest that the very notion of the centre has collapsed, leaving only a centrifugal dissemination of debris. The poem teems with urban waste, butt-ends of the city's days and ways: 'empty bottles, sandwich papers,/silk handkerchiefs, cardboard boxes, cigarette ends' (177–8). Abortions, broken fingernails, carious teeth, and 'female smells' betoken cultural decay as well as bodily decrepitude. The filth without insinuates defilement within.

It is waste *paper*, however, which particularly fascinates the text, the written detritus which drifts among its idioms as randomly as picnics sink into the Thames (177–8). Like many modernist writers, Eliot scavenges among the relics of the literary past, recycling its 'once current puns' and 'quashed quotatoes', in Joyce's words. But whereas Joyce treats the rubbish heap of literature as a fund of creativity, Eliot regards it as the corpse of speech and strews his poem with its bones. In a lugubrious version of Joyce's jubilant 'recirculation' of the past, all waste becomes unbiodegradable: 'Men and bits of paper, whirled by the cold wind

. . .' (BN, III, 15). Indeed, *The Waste Land* is one of the most abject texts in English literature: for abjection, according to Bataille, is 'the inability to assume with sufficient strength the imperative act of excluding abject things,' an act that 'establishes the foundations of collective existence.'[6] Waste is what a culture casts away in order to determine what is not itself, and thus to establish its own limits. In the same way, the subject defines the limits of his body through the violent expulsion of its own excess. Ironically, it is this division between self and not-self which institutes the very notion of the excremental. As Paul Ricoeur has pointed out, 'impurity was never literally filthiness' and 'defilement was never literally a stain', for the notion of the impure is 'primordially symbolic'. It is created by the very rituals of its purgation. For these ceremonies, such as burning, chasing, throwing, spitting out, covering up, and burying, continuously name and reinvent the waste they exorcize.[7]

The word 'abject' literally means 'cast out', though commonly it means downcast in spirits: but 'abjection' may refer to the waste itself as well as to the act of throwing it away. It is the ambiguity of the 'abject' that distinguishes it from the 'object', which the subject rigorously jettisons (ob-jects). The abject emerges when exclusions fail, in the sickening collapse of limits. According to Julia Kristeva, the abject is that which 'disturbs identity, system, order': it is the 'in-between, the ambiguous, the composite'.[8] An example might be found in the 'brown fog' of *The Waste Land* (61, 208); or in the yellow fog of 'Prufrock', where the in-between grows animate, rubbing its back upon the window-pane and licking its synecdochic tongue into the corners of the evening like an abject Cheshire cat. It is to avoid abjection, too, that Madame Sosostris warns her client to fear death by water, for although water promises rebirth it also causes the erosion of distinctions: 'The river's tent is broken; the last fingers of leaf/Clutch and sink into the wet bank' (173–4). In the semantic landscape of the text, sinking banks imply dissolving definitions. In fact, the horror of *The Waste Land* lies in its osmoses, exhalations, and porosities, for this miasma is the symptom of disintegrating boundaries. Likewise, the proliferating corpses signify the 'utmost of abjection', in Kristeva's phrase, because they represent 'a border that has encroached upon everything': an outside that irrupts into the inside, eroding the parameters of life.[9] It is impossible to keep

them underground, for they are always just about to 'sprout': Stet-
son's garden is an ossuary, while the dull canals, the garrets, and
the alleys are littered with unburied bones. 'Tumbled graves' (387)
have overrun the city, and the living have changed places with the
dead: 'A crowd flowed over London Bridge, so many,/I did not
know death had undone so many' (62–3). Yet *The Waste Land*
does not fear the dead themselves so much as their invasion of the
living and this betweenness eats away at its distinctions, like the
teeming rats that gnaw the city's walls.

Horkheimer and Adorno argue that 'the history of civilization is
the history of the introversion of the sacrifice'.[10] *The Waste Land*
confirms this principle, because obsessive, private, bourgeois
rituals supplant the sacrificial rites which formerly expelled the
scapegoats of defilement. Thus, dressing tables take the place of
altars; fortune-tellers take the place of priests; and the voice of the
prophet is drowned in the garrulity of neurasthenia. Similarly, Mrs
Porter and her daughter wash their feet in soda water, to travesty
the ritual of baptism. However, *The Waste Land*, too, is an
obsessive rite, and as such it is compelled to re-inscribe the waste
that it is struggling to cast away. This contradiction grows
particularly acute in the poem's agon with its own precursors, the
dead who constitute its literary canon. For *The Waste Land*
vandalizes its tradition, as if desecration were the last remaining
ritual of reverence. Eliot once argued that 'no one can possibly
blaspheme . . . unless he profoundly believes in that which he
profanes' (ASG, p. 52). In this sense, *The Waste Land* is a
blasphemy against tradition, an affirmation masked as a denial. As
Terry Eagleton argues:

behind the back of this ruptured, radically decentred poem runs an alternative text which is nothing less than the closed, coherent, authoritative
discourse of the mythologies which frame it. The phenomenal text, to use
one of Eliot's own metaphors, is merely the meat with which the burglar
distracts the guard-dog while he proceeds with his stealthy business.[11]

At the same time, however, the poem uses its nostalgia to conceal
its infidelities to the tradition, in an impish parody of its own
pieties. Cleopatra's burnished throne becomes a vanity, time's
winged chariot a grinning skull (77, 186): but there are many
subtler deformations.

Take, for example, the opening words. 'April is the cruellest month' could be seen in Eliot's terms as a blasphemy against the first lines of *The Canterbury Tales*, which presented April's showers as so sweet. At once a nod to origins and a flagrant declaration of beginninglessness, this allusion grafts the poem to another text, vaunting its parasitic in-betweenness. The author's individuality dissolves in the citational abyss. It is this technique which prompted Conrad Aiken to complain that Eliot had created ' "a literature of literature" ... a kind of parasitic growth on literature, a sort of mistletoe. . .'.[12] For *The Waste Land* poaches on the past, caught in a perpetual allusion to the texts that it denies. In fact, the poem shows that it is writing which necessarily engenders blasphemy, just as the law is the prerequisite to crime. Yet it is by corrupting Chaucer's writings that the poem grieves the passing of his world:

> *April is the cruellest month, breeding*
> *Lilacs out of the dead land, mixing*
> *Memory and desire, stirring*
> *Dull roots with spring rain.*
> *Winter kept us warm, covering*
> *Earth in forgetful snow, feeding*
> *A little life with dried tubers (1–7).*

Because these lines allude to Chaucer, they invoke the beginning of the English literary tradition as well as the juvescence of the year. However, words like 'stirring', 'mixing', and 'feeding' blaspheme against beginnings, be they literary or organic, for the passage whispers of the words *its* words deny, sorrowing for things it cannot say. Most of the lines stretch beyond the comma where the cadence falls, as if the words themselves had overflowed their bounds, like the dull roots that hesitate between two states of being. The passage typifies the poem's own 'abjection', as it aspires towards the many poems which have already been written ('I did not know death had undone so many') – or another poem which has yet to be composed.

The speaker, too, succumbs to this betweenness, as the first-person pronoun roams from voice to voice.[13] The 'us' in 'Winter kept us warm' glides into the 'us' of 'Summer surprised us', without alerting 'us', the readers, of any change of name or locus. At last, the 'us' contracts into the couple in the Hofgarten, after having spoken for the human, animal, and vegetable worlds. What begins as an editorial 'we' becomes the mark of a migration, which restlessly displaces voice and origin. However, Eliot insisted in the Notes to *The Waste Land* that Tiresias should stabilize this drifting subject, and rally the nomadic voices of the text:

218.   Tiresias, although a mere spectator and not indeed a 'character,' is yet the most important personnage in the poem, uniting all the rest. Just as the one-eyed merchant, seller of currants, *melts into* the Phoenician Sailor, and the latter is *not wholly distinct* from Ferdinand Prince of Naples, so all the women are one woman, and the *two sexes meet* in Tiresias. What Tiresias *sees*, in fact, is the substance of the poem. (CPP, p. 52)

But what *does* Tiresias see? Blind as he is, the prophet has a single walk-on part, when he spies on the typist and her lover indulging in carbuncular caresses. In this Note, moreover, Eliot emphasizes the *osmosis* of identities more than their reunion in a central consciousness. Within the poem, likewise, Tiresias plays the double part of the voyeur, hovering between the roles of actor and spectator:

> *I Tiresias, though blind, throbbing between two lives,*
> *Old man with wrinkled female breasts, can see*
> *At the violet hour, the evening hour that strives*
> *Homeward, and brings the sailor home from sea,*
> *The typist home at teatime, clears her breakfast, lights*
> *Her stove, and lays out food in tins.*
> *Out of the window perilously spread*
> *Her drying combinations touched by the sun's last rays,*
> *On the divan are piled (at night her bed)*
> *Stockings, slippers, camisoles, and stays.*
> *I Tiresias, old man with wrinkled dugs*
> *Perceived the scene, and foretold the rest –*
> *I too awaited the expected guest*
> *He, the young man carbuncular, arrives . . . (218–31).*

'Throbbing between two lives', Tiresias could be seen as the very prophet of abjection, personifying all the poem's porous membranes. For he not only confounds the sexes but undermines the difference between the living and the dead. The Notes which dignify him retrospectively could be seen as 'abject', too, because they represent a kind of supplement or discharge of the text that Eliot could never get 'unstuck' (to use his own word), although he later wished the poem might stand alone (PP, p. 110). As a whole, *The Waste Land* throbs between two authors and three lives – the Notes, the published poem, and the manuscript that Pound pruned so cunningly – not to mention all the other poems that it weaves into its fabric. Thus the text's integrity dissolves under the invasion of its own disjecta.

In the passage above, the typist, like Tiresias, personifies the poem's in-betweenness. Her profession parodies the poet's demoted as he is to the typist or amanuensis of the dead. Too untidy to acknowledge boundaries, she strews her bed with stockings, slippers, camisoles, and stays, and even the bed is a divan by day, in a petty-bourgeois disrespect for definition. She resembles the neurotic woman in 'A Game of Chess', who cannot decide to go out or to stay in, as if she were at enmity with their distinction. Eliot himself declares that all the women in *The Waste Land* are one woman, and this is because they represent the very principle of unguency. For Eliot, 'pneumatic bliss' implies emulsive demarcations.[14] Yet the misogyny is so ferocious, particularly in the manuscript, that it begins to turn into a blasphemy against itself. For the text is fascinated by the femininity that it reviles, bewitched by this odorous and shoreless flesh. 'Woman', as the text conceives her, is the very spirit of its own construction, the phantom of its own betweennesses. In 'The Fire Sermon', for example, it is a woman's nameless, bruised, defiled body that personifies the poem and its broken images:

'*Trams and dusty trees.*
Highbury bore me. Richmond and Kew
Undid me. By Richmond I raised my knees
Supine on the floor of a narrow canoe.'

'*My feet are at Moorgate, and my heart*
Under my feet. After the event
He wept. He promised "a new start".
I made no comment. What should I resent?'

'*On Margate Sands.*
I can connect
Nothing with nothing.
The broken fingernails of dirty hands.
My people humble people who expect

Nothing.'

   la la

To Carthage then I came

Burning burning burning burning
O Lord Thou pluckest me out
O Lord Thou pluckest

burning (292–311)

Here, the city and the woman's body melt together, no longer themselves but not yet other, transfixed in an eternal in-betweenness. Both the woman and the city have been raped, but the 'he' seems passive in his violence, weeping at his own barbarity. The victim, too, consents to degradation as if it were foredoomed: 'I raised my knees/Supine . . . What should I resent?' (As Ian Hamilton observes, 'no one in *The Waste Land* raises her knees in any other spirit than that of dumb complaisance.'[15]) 'Undone', the woman's body disintegrates into a synecdochic heap of knees, heart, feet, weirdly disorganized: 'my feet are at Moorgate, and my heart/Under my feet.' But the city which undid her decomposes, too, into a random concatenation of its parts – Highbury, Richmond, Kew, Moorgate – and ends in broken fingernails on Margate Sands. Itinerant and indeterminate, the 'I' meanders from the woman to the city, and then assumes the voice of Conrad's Harlequin in *Heart of Darkness*, who speaks for the exploited natives of the Congo: 'My people humble people who expect/Nothing' (304). Finally, the speaker coalesces with the 'I' who came to Carthage in Augustine's *Confessions*. As the last falter-ing words suggest, it is impossible to 'pluck' the speaking subject out of the conflagration of the poem's idioms. The 'I' cannot preserve its own identity intact against the shrieking voices which assail it, 'Scolding, mocking, or merely chattering' according to their whim (BN, IV, 28). In *The Waste Land*, the only voice which *is* 'inviolable' is the voice beyond articulated speech, the lamenta-tions of the daughters of the Thames: 'la la'.

This tragic melody recalls the warblings of Philomela the nightingale, who filled the desert with 'inviolable voice' in 'A Game of Chess' (101). Like the Thames daughters, however, her voice was born in violation. In Ovid's *Metamorphoses*, Tereus, 'the barbarous king' (109), raped Philomela and cut out her tongue to prevent her from accusing him as her defiler. (In *The Waste Land*, she can only twitter 'Tereu . . .' (206).) The gods, however, took pity on her, transforming her into a nightingale to compensate her loss of speech with wordless song. For all her purity, however, the nightingale is secretly in league with the degraded women of the text, who also empty language of its sense through darker means. The scolding voice of the neurotic vamp is not so very different from the desolate music of the nightingale, for both, in their own ways, obliterate semantics with acoustics. In Kristeva's terms, the semiotic overpowers the symbolic. It is this severance of sound from sense that Eliot calls the 'dissociation of sensibility', and regards as the linguistic fall of man (SE, p. 288). Milton is his prime culprit, because his poetry obeys the witchery of music rather than the laws of sense, forsaking meaning for mellifluence. The pleasure, Eliot complains, 'arises from the *noises*': from a language which refuses to efface itself, delighting in the 'mazes' of its own sonority (SP, pp. 261–3). Yet *The Waste Land* treats the semiotic as both the most exalted and the most contemptible extreme of language. In the 'la la' of the Thames daughters, or the 'jug, jug' of the nightingale, language is purified as pain, conveying no semantic content but the feeling of some infinitely gentle, infinitely suffering thing. But these forlorn notes also correspond to other meaningless sounds, like the rattle of the bones and the hollow echo of obsolescent rituals. In *The Waste Land*, songs without words are the only refuge for a speaker violated by the writings of the dead and seized in a cacophony beyond control.

Prince of Morticians

Curious, is it not, that Mr. Eliot
Has not given more time to Mr Beddoes
    (T.L.) prince of morticians (Pound, Canto LXXX)

In 'Tradition and the Individual Talent', Eliot extends a welcome to the very voices of the dead which lie in ambush for the speaker of *The Waste Land*. In the essay, he claims that 'not only the best, but the most individual parts of [a poet's] work may be those in which dead poets, his ancestors, assert their immortality most vigorously' (SE, p. 4). By this logic, the poet is most himself when he is least himself; most individual when he is most bespoken; most intimate when he is serving as amanuensis for the dead. Eliot published 'Tradition and the Individual Talent' in 1919, immediately after the First World War, and in the same year that Freud composed *Beyond the Pleasure Principle*. As Peter Middleton has pointed out, both essays are negotiating with the same material: the unprecedented death toll of the First World War.[16] Like Freud's theory of repetition, Eliot's account of influence attempts to salvage something of a past that had never been so ruthlessly annihilated – however fearsome its reanimation from the grave. Now, according to Freud, human beings first acknowledged death when they invented ghosts, yet this is also when they first defied it, by asserting that the dead return. Eliot's conception of tradition involves the same uneasy compromise. 'What is dead', says Eliot, is really 'what is already living'; and by the same principle, the living are already dying, for they undergo 'continual extinction' in the act of writing, reduced to the phantoms of their own precursors: 'The progress of the artist is a continual self-sacrifice, a continual extinction of personality' (SE, pp. 22, 17). Writing, in the words of Yeats, is death-in-life and life-in-death. Whereas Freud discovers the death drive in the compulsion to repeat, *The Waste Land* stages it in the compulsion to citation. Yet both compulsions invest death with the strange insistence and vitality that might be called its 'vigour mortis'.[17]

In 1919 Freud also wrote his famous essay on 'The "Uncanny"', where he extends his theory of the death drive into literature. Here he defines the uncanny as 'whatever reminds us of this inner compulsion to repeat', a compulsion which always bears the mark of Thanatos (SE, XVII, p. 238). *The Waste Land* is 'uncanny' in a double sense: for not only is it haunted by the repetition of the dead, in the form of mimicry, quotation, and pastiche, but it also teems with Hammer horror: bats with baby faces, whisper music; violet light, hooded hordes, witches, death's heads, bones, and zombies (378–81). Freud demonstrates in an ingenious etymology that the German word '*Heimlich*' literally means 'homely' or familiar, but that it has developed 'in the direction of ambivalence' until it has converged with its antithesis, '*Unheimlich*', meaning 'unhomely' or uncanny (SE, XVII, pp. 222–6). In this way the very word has grown uncanny to itself.

This ambiguity between the strange and the familiar may also be detected in Eliot's uncanny imagery, particularly in the passage he misquotes from *The White Devil*:

> O keep the Dog far hence, that's friend to men,
> Or with his nails he'll dig it up again! *(74–5)*

Since these lines have been lifted from Webster, the very words are ghostly revenants, at once remembered and unknown. It is significant that ghosts and quotations often come together in *The Waste Land*, for they are both 'extravagant and erring spirits', unleashed from the dead they represent. In fact, *The Waste Land* hints that writing, in so far as it is quotable, institutes the very possibility of errancy, which in its turn engenders the possibility of ghosts. In this passage, however, Eliot writes Dog where Webster wrote Wolf, and friend where Webster wrote foe: and thus he tames the hellhound in the same misprision that domesticates the discourse of the past. Friendly pet and wild beast, the Dog embodies the literary necrophilia of the text itself, and the familiar strangeness of the past it disinters.

If a quotation is the ghost of a dead speech, a prophecy is the ghost of an unborn event. It is prophets, therefore, who personify the poem's temporality, caught between an undead future and a posthumous past. For prophecy means that we hear about a thing before it happens. The report precedes the event. The bell echoes before it rings. Tiresias, for instance, is a human misquotation, having foreseen and 'foresuffered all'. Even in *The Odyssey*, he represents the principle of repetition, for the hero's deeds become the mere reiteration of his words. His alter ego, Madame Sosostris, fears the very repetition that she represents, nervous that her words may go astray: 'Tell her I bring the horoscope myself', she says, 'One must be so careful these days' *(58–9)*. Her fear of plagiarizers parodies the inner struggle of the text itself, torn between originality and verbal keptomania. Mr Eugenides also stands for repetition and dissemination. A Turkish merchant in London, he propositions the narrator in demotic French: and the word 'demotic', Greek in etymology, pertains to Egyptian hieroglyphics. Being a merchant, he is not only the produce but the sinister conductor of miscegenation, intermingling verbal, sexual, and monetary currencies. Even his pocketful of currants could be heard as 'currents', which dissolve identities and definitions, like the 'current under sea' that picks the bones of Phlebas, his Phoenician alter ego. His reappearances suggest that repetition has become an epidemic, unwholesome as the very personages who recur. But it is writing which induces repetition, because it necessarily deserts its author and can be quoted anywhere, by anyone. A plague of echoes, writing is the source of the 'abjection' of *The Waste Land*, its inability to close its boundaries or to void itself of other texts. For any set of written signs may fall into bad company, into contexts which pervert their sense and genealogy.

The worst company in *The Waste Land*, both socially and rhetorically, is the London pub where Lil is tortured by her crony for her bad teeth and her abortion. While Eliot attempts to give the dead a second life by quoting them, Lil inverts this trope by killing what is yet unborn. It is curious in this respect that Eliot should have thanked Pound for the 'Caesarian section' he performed upon *The Waste Land*, as if the poem too had been aborted or at least unnaturally born.

> *You ought to be ashamed, I said, to look so antique.*
> *(And her only thirty-one)*
> *I can't help it, she said, pulling a long face,*
> *It's them pills I took, to bring it off, she said.*
> *(She's had five already, and nearly died of young George.)*
> *The chemist said it would be all right, but I've never been the same.*
> *You are a proper fool, I said.*
> *Well, if Albert won't leave you alone, there it is, I said,*
> *What you get married for if you don't want children?*
> *HURRY UP PLEASE ITS TIME*
> *Well, that Sunday Albert was home, they had a hot gammon.*
> *And they asked me to dinner, to get the beauty of it hot*
> *HURRY UP PLEASE ITS TIME*
> *HURRY UP PLEASE ITS TIME*
> *Goonight Bill, Goonight Lou, Goonight May, Goonight.*
> *Ta ta. Goonight. Goonight.*
> *Good night, ladies, good night, sweet ladies, good night,*
>   *good night. (156–72)*

As Peter Middleton has pointed out, there is a repressed allusion in this passage to contemporary feminist demands for birth control.[18] Ezra Pound's invectives against 'usury' in the same era reveal a similar anxiety, for he fulminates specifically against its *contraceptive* powers. *The Waste Land*, on the other hand, interprets women's pleas for control over their reproductive systems as frigidity: 'Exploring hands encounter no defence . . . And [make] a welcome of indifference' (240–2). In contrast to the ghost-raising that dominates the text, women become corpses, moribund in their passivity: 'You ought to be ashamed . . . to look so antique', says May to Lou (156). Yet in the pub scene, the ghost of Shakespeare is revived as Lil declines. Just as the dialogue is closing, Ophelia's poignant voice joins into the chorus of insouciant good-byes: 'Good night, ladies, good night, sweet ladies, good night, good night.' It is before she drowns herself that Ophelia utters these adieux, and the allusion dignifies Lil's slower suicide. On the other hand, *The Waste Land* challenges the sanctity of the tradition by suturing Ophelia's words to Lil's, reducing Shakespeare to graffiti.

This passage typifies the text's ambivalence towards the tradition. Afraid to remember and afraid to forget, it savages the very ghosts it summons from their literary graves. On the one hand it struggles to transcend the past and to introduce a new poetic idiom, invigorated by the pungency of common speech: but on the other hand it can only justify its present by deferring to the icons of the past. Potentially revolutionary, it retreats into conservatism, dazed by the vertigo of its own insights. As Marx puts it in another context:

The tradition of all the dead generations weighs like a nightmare on the brain of the living. And just when [men] seem engaged in revolutionizing themselves and things, in creating something that has never yet existed, precisely in such periods of revolutionary crisis they anxiously conjure up the spirits of the past to their service and borrow from them names, battle cries and costumes in order to present the new scene of world history in this time-honoured disguise and this borrowed language.[19]

Freud argues that taboos against the dead reveal a conflict between veneration and horror, similar to the divided impulses which *The Waste Land* expresses towards its past (SE, XIII, p. 25). These taboos, Freud says, are 'expressions of mourning; but on the other hand they clearly betray – what they seek to conceal – hostility against the dead . . .' (SE, XIII, p. 61). But he stresses that it is not the dead themselves so much as their 'infection' which is feared, their insidious invasions of the living (SE, XIII, pp. 20–2, 41). Thus, taboos arise to reassert the boundary between the living and the dead. Strangely, however, it is the taboo itself which grows infectious, because the rites and sacred objects which represent the dead gradually become forbidden by contagion. Freud compares these forbidden rites to those of obsessional neurotics, whose ceremonials eventually become a source of guilt because they raise unconscious wishes by denying them. Eventually, 'the whole world lies under an embargo'. According to Freud, there are two ways in which taboo can spread, through resemblance or through contiguity. To touch a sacred object is to fall under its interdict, which is an instance of *contiguous* infection. But the offender must also be tabooed because of 'the risk of imitation', for others may follow his example. These two forms of transference operate like rhetorical tropes, because the first, like metonymy, depends on contiguity, the second on similitude, like metaphor. Freud adds that 'the prohibitions lack any assignable motive', and that they are 'easily displaceable'. In this sense the taboos compare to language, for it is the unmotivated nature of the signifier that enables it to slide over the signified, as 'easily displaceable' as a contagion. In fact, the spread of the taboo depends upon rhetorical displacement, and underneath the fear of death lies the fear of tropes, of the death-dealing power of figuration (SE, XIII, pp. 27–33).

Now, much of Eliot's prose consists of a crusade against displacement, in the realms of culture, politics, literature, and religion. He denounces Matthew Arnold, for example, for allowing literature to 'usurp the place of religion', and for instituting the idolatry of 'culture'. Arnold, he says, 'discovered a new formula: poetry is not religion, but it is a capital substitute for religion – not invalid port, which may lend itself to hypocrisy, but coffee without caffeine, or tea without tannin' (UPUC, p. 26). Similarly, Milton's poetry neglects the *meaning* of the language for its *art*. Eliot's arguments imply that all these 'heresies' begin with the fetishism of the signifier – of the written or acoustic tissues of the word – where literary pleasure overwhelms the stern demands of sense, replacing sound for meaning, form for content, rite for faith. Yet although Eliot accuses Milton of dividing sound from sense and bequeathing a fallen language to posterity, his own techniques of theft and bricolage entail the same displacements. In fact, the abjection of *The Waste Land* arises out of the displacements which haunt it from within: the mutual contaminations of the past and present, of the dead letter and the living voice. Eliot's quotations demonstrate how written signs are necessarily displaceable, orphaned from their origins and meanings. Moreover, *The Waste Land* shows a Miltonic and perverse delight in the semiotic side of language, in the asemantic echolalias of words. Beneath the meaningful connections of the text a parodic underlanguage opens forth, based on the contagion between sounds.

Aptly, it is the rats who carry this contagion, for the echoes between rat and rattle constitute a musical recurrent theme. They make their first appearance in 'rats' alley', where the dead men lost their bones; but later on more rats appear, and the bones begin to rattle too:

> *But at my back in a cold blast I hear*
> *The* rattle *of the bones, and chuckle spread from ear to ear.*

> *A* rat *crept softly through the vegetation*
> *Dragging its slimy belly on the bank*
> *While I was fishing in the dull canal*
> *On a winter evening round behind the gashouse*
> *Musing upon the king my brother's wreck*
> *And on the king my father's death before him.*
> *White bodies naked on the low damp ground*
> *And bones cast in a little low dry garret,*
> *Rattled by the rat's foot only, year to year (III, 185–95; my emphases)*

It is the sound, here, which connects the rattle to the rat, as opposed to a semantic continuity. In fact, the rattle of the words controls their combinations, for they proceed according to their sounds rather than their sense. It is important, moreover, that the text associates the rattle of the rats with 'the king my brother's wreck' and 'the king my father's death before him'. For the contiguity suggests a link between the rattle and these royal deaths. Borrowed from *The Tempest*, these shipwrecked kings imply the downfall of the paternal sovereignty, as do the stories of the Fisher King that Eliot discovered in Jessie Weston's study of the Grail romance.[20] According to these legends, the Fisher King has fallen impotent, and his sterility has brought a blight upon his lands. Eliot connects the Fisher King with Christ, the fisher of men, and also with 'the man with three staves' in the Tarot pack. The emasculation of these symbolic figures corresponds to the impotence that Eliot detects in language, in the inability of words to reach the Word: 'The word within a word, unable to speak a word,/Swaddled with darkness' ('Gerontion'). Thus, the death of kings implies that meaning is evacuated from the word, eliciting the 'rattle' – the verminous proliferation of the signifier – which the poem thematizes in the form of rats.

This semantic crisis is more baldly stated in *The Waste Land* manuscript. For here the pilgrim seeks 'the one essential word that frees' because he is entrammeled in 'concatenated words from which the sense seemed gone'.[21] In the finished poem, all that remains of the lightning of the Word is the 'dry sterile thunder' of the desert: the belated rattle of concatenated signs (342). And this is why *The Waste Land* is obsessed with afterness: even the word 'after' rattles through the text as it bemoans its irremediable belatedness:

> *After the torchlight red on sweaty faces*
> *After the frosty silence in the garden*
> *After the agony in stony places . . . (V, 322–4)*

Here the poem breaks off, but the manuscript goes on to deplore the time lag between its own conception and its execution: 'After the ending of this inspiration',[22] The act of writing always comes too late, the wake of inspiration and its obsequies. As Prufrock is forever halting at the threshold, caught in a perpetual before, so *The Waste Land* is transfixed in an eternal afterwards: but in both cases the experience is always missed. The present is eclipsed, laying time as well as space to waste: 'Ridiculous the waste sad time/Stretching before and after' (BN, IV, 48–9).

Yet *The Waste Land* uses this nostalgia to conceal the *now* which constantly irrupts within, unsettling its carefully caught regrets. The present which Eliot is trying to abject resurges in the form of poverty, abortion, demobbed men and neurasthenic women, whose human voices drown the etherizing music of the past. The dead the poem cannot name and the women that it cannot bury re-emerge in the miasma of its failed exclusions. For the text is full of odours, particularly 'female smells'. This 'hearty female stench' coalesces with the odour of mortality, because they both exude from writing, from the violated corpse of speech. All these effluvia are symptoms of displacement, and displacement is the symptom of the errancy of writing, of the unavoidable diaspora of written signs. To paraphrase the text's sexology, writing and the after-smell of femininity have overpowered the immediate priapic realm of speech. Eliot to some extent repressed the 'hearty female stench' when he excised it from the manuscript: but it lingers in the strange synthetic perfumes of the lady in 'A Game of Chess', which 'troubled, confused/And drowned the sense in odours'. 'Sense', here, implies the sense of words as well as the pleasures of the senses, for both are overcome by the narcotic scents of femininity.

The reason that the text's misogyny takes the form of smell is that the subject smelling actually imbibes the object smelt, bearing witness to invisible displacements. In vision, by contrast, the seer and the seen maintain their distance and integrity. As stench, the feminine dissolves the limits of the private body, so that the very notion of identity subsides into pneumatic anarchy. In *Moses and Monotheism*, Freud says that the displacements of a text resemble a murder, because the difficulty is not in perpetrating the deed but in getting rid of its traces. There is a murder in *The Waste Land* too, but only the traces of the deed remain: the dead kings, the castrated gods, the silent Word, unspeakable and disincarnate. These absences unleash the sexual, linguistic, and geographical displacements which constitute the text's aesthetic but also drive it to its frenzied abjection of itself. And this murder – of the father, the phallus, or the Logos – entails at last the dissolution of identity itself, imaged as asphyxiation in the body of the feminine.

At the end of the poem, Eliot explodes the discourse of the west, petitioning the east for solace and recovery.

> *London Bridge is falling down falling down falling down*
> Poi s'ascose nel foco che gli affina
> Quando fiam uti chelidon – *O swallow swallow*
> Le Prince d'Aquitaine à la tour abolie
> *These fragments I have shored against my ruins*
> *Why then Ile fit you. Hieronymo's mad againe.*
> Datta. Dayadhvam. Damyata.
> *Shantih shantih shantih (426–33)*

Here at last the poem silences its western noise with eastern blessings. By striving towards a universal language, the poem is trying to recover the totalizing spirit of imperialism from the savage scramble of the First World War. But the text changes its exhausted English only for the jabber of miscegenated tongues, stammering its orisons in Babel. One of Eliot's earliest and canniest reviewers said that '"Words, words, words" might be his motto, for in his verse he seems to have them and to be always expressing his hatred of them, in words.'[23] Because the poem can only abject writing with more writing, it turns into the infection it is struggling to purge, and implodes under the pressure of its own contradictions.

The Violet Hour

It is in another abject ceremonial that Freud discovered the death drive, in his grandchild's ritual expulsion of his toys. In *Beyond the Pleasure Principle*, he explains how this little boy would fling a cotton-reel in the abyss beyond his cot and retrieve it with an 'aaaa' of satisfaction, only to cast it out again, uttering a forlorn 'oooo'. Freud interprets these two syllables as primitive versions of the German words '*fort*' (gone) and '*da*' (here), and he argues that the child is mastering his mother's absences by 'staging' them in the manipulation of a sign (SE, XVIII, p. 28). Indeed, Freud compares this theatre of abjection to the catharses of Greek tragedy, and he sees the child's pantomime renunciation as his first 'great cultural achievement'.

It is important, however, that the *drama* fascinates the child rather than the toy itself, for the bobbin belongs to a series of objects which he substitutes indifferently for one another.[24] While the cotton-reel stands for the mother, re-enacting her intermittencies, it also represents the child himself, who sends it forth like an ambassador. As if to emphasize this point, he tops his first act by staging his own disappearance. Hiding from his own reflection in a mirror, he lisps, 'Baby o-o-o-o!' [Baby gone!]: like an abject Narcissus, fascinated by his absence rather than his image. Casting *himself* out, the child founds his subjectivity by rehearsing his annihilation in a game that can only end in death. As Kristeva writes: 'I expel *myself*, I spit *myself* out, I *abject* myself within the same motion through which "I" claim to establish *myself*.'[25] Moreover, by attempting to control his world with signs, the child has become a function of the sign, *subjected to* its ineluctable trajectory.

In this scenario, Freud intervenes between the mother and the child, bearing the law of language. For it is he who transforms the oscillation of the child's vowels into intelligible speech. But he neglects the vengeful pleasure that the infant takes in the semiotic rattle of their sounds. It is significant, moreover, that the little boy never changed his 'o-o-o-o' into the neutral *'fort'* when he acquired the command of language. Instead, he sent his bobbin to the trenches. 'A year later', Freud writes:

the same boy whom I had observed at his first game used to take a toy, if he was angry with it, and throw it on the floor, exclaiming: 'Go to the fwont!' He had heard at that time that his absent father was 'at the front', and was far from regretting his absence . . . . (SE, XVIII, p. 16)

Thus it is not just any absence which the child is trying to control but the specific desolation of the war. *The Waste Land* confronts this silence, too, evincing both the dread and the desire to hear the voices at the 'fwont' again. Its ruling logic is 'prosopopeia', as Paul de Man defines the trope:

the fiction of an apostrophe to an absent, deceased, or voiceless entity, which posits the possibility of the latter's reply and confers upon it the power of speech. Voice assumes mouth, eye and finally face, a chain that is manifest in the etymology of the trope's name, *prosopon poien*, to confer a mask or face (*prosopon*).[26]

The many ghosts that haunt *The Waste Land* – like the spirits flowing over London Bridge, the restless corpses and the hooded hordes – bespeak the need to give a face and voice to death. But it is significant that these figures have no faces, remaining voiceless and unrecognizable:

Who is the third who walks always beside you?
When I count, there are only you and I together
But when I look ahead up the white road
There is always another one walking beside you
Gliding wrapt in a brown mantle, hooded
I do not know whether a man or a woman
– But who is that on the other side of you? (V, 360–6)

Here, these nervous efforts to reconstitute the face only drive it back into the darkness. This nameless third is Christ, of course, but it also embodies the anxiety of influence, the tradition of the past that weighs like a nightmare on the living: 'There is always another one walking beside you.' Neither absent nor present, this figure signifies the failure of prosopopoeia to overcome the poem's equally indomitable drive to disincarnate and deface the dead. Indeed, Eliot hints in *Little Gidding* that to give a face to death is necessarily to sacrifice one's own identity. For the ghost of *Little Gidding* stands for memory but also for oblivion, forgotten in the moment that he is recalled. Caught between 'next year's words' and 'last year's language', he marks a rift in memory where speech itself dissolves into amnesia (LG, II, 65–6). 'I may not comprehend, may not remember', cries the speaker; and the ghost himself is 'known, forgotten, half-recalled', obsolescing as he shapes his 'down-turned face': 'And he a face still forming' (LG, II, 57, 40, 36, 48). Yet the speaker also loses face and voice, suggesting that the ghost can only rise by reducing his ephebe to unbeing. Knowing himself yet 'being someone other', and hearing his own exclamations in 'another's voice', the speaker plays a 'double part', staging his own death and watching his identity disfeaturing (LG, 44–7). The struggle ends in the disappearance of the ghost, and the evacuation of his 'figure' from the text:

> The day was breaking. In the disfigured street
> > He left me, with a kind of valediction,
> > And faded on the blowing of the horn (LG, II, 94–6)

The word 'disfigured' commonly means 'mutilated', and it implies unfaced, unrecognizable. But in this context it literally means *figureless* – emptied of persona, phantom, shape, face, rhetoric. For it is only by banishing the 'figures' of the dead that the poet can establish an originary voice.

The speaker of *The Waste Land* also stages his own death when he conjures up the writings of the dead, sacrificing voice and face to their ventriloquy. In this sense he resembles the child in *Beyond the Pleasure Principle*, who stages his extinction in the mirror. Freud compares his grandchild to the victims of shell-shock, who relive their terrors in their dreams, repeating death as if it were desire. This is the game *The Waste Land* plays, and the nightmare that it cannot lay to rest, as it stages the ritual of its own destruction.

Notes

1 Oscar Wilde, 'A Sphinx without a Secret', *Complete Writings*, London, vol. VIII, pp. 121–32.

2 All references to Eliot's poetry are cited from T.S. Eliot, *The Complete Poems and Plays*, London, Faber, 1969: henceforth CPP. Unless otherwise designated, line numbers in the text refer to *The Waste Land*. Other abbreviations of Eliot's works include:

ASG   *After Strange Gods: A Primer of Modern Heresy*, London, Faber, 1934.

BN   *Burnt Norton* (1935 – *Four Quartets* Part I).

LG   *Little Gidding* (1942 – *Four Quartets* Part IV).

PP   *On Poetry and Poets*, London, Faber, 1957.

SE   *Selected Essays*, London, Faber, 1932.

SP   *Selected Prose*, ed. Frank Kermode, London, Faber, 1975.

UPUC   *The Use of Poetry and the Use of Criticism*, 1933, reprinted London, Faber, 1964.

WL Fac   *The Waste Land: A Facsimile and Transcript of the Original Drafts Including the Annotations of Ezra Pound*, ed. Valerie Eliot, London, Faber, 1971.

3 See *Hegel's Aesthetics: Lectures on Fine Art*, translated by T.M. Knox, Oxford, Clarendon, 1975, pp. 360–1.

4 For the Holy Grail interpretation, see Grover Smith, *T.S. Eliot's Poetry and Plays: A Study in Sources and Meaning*, Chicago, University of Chicago Press 1956, pp. 69–70, 74–7; and Edmund Wilson, *Axel's Castle: A Study in the Imaginative Literature of 1870–1930*, New York and London, Scribner's, 1931, pp. 104–5. Helen Gardner subscribes to this position with some qualifications in *The Art of T.S. Eliot*, London, Cresset Press, 1949, p. 87. George Williamson reconstructs *The Waste Land* ingeniously in *A Reader's Guide*, especially pp. 129–30. See also John Peter, 'A New Interpretation of *The Waste Land*', *Essays in Criticism*, 2, 1952, especially p. 245; and James E. Miller, *T.S. Eliot's Personal Waste Land: Exorcism of the Demons*, University Park, Pennsylvania State University Press, 1977, *passim*.

5 Joseph Breuer and Sigmund Freud, *Studies on Hysteria* (1893–5), in *The Standard Edition of The Complete Psychological Works of Sigmund Freud* (henceforth SE), translated by James Strachey, London, Hogarth, 1953–74, vol. II, p. 7.

6 Quoted in Julia Kristeva, *Powers of Horror. An Essay on Abjection*, translated by Leon S. Roudiez, New York, Columbia University Press, 1982, p. 56.

7 See Paul Ricoeur, *The Symbolism of Evil*, translated by Emerson Buchanan, Boston, Beacon Press, 1967, pp. 35, 39.

8 Kristeva, *Powers of Horror*, p. 4; see also p. 9.

9 Ibid., pp. 4, 3.

10 Max Horkheimer and Theodor W. Adorno, *Dialectic of Enlightenment*,

translated by J. Cumming, 1944, reprinted New York, Seabury Press, 1972, p. 55.

11 Terry Eagleton, *Criticism and Ideology*, London, Verso, 1978, pp. 149–50.

12 See Conrad Aiken, 'An Anatomy of Melancholy', 1923, reprinted in *A Collection of Critical Essays on The Waste Land*, ed. J. Martin, Englewood Cliffs, NJ, Prentice Hall, 1968, p. 54.

13 Alick West pointed this out long ago: see *Crisis and Criticism*, London, Lawrence & Wishart, 1937, pp. 5–6, 28.

14 See Eliot, 'Whispers of Immortality':

> *Grishkin is nice: her Russian eye*
> *Is underlined for emphasis;*
> *Uncorseted, her friendly bust*
> *Gives promise of pneumatic bliss. (17–20)*

15 Ian Hamilton, '*The Waste Land*', in *Eliot in Perspective*, ed. Martin, p. 109.

16 Peter Middleton, 'The Academic Development of *The Waste Land*', in *Demarcating the Disciplines*, Glyph Textual Studies I, ed. Samuel Weber, Minneapolis, University of Minnesota Press, 1986, pp. 153–80.

17 Richard Rand used this phrase as the title of his unpublished essay on Paul de Man.

18 Middleton, 'The Academic Development of *The Waste Land*', pp. 166–9.

19 Karl Marx, *The Eighteenth Brumaire of Louis Bonaparte*, New York, International Publishers, 1963, p. 15.

20 See Jessie Weston, *From Ritual to Romance*, 1920, reprinted Garden City, NY, Doubleday, 1957, Ch. 9, pp. 113–36.

21 WL Fac, 109, 113.

22 WL Fac, 109.

23 Anon., Review of *Ara Vos Prec*, TLS, no. 948, 1920, p. 184. See also Gabriel Pearson, 'Eliot: An American Use of Symbolism', in *Eliot in Perspective*, ed. Martin, pp. 83–7, for an illuminating discussion of 'the social as well as verbal logic' of 'the conversion of words into the Word'.

24 In the same way, Ricoeur argues that defilement is acted out through 'partial, substitutive and abbreviated signs' which 'mutually symbolise one another' (*The Symbolism of Evil*, p. 35).

25 Kristeva, *Powers of Horror*, p. 3.

26 Paul de Man, 'Autobiography as De-facement', *Modern Language Notes*, 94, 1979, 926, reprinted as Ch. 4 in *The Rhetoric of Romanticism*, New York, Columbia University Press, 1984.

Index

Roland 13; *Song of Roland* 13
romanticism 117
romantic theory of texts 124, 128, 133
Rose, J.: 'The Imaginary' 109–10, 133
Roudiez, L. 66
Rousseau, J.J. 8, 15–17, 133; *Emile* 8, 15; *The Fairy Queen* 16–17; *Letter to d'Alembert on Theatre* 16
Russian futurism 107
Ryan, J. 51

sacred 99, 154
sacrifice 59
sacrificial role 73
Sade, Marquis de 150
Same, the 42
Sand, G. 15
Sartre, J.-P. 112, 118; *Being and Nothingness* 111, 142, 152; *Between Existentialism and Marxism* 156n; *Reflexions sur la question juive (Portrait of the Anti-Semite)* 152, 156n; *Saint Genet* 147
Sartrean engagement 140; 'the look' 111
Saussure, F. de 98, 131, 140, 167; *Anagrammes* 129
Schilder, P. 84; *The Image and the Appearance of the Human Body* 102n
science 38, 107
seduction 124–5
self 31, 84, 92, 164, 169, 172, 181; consciousness of 43; corporeal limits of 90; dispersed 163; fragmentation of 170; knowledge of 44; not- 181; self/other 101; unitary 159
semiosis: and symptoms 159
semiotic 3, 6, 22, 27–8, 36, 39, 45, 65–7, 88, 94, 96, 98–100, 130, 144–5, 148–9, 158, 161–3, 165–6, 173–6, 187, 192, 197;

and aesthetic 28; and the biological 66; and the body 6, 145, 174; chora 4, 27–32, 99, 145, 147, 163, 173, 175; and conscious/unconscious 66; difference 32; dissolution 164; drives 86; energy 28; and id/superego 66; mobility 166; as music 149–50; and nature/culture 66; and negativity 144; as other to symbolic 149; practice 10; process 4, 129, 145; psychotic 80; relation 45; and symbolic 46, 66, 80, 147–9, 164; *see also* body, dialectic, mother, practice, subject
semiotics 1, 109, 140, 154
sex 14–17, 97; *see also* gender
sexism 72, 77
sexuality 6, 50–1, 94, 101, 115, 129, 145, 179; infantile 80; *see also* female
Shaftesbury 117
Shakespeare, W. 191; *Cymbeline* 164; *The Tempest* 193
Shandy, Tristram 22
Shaw, M.: 'Feminism and Fiction between the Wars' 64
Showalter, E. 165
sign 9, 11, 21, 25, 34–7, 125, 127–30, 132, 134, 190, 193–4; arbitrary 35; and body 25; materiality of 130; and other 128, 131; and signifying practices 29, 81; and signifying process 50
significance 27
signification 55–6, 67, 80, 82, 125–6, 130–2, 149, 158, 164
signified 125, 130–2, 173–4, 192
signifier 47, 86, 125, 130, 132, 145, 167, 172, 174, 192, 194
signifying 167; practice 81, 85, 169; process 36, 45, 50, 66, 145, 158, 163; *see also* body, sign
Smith, G. 199n

women 94, 194; of China 69;
European 68, 72; specificity of
59, 72, 92

Woolf, V. 4, 157–77; *Between the
Acts* 173–5; *Collected Essays*
159, 164, 166, 171; *A Haunted
House and Other Stories* 161,
168; *Jacob's Room* 158; *Mrs
Dalloway* 160, 163–4, 166;
Orlando 161–3, 165, 171, 173;
A Room of One's Own 157, 160,
165; *To the Lighthouse* 161; *The
Voyage Out* 172; *The Waves* 4,
159–60, 165–73; *A Writer's
Diary* 161, 163, 166, 171, 173–4

Wordsworth, W. 128, 133, 134;
The Prelude 133

writing 22, 188–90; abject 196; act
of 194; adolescent 8–11; errancy
of 194; experimental 150; fascist
152; feminine 157–8; imaginary
11; laws of 160, 175; novelistic
11, 22; in modernity 154;
practice of 143–6; productive
potential of 142; transgressive
139, 150–2, 156; women's 175

Yeats, W.B. 188

Zedong, Mao 138